MW00892703

THE CFO GUIDE TO FORECASTING IN FP&A

Hayden Van Der Post

Reactive Publishing

CONTENTS

PREFACE

In the rapidly evolving landscape of corporate finance, the ability to forecast accurately is more than a skill—it's an essential tool for survival and success. "The CFO Guide to Forecasting in FP&A - Guide for Advanced Forecasting" is crafted as a beacon for those who have already navigated the basics of financial planning and analysis (FP&A) and are ready to elevate their forecasting capabilities. This book is the culmination of years of expertise, research, and real-world experience, designed to bridge the gap between traditional methodologies and the cutting-edge techniques that are shaping the future of corporate finance.

The purpose of this guide is twofold. Firstly, to arm Chief Financial Officers (CFOs), senior finance professionals, and advanced practitioners with the knowledge and tools to implement sophisticated forecasting models that can enhance decision-making processes, financial stability, and strategic planning. Secondly, it serves to elucidate the complexities of modern financial forecasting, offering clarity and actionable strategies amidst the myriad of tools and theories that often cloud the field.

Our target audience is the seasoned financial professional who is no stranger to FP&A but seeks to deepen their understanding and application of advanced forecasting techniques. Whether you are a CFO looking to refine your organization's financial trajectory, a senior finance manager aiming to leverage forecasting for competitive advantage, or an FP&A professional seeking to solidify your expertise and contribute more strategically to your organization, this guide promises to be an invaluable resource.

Within these pages, you will find a comprehensive exploration of the latest trends, technologies, and methodologies in forecasting. From the integration of artificial intelligence and machine learning to the nuances of scenario planning and risk management, this guide traverses the breadth and depth of advanced forecasting. Each chapter is meticulously designed to not only impart knowledge but also to inspire innovation and creativity in your forecasting endeavors.

As you embark on this journey through "The CFO Guide to Forecasting in FP&A - Guide for Advanced Forecasting," remember that the landscape of corporate finance is perpetually shifting. The models and strategies discussed herein are not endpoints but stepping stones. The true measure of success in forecasting lies not in the accuracy of predictions but in the agility and adaptability of your approach to the unforeseen.

We welcome you to this exploration of advanced forecasting in FP&A and invite you to challenge the boundaries of your understanding. Let this book be your guide as you navigate the complexities of the financial future, armed with insight, foresight, and the readiness to redefine the possibilities of corporate finance.

CHAPTER 1:
INTRODUCTION
TO FORECASTING
IN FP&A

Forecasting, within Financial Planning and Analysis (FP&A), is not merely a process of predicting numbers; it embodies the art and science of foreseeing the financial future of an organization. This critical function serves as the compass by which companies navigate the uncertain waters of economic shifts, market volatility, and emerging industry trends. Its strategic importance cannot be overstated, as it directly influences decision-making at the highest levels, shaping the course of investments, operational expansions, cost management, and strategic planning.

In the ever-evolving marketplace, the ability to anticipate and effectively prepare for future possibilities gives businesses a formidable competitive edge. Forecasting enables enterprises to move from reactive measures to a proactive stance, where strategic decisions are informed by data-driven insights rather than mere speculation or historical precedent. This shift not only enhances efficiency but also significantly mitigates risk, allowing organizations to allocate resources more effectively and pursue opportunities with greater precision.

forecasting acts as a foundational element in budgeting activities. While closely related, it's essential to distinguish between these functions. Budgeting outlines the financial plan for a business over a specific period, based on the goals and strategies set forth. Forecasting, however, extends beyond this static framework, offering a dynamic outlook that assists in adjusting strategies in response to unforeseen challenges or opportunities. This dynamic nature of forecasting allows for a more flexible approach to financial planning, adapting to real-time economic conditions and market dynamics.

Furthermore, forecasting plays a pivotal role in performance evaluation. By setting benchmarks and financial targets, businesses can monitor actual performance against forecasted figures, allowing for timely interventions when discrepancies arise. This continuous loop of planning, monitoring, and adjusting forms the backbone of effective financial management, driving businesses towards their strategic objectives while preserving financial health.

The methodology employed in forecasting ranges from quantitative models, leveraging historical data and statistical analyses, to qualitative techniques that incorporate expert judgments and market sentiment. The amalgamation of these approaches provides a robust framework for predicting future financial outcomes, taking into account a wide array of variables including sales trends, market conditions, and external economic factors.

The role of forecasting in FP&A transcends mere number crunching. It embodies the synthesis of data analysis, market intuition, and strategic vision. As businesses operate in an increasingly complex and fast-paced world, the importance of developing accurate, timely, and insightful forecasts has never been more critical. It not only informs strategic planning and decision-making but also equips leaders with the foresight necessary to steer their organizations towards sustainable growth and success. Through the lens of forecasting, businesses can envision their future with greater clarity, charting a path that is both ambitious and attainable.

The Strategic Importance of Forecasting in Decision-Making

Any successful organization lies a strategic decision-making process enriched by accurate and forward-looking financial forecasting. This indispensable tool in Financial Planning and Analysis (FP&A) serves as a linchpin for crafting strategies that not only withstand the test of time but also capitalize on emerging opportunities and navigate through the vicissitudes of the marketplace.

The strategic importance of forecasting in decision-making is multifaceted, impacting various aspects of an organization's operations. Firstly, it enables a proactive approach to risk management. By anticipating potential financial downturns or identifying lucrative opportunities ahead of the competition, companies can devise contingency plans, thereby minimizing risks and maximizing returns. This foresight is crucial in today's volatile market conditions, where businesses must remain nimble and responsive to external pressures.

Moreover, forecasting influences capital allocation and investment decisions, guiding leaders on where to channel resources for the highest potential yield. In an era where capital efficiency can set leading enterprises apart from their counterparts, the ability to predict future financial outcomes with a degree of accuracy becomes a critical competitive advantage. It ensures that investments are made not only in growth areas but also in initiatives that bolster resilience against market uncertainties.

The strategic planning process, too, is inextricably linked with proficient forecasting. It provides a roadmap that aligns with the company's long-term vision, taking into account anticipated financial trends, market dynamics, and industry shifts. Without the insights derived from effective forecasting, strategic plans would be mere conjectures devoid of any actionable intelligence. It is forecasting that transforms these plans into viable, strategic initiatives poised to drive sustainable growth.

Furthermore, forecasting plays a vital role in stakeholder communication and relations. Shareholders, investors, and partners seek assurance that their interests are managed judiciously. A well-founded forecast demonstrates a company's commitment to due diligence and its capability to navigate future challenges, thereby fostering trust and confidence among stakeholders. It also ensures that stakeholder expectations are aligned with the company's strategic objectives, paving the way for more harmonious and productive engagements.

The strategic importance of forecasting in decision-making extends beyond mere numerical predictions; it is about understanding the narrative behind the numbers. It involves discerning patterns, interpreting market signals, and anticipating changes in the economic landscape. This comprehensive view allows businesses to make informed decisions that are not reactive but strategic, ensuring long-term viability and success.

Incorporating advanced technologies, such as AI and machine learning, into forecasting processes has further elevated its strategic value. These technologies enable more accurate predictions by analyzing vast datasets, recognizing trends that elude human analysts, and providing insights at a speed and scale unprecedented in traditional forecasting. As such, they augment the decision-making process, allowing for more nuanced and sophisticated strategic planning.

The strategic essence of forecasting, therefore, is not just in its ability to predict the future but in empowering leaders to shape it. It is a dynamic, iterative process that requires continual refinement and adjustment as new information unfolds. By integrating robust forecasting into their strategic decision-making processes, organizations can not only anticipate the future but also actively participate in its creation, steering toward a horizon of growth, innovation, and resilience.

How Accurate Forecasts Impact FP&A

The precision of forecasts within Financial Planning and Analysis (FP&A) exerts a profound influence on an organization's strategic agility and financial health. Accurate forecasts serve as a compass that guides financial strategy, operational efficiency, and overall organizational resilience. Their impact is far-reaching, affecting everything from day-to-day operations to long-term strategic initiatives.

Enhanced Strategic Decision Making

Accuracy in forecasting equips leaders with the clarity

needed to make informed strategic decisions. When financial predictions closely align with eventual outcomes, organizations can confidently allocate resources, invest in new ventures, or scale back operations to mitigate anticipated downturns. This precision reduces the speculative nature of decision-making, ensuring that investments and strategic shifts are based on solid data rather than conjecture.

Resource Optimization

One of the most tangible impacts of accurate forecasting is the effective allocation and optimization of resources. Organizations can channel their assets—be it capital, labor, or technology—towards initiatives that are predicted to yield the best returns. Conversely, accurate forecasts can highlight areas where resources may be overallocated, preventing wasteful expenditure and focusing efforts on more productive areas.

Risk Management

In the dynamic landscape of business, risk is an ever-present factor. Accurate financial forecasts play a pivotal role in identifying potential risks before they manifest into full-blown crises. By foreseeing financial shortfalls, market downturns, or shifts in consumer behavior, organizations can proactively develop strategies to cushion the impact. This proactive approach to risk management is only possible with forecasts that reliably predict future financial states.

Stakeholder Assurance

Accuracy in FP&A forecasting also has significant implications for stakeholder confidence. Investors, lenders, and shareholders rely on forecasts to assess an organization's future viability and profitability. When forecasts are consistently accurate, it builds trust and confidence among these stakeholders, leading to more favorable financing conditions, increased investment, and overall supportive stakeholder relations.

Market Competitiveness

In competitive markets, the ability to forecast accurately provides a distinct advantage. It allows organizations to anticipate market trends, adapt to consumer demands, and innovate ahead of competitors. Accurate forecasts enable businesses to seize opportunities and avoid pitfalls, positioning them as leaders rather than followers in their respective industries.

Operational Efficiency

On an operational level, the impact of accurate forecasting cannot be overstated. It enables detailed planning of inventory levels, workforce management, and production schedules. This ensures that operations are lean and agile, capable of scaling up or down in response to accurately anticipated demand fluctuations. Without the guidance of precise forecasts, operations may become either bloated with excess inventory or underprepared to meet customer demand, both of which can erode profit margins.

Financial Stability

Ultimately, the culmination of these impacts leads to enhanced financial stability. Accurate forecasting enables better control over cash flow, ensuring that the organization can meet its financial obligations while also investing in growth opportunities. It reduces the likelihood of financial distress by providing early warnings of potential shortfalls, allowing for corrective action to be taken.

Accurate forecasts are not a panacea for all financial challenges; they are, however, a critical component of a robust FP&A function. Their influence extends throughout the organization, embedding a culture of data-driven decision-making, strategic foresight, and operational efficiency. As such, the quest for accuracy in forecasting should be a continual endeavor, leveraging the latest technologies, methodologies, and data analytics to refine and improve the forecasting process. In doing so, organizations can navigate the complexities of the business world with confidence, grounded in the insights that accurate forecasts provide.

Differences between Forecasting and Budgeting

Understanding the nuanced distinctions between forecasting and budgeting is pivotal for any Financial Planning and Analysis (FP&A) professional. While both are essential financial management tools, they serve markedly different purposes and are utilized in diverse strategic contexts.

Definition and Purpose

Budgeting is the process of creating a financial plan for a future period. It is prescriptive in nature, detailing where a company intends to allocate its resources. Budgets are often set annually and serve as a financial blueprint that guides spending, investment, and revenue targets for the forthcoming year. The primary purpose of budgeting is to impose financial discipline, ensuring that resources are allocated in alignment with strategic priorities.

Forecasting, on the other hand, is predictive. It is the art and science of predicting future financial outcomes based on historical data, current market trends, and forward-looking projections. Unlike budgeting, forecasting is dynamic and can be updated regularly to reflect changes in the business environment or company performance. The objective of forecasting is to provide insight into future financial conditions, helping organizations navigate uncertainty and make informed strategic decisions.

Time Frame and Flexibility

Budgets are typically fixed for the budgeted period—usually a fiscal year. Once established, budgets are not easily changed, as they reflect a commitment to a set of financial targets and expenditures. This rigidity is necessary for financial control and planning but can be a limitation if the business environment changes significantly.

Forecasts are more flexible and can be updated as new information becomes available. They often cover various time frames, from short-term forecasts that look at the next quarter to long-term forecasts projecting years into the future. This flexibility allows forecasts to adapt to changing circumstances, providing a more accurate picture of the company's financial trajectory.

Function and Use

The function of budgeting is predominantly to control and manage resources. It sets limits on spending and establishes financial targets that departments and teams must adhere to. Budgets are used as benchmarks against which actual performance is measured, and variances are analyzed for better control.

Forecasting, however, is used for strategic planning and decision-making. It enables companies to anticipate results and financial conditions, allowing them to strategize around growth, investments, and risk management. Forecasts guide strategic decisions such as entering new markets, launching new products, or adjusting operations to meet future demand.

Detail and Scope

Budgets are detailed and specific, breaking down expected income and expenditures by department, project, or activity. This level of detail is necessary to ensure that financial resources are allocated efficiently and that spending aligns with organizational priorities.

Forecasts may not always dive into the same level of granularity as budgets. Instead, they provide a broader view of the financial landscape, focusing on key metrics such as revenue growth, cash flow, and profitability. The scope of forecasting is more about identifying trends and potential financial outcomes than about allocating resources.

Stakeholders and Communication

The process of budgeting is a collaborative effort that involves input from various departments within an organization. It requires buy-in from department heads and is often subject to approval by the board of directors. The finalized budget becomes a document that communicates the company's financial priorities and constraints to all stakeholders.

Forecasts, while also a collaborative effort, are primarily used by senior management and the finance team to guide strategic planning and decision-making. While forecasts are shared with stakeholders, they are more fluid and subject to change, reflecting ongoing adjustments to the company's strategic direction.

The differences between forecasting and budgeting lie in their purpose, flexibility, scope, and use within an organization. Both are indispensable to effective financial management and strategic planning in FP&A. By recognizing their distinct roles and leveraging each appropriately, companies can ensure financial discipline while navigating the complexities and uncertainties of the business environment with agility and foresight.

Types of Financial Forecasts

In the dynamic realm of Financial Planning and Analysis (FP&A), mastering the art of financial forecasting is akin to possessing a navigational compass in the vast ocean of commerce. Financial forecasts serve as pivotal tools, guiding businesses through the ebbs and flows of economic conditions and market volatility. They are not monolithic; rather, they come in various forms, each tailored to specific strategic needs and time horizons. Understanding these types is crucial for FP&A professionals as they seek to steer their organizations towards financial stability and growth.

Short-term Forecasts

Short-term forecasts are the sprinters of the financial forecasting world, covering a period of up to one year. They are instrumental in managing daily operations, addressing immediate financial needs, and capitalizing on near-term opportunities. These forecasts focus on liquidity planning, cash flow management, and short-term financial health. They enable businesses to maintain operational efficacy, ensuring that they can meet payroll, supplier payments, and other short-term liabilities.

Long-term Forecasts

Long-term forecasts, on the other hand, are the marathon runners, extending beyond a year and sometimes reaching five to ten years into the future. These are essential for strategic planning, capital investment decisions, and long-term financial planning. Long-term forecasts provide a vision of the company's future financial trajectory, including potential revenue growth, market expansion, and major capital expenditures. They help businesses prepare for future challenges and opportunities, guiding long-range strategic initiatives.

Rolling Forecasts

Rolling forecasts represent a hybrid approach, combining the immediacy of short-term forecasting with the strategic outlook of long-term forecasts. Unlike traditional forecasts, which are fixed in time, rolling forecasts are continuously updated throughout the year to reflect new financial data and market conditions. This approach provides businesses with the flexibility to adapt to changes and make informed decisions in real-time. Rolling forecasts typically cover a period of 12 to 18 months, constantly extending the forecast horizon as time progresses.

Scenario Forecasts

Scenario forecasts are designed to explore various future states based on differing assumptions and external factors. These forecasts create a range of possible outcomes, from best-case to worst-case scenarios, enabling businesses to assess potential risks and opportunities. Scenario planning is particularly useful in volatile markets or industries undergoing rapid change. It allows companies to prepare contingency plans and strategies to navigate uncertainties effectively.

Cash Flow Forecasts

Cash flow forecasts are focused on predicting the flow of cash into and out of the business over a specific period. These forecasts are critical for ensuring liquidity and solvency, helping businesses to anticipate cash shortages and surpluses. Cash flow forecasting is vital for day-to-day operational planning, debt management, and investment planning. It provides a detailed view of the company's financial position, enabling timely decision-making regarding expenditures, investments, and financing activities.

Project-specific Forecasts

Project-specific forecasts are tailored to individual projects or initiatives within the organization. These forecasts evaluate the financial viability and expected outcomes of specific projects, considering costs, revenues, and potential return on investment. Project-specific forecasting is essential for project selection, budgeting, and management, ensuring that resources are allocated to projects that align with strategic goals and offer acceptable returns.

Each type of financial forecast serves a distinct purpose, contributing to a comprehensive financial planning and analysis framework. By leveraging these different types of forecasts, FP&A professionals can equip their organizations with the insights needed to navigate financial uncertainties, capitalize on opportunities, and drive strategic decision-making. Understanding and applying these forecasts effectively is paramount for fostering financial health and achieving long-term success in the competitive business landscape.

Short-term vs. Long-term Forecasts

Short-term forecasts, often delineated for a period extending up to one year, serve as the tactical arsenal in a company's financial toolkit. These forecasts are grounded in the present, meticulously crafted from the latest financial data and market intelligence to provide a near-term financial outlook. The primary aim is to ensure operational fluidity and financial health, focusing on cash flow management, budget control, and the tactical allocation of resources.

The granularity of short-term forecasts is their hallmark, offering a detailed lens through which immediate revenue and expenditure trends can be scrutinized. These forecasts are instrumental in identifying potential cash flow crunches, enabling businesses to enact preemptive strategies to mitigate liquidity risks. For instance, a sudden market downturn or an unexpected operational hiccup can significantly impact a company's cash flow. Short-term forecasts, with their pulse on the immediate financial horizon, allow businesses to navigate through these turbulent waters with agility and precision.

The Visionary Scope of Long-term Forecasts

Long-term forecasts, projecting three to five years or sometimes even a decade into the future, embody the strategic compass of a business. These forecasts are less about the minutiae of daily financial operations and more about charting a course towards the company's long-range goals and aspirations. They encompass broad financial projections, including revenue growth, capital investments, and market expansion strategies, serving as the blueprint for sustainable growth and competitive positioning.

The development of long-term forecasts requires a blend of historical financial data, industry trends analysis, and forward-looking market insights. This type of forecasting is inherently speculative, embracing the uncertainties of the future while striving to outline a plausible financial trajectory for the organization. For example, a company planning to enter new markets or launch new product lines would rely on long-term forecasts to evaluate the financial implications and strategic viability of these initiatives.

Interplay and Integration: Bridging Short-term and Long-term Forecasts

While short-term and long-term forecasts may seem like distinct entities, their greatest value lies in their integration. The strategic depth of long-term forecasts gains practical relevance when aligned with the tactical agility of short-term forecasts. This synergistic approach allows businesses to maintain a steady course towards their long-term objectives while adeptly navigating the short-term financial ebbs and flows.

For instance, a company's strategic plan to expand its operational capacity over the next five years necessitates significant capital investments. Long-term forecasts would outline the financial implications of this expansion, while short-term forecasts would ensure that the company maintains adequate liquidity and cash flow to support the initial stages of this strategic initiative.

the art of financial forecasting in FP&A is not confined to the binary choice between short-term and long-term perspectives but lies in mastering the dynamic dance between them. Short-term forecasts provide the immediate financial bearings, while long-term forecasts chart the strategic horizon. Together, they form a comprehensive financial planning framework that empowers businesses to pursue their short-term operational imperatives and their long-term strategic ambitions with confidence and clarity. The adept navigation of this temporal spectrum ensures that businesses can thrive amidst the uncertainties of the present while steadfastly pursuing their vision for the future.

Rolling Forecasts and Their Significance

A rolling forecast is an iterative, continuously updated process of financial forecasting that extends beyond the static confines of traditional fiscal year boundaries. Unlike annual forecasts, which offer a fixed outlook, rolling forecasts evolve with the passage of time, incorporating the latest market trends, operational data, and financial insights to provide a constantly refreshing financial horizon.

Typically structured on a quarterly or monthly basis, rolling forecasts maintain a constant projection window—often looking forward 12 to 18 months—thereby ensuring that the financial forecast horizon moves forward with each passing period. This dynamic nature allows organizations to remain perpetually attuned to the financial implications of their operational performance and market conditions, enabling more informed decision-making.

The Significance of Rolling Forecasts in Modern FP&A

The adoption of rolling forecasts signifies a paradigm shift towards a more adaptive, resilient approach to financial planning. In today's fast-paced, uncertain business environment, the ability to anticipate and respond to change is paramount. Rolling forecasts emerge as a beacon of adaptability, empowering businesses to pivot their strategies in alignment with emerging opportunities and risks.

1. Enhanced Agility: Rolling forecasts enable a degree of agility unseen in traditional forecasting models. By continuously updating the financial outlook, organizations can swiftly adjust their strategies and operations in response to changing market dynamics.

2. Strategic Alignment: With a forward-looking stance, rolling forecasts facilitate a tighter alignment between strategic objectives and financial planning. This alignment ensures that every financial decision is made with a clear understanding of its impact on the organization's strategic direction.

3. Risk Management: The iterative nature of rolling forecasts provides a framework for proactive risk management. By constantly refreshing the forecast, businesses can better anticipate potential financial pitfalls and devise strategies to mitigate them.

4. Resource Optimization: By offering a continuously updated view of financial resources, rolling forecasts guide organizations in optimizing their allocation of capital, labor, and other resources. This optimization supports operational efficiency and strategic investment in growth opportunities.

Implementing Rolling Forecasts: Considerations and Challenges

While the benefits of rolling forecasts are compelling, their implementation is not without challenges. Transitioning from a traditional annual forecasting process to a rolling forecast model requires a cultural shift, embracing flexibility, and continuous planning. Key considerations include:

- Data Integration: Effective rolling forecasts hinge on the seamless integration of financial and operational data. Organizations must invest in systems and technology that facilitate real-time data access and analysis.

- Process Redesign: Adopting rolling forecasts may necessitate a redesign of existing financial processes and systems. This redesign involves training finance teams, establishing new workflows, and integrating rolling forecasts into the decision-making fabric of the organization.

- Stakeholder Engagement: Ensuring the buy-in of key stakeholders is crucial. This engagement involves clear communication of the benefits of rolling forecasts and addressing concerns related to the shift from traditional forecasting methods.

rolling forecasts represent not just a financial tool but a strategic imperative for organizations aiming to navigate the uncertainties of the modern business landscape. By embedding agility, strategic alignment, and proactive risk management into the financial planning process, rolling forecasts pave the way for organizations to seize opportunities, mitigate risks, and steer towards a resilient, prosperous future. As businesses continue to confront rapid changes and heightened uncertainties, the significance of rolling forecasts in shaping agile, robust financial strategies becomes ever more pronounced.

Scenario Planning and Its Application

Scenario planning, distinct from forecasting, involves the construction of several plausible futures based on varying assumptions about how key external variables could evolve over time. It transcends traditional predictive models by acknowledging the inherent unpredictability of the future and instead focuses on understanding how different scenarios could impact organizational strategy and operations. This approach fosters a mindset of preparedness, encouraging businesses to consider a broad spectrum of possibilities and develop flexible strategies.

Strategic Application in FP&A

The application of scenario planning within financial planning and analysis (FP&A) serves as a strategic lever, enhancing the organization's adaptability and strategic agility. By integrating scenario planning into the FP&A process, businesses can reap several strategic benefits:

1. Informed Decision-Making: Scenario planning equips decision-makers with a comprehensive understanding of potential risks and opportunities. By evaluating the financial implications of various scenarios, organizations can make informed choices, prioritizing investments and initiatives that are resilient across multiple futures.

2. Risk Mitigation: Through the examination of adverse scenarios, businesses can identify potential threats and vulnerabilities. This proactive risk assessment enables the formulation of contingency plans, ensuring that the organization can respond swiftly and effectively to mitigate impacts.

3. Strategic Flexibility: By preparing for a range of outcomes, businesses can develop flexible strategies that can be adapted as the external environment changes. This flexibility ensures that the organization remains aligned with its strategic objectives, even as it navigates through uncertainties.

4. Stakeholder Communication: Scenario planning facilitates clear and effective communication with stakeholders by providing a structured framework for discussing potential risks and strategies. This transparency supports stakeholder engagement and fosters trust in the organization's strategic direction.

Implementing Scenario Planning: Key Considerations

The successful implementation of scenario planning within the FP&A process involves several key considerations:

- Identifying Critical Uncertainties: The first step is

to identify the external factors that could significantly impact the organization. These may include economic indicators, regulatory changes, technological advancements, and competitive dynamics.

- Developing Plausible Scenarios: For each critical uncertainty, develop a range of plausible scenarios, from the most optimistic to the most pessimistic. Each scenario should be coherent and internally consistent, with a narrative that explains how and why the future might unfold in that particular way.

- Financial Modelling: For each scenario, construct detailed financial models to assess the potential impacts on revenue, expenditures, cash flow, and other key financial metrics. This modelling should take into account the interdependencies between different areas of the business.

- Strategic Response Planning: Based on the financial implications of each scenario, develop strategic response plans that outline how the organization would adjust its strategy, operations, and resource allocation in response to each potential future.

- Regular Review and Reassessment: Scenario planning is not a one-time exercise but a dynamic process that requires regular review and reassessment. As the external environment evolves, scenarios should be updated, and response plans refined to ensure ongoing relevance and effectiveness.

Embracing Uncertainty with Strategic Foresight

Scenario planning represents a paradigm shift in how organizations approach the future, moving from a predictive to a preparative mindset. By embracing the uncertainties of the business environment and preparing for a range of possible futures, businesses can bolster their resilience, adaptability, and strategic foresight. In the ever-changing landscape of FP&A, scenario planning emerges as a critical tool, enabling organizations to chart a course through the complexities of the future with confidence and strategic agility. Through its thoughtful application, businesses can unlock new avenues for growth, innovation, and competitive advantage, securing their place in the annals of success amidst the unpredictable tides of change.

Key Components of an Effective Forecast

Central to the craft of forecasting is the collection of comprehensive, accurate, and up-to-date data. This data spans across various dimensions of the business, encompassing sales performance, market trends, customer behavior, and operational capabilities. In FP&A, precision in data collection equates to the clarity of the lens through which future possibilities are viewed. It's not just about gathering quantities but about curating quality insights that reflect the true state of affairs and potential market dynamics.

Integration of Financial and Non-Financial Factors

The tapestry of forecasting is woven with threads of both financial and non-financial factors. Revenue, expenditures, and cash flow constitute the financial threads, essential for plotting the numerical trajectory of the organization. However, an effective forecast also integrates non-financial factors such as market conditions, regulatory changes, technological advancements, and competitive landscape. These elements provide context, allowing for a forecast that is both nuanced and comprehensive, reflecting the multifaceted nature of business operations.

Analytical Models and Methodologies

forecasting lies the selection of appropriate analytical models and methodologies. This involves a balancing act between the sophistication of statistical techniques and the practicality of their application within the business context. Time series analysis, regression models, and econometric methods are among the quantitative tools that can dissect historical data to unveil patterns and relationships. Meanwhile, qualitative insights from expert judgement and market analysis enrich the forecast with perspectives that numbers alone cannot reveal.

Adjustment for Seasonality and Market Trends

An effective forecast acknowledges and adjusts for the rhythmic pulse of seasonality and the undercurrents of market trends. Seasonal variations in demand, supply chain disruptions, and emerging market trends can significantly influence business performance. By incorporating adjustments for these factors, a forecast transforms into a dynamic instrument, attuned to the ebb and flow of the market and capable of providing actionable insights across different time horizons.

Scenario Analysis and Sensitivity Testing

A robust forecast is not a monolith but a spectrum of possibilities. Scenario analysis and sensitivity testing introduce flexibility into forecasting, allowing businesses to explore the potential impacts of varying assumptions and external factors. This component of forecasting equips decision-makers with the agility to pivot strategies, reallocate resources, and mitigate risks, ensuring that the organization remains resilient in the face of uncertainty.

Continuous Review and Revision

The final and perhaps most crucial component of an effective forecast is the commitment to continuous review and revision. The landscape of business and finance is ever-evolving, and a forecast must evolve alongside it. This entails regular assessments of forecasting accuracy, adjustments based on new information, and recalibrations in response to internal and external changes. It is through this iterative process that a forecast maintains its relevance, accuracy, and strategic value.

Charting the Course with Precision and Insight

The key components of an effective forecast – comprehensive data collection, the integration of financial and non-financial factors, analytical models and methodologies, adjustments for seasonality and market trends, scenario analysis and sensitivity testing, and continuous review and revision – together form the sextant by which businesses navigate the vast ocean of FP&A. This detailed exploration underscores the importance of a meticulously constructed forecast, one that not only predicts the future but also prepares the organization to meet it with confidence, agility, and strategic foresight. Through the diligent application of these components, businesses can chart a course towards sustainable growth and resilience, capable of weathering the storms and capitalizing on the winds of opportunity.

Revenue, Expenditures, and Cash Flow Considerations

Revenue forecasting stands at the forefront, serving as a barometer for the company's financial vitality. It is an process that involves analyzing past sales data, market trends, industry dynamics, and the potential impact of new products or services. The goal is to project future sales volumes and revenue streams, taking into consideration factors such as seasonal fluctuations, promotional activities, and changes in consumer behavior. This projection not only informs budget allocations and investment strategies but also helps in setting realistic targets for sales teams.

Key Strategies for Effective Revenue Forecasting

- Market Analysis: Thoroughly understanding market trends and consumer behavior to anticipate changes in demand.

- Historical Data Analysis: Utilizing time series analysis to identify patterns and predict future sales based on historical performance.

- Product Lifecycle Considerations: Accounting for the stages of each product or service lifecycle, from introduction to decline, and adjusting forecasts accordingly.

Expenditure Forecasting: Navigating the Cost Landscape

Expenditure forecasting is crucial for managing the outflows of cash that sustain the business operations. It encompasses all costs associated with running the business, including but not limited to, direct costs (cost of goods sold), operating expenses (salaries, rent, utilities), and capital expenditures (investments in equipment or infrastructure). Precision in forecasting expenditures is vital for maintaining liquidity, ensuring profitability, and planning for expansion or contractions in business operations.

Effective Techniques for Expenditure Forecasting

- Zero-Based Budgeting: Building the expenditure forecast from scratch to ensure all costs are justified for each new period.

- Variance Analysis: Comparing actual expenses against budgeted figures to identify and analyze discrepancies.

- Trend Analysis: Leveraging historical expenditure data to predict future spending patterns and adjustments needed.

Cash Flow Forecasting: The Lifeline of the Business

Cash flow forecasting is arguably the most critical component, providing a snapshot of the financial health of the business in terms of liquidity. It involves predicting the inflow and outflow of cash over a specific period, allowing businesses to ensure that they maintain adequate liquidity to meet their obligations. Accurately forecasting cash flow enables strategic decision-making regarding investment opportunities, debt management, and dividend policies.

Strategies for Robust Cash Flow Forecasting

- Direct and Indirect Methods: Utilizing both methods for short-term and long-term forecasting to capture a comprehensive view of cash movements.

- Scenario Planning: Preparing for various scenarios, including best case, worst case, and most likely case, to understand potential impacts on cash flow.

- Regular Monitoring: Continuously updating the cash flow forecast to reflect actual cash movements and adjusting for unforeseen changes in the business environment.

Integrating Revenue, Expenditures, and Cash Flow into Financial Forecasting

Integrating these three components into the financial forecasting process demands a holistic view of the business. The interplay between revenue, expenditures, and cash flow provides critical insights into the operational efficiency, profitability, and financial stability of the organization. It requires a collaborative effort across departments, leveraging both financial and non-financial data, to construct a cohesive and realistic financial forecast.

Leveraging Technology in Forecasting

Adopting advanced financial planning and analysis (FP&A) software can significantly enhance the accuracy and efficiency of forecasting these key financial elements. These tools offer sophisticated data analysis capabilities, real-time data integration, and scenario planning features, enabling finance teams to generate more accurate and dynamic forecasts.

The Triad of Financial Foresight

revenue, expenditures, and cash flow considerations are intertwined strands that form the core of financial forecasting. Their meticulous analysis and integration facilitate strategic planning, risk management, and decision-making processes. By adopting a comprehensive approach to forecasting these key components, businesses can navigate the complexities of the financial landscape with greater agility and foresight, ensuring sustained growth and resilience in the face of uncertainty.

The Importance of Incorporating Non-Financial Data

Non-financial data encompasses a wide array of metrics outside the traditional financial statements, including customer satisfaction scores, employee engagement levels, market penetration rates, and even social media engagement statistics. These metrics, though not directly tied to financial outcomes, have profound implications for revenue growth, cost management, and risk assessment.

Customer Satisfaction: The Unseen Revenue Driver

High customer satisfaction not only augments customer loyalty but also increases the likelihood of positive word-of-mouth, significantly impacting revenue growth. By integrating customer satisfaction scores into the forecasting model, businesses can predict future sales trends more accurately, identifying potential areas for improvement or investment.

Employee Engagement: A Catalyst for Efficiency

Engaged employees are the cornerstone of operational

efficiency and innovation. High engagement levels correlate with lower absenteeism, higher productivity, and reduced turnover rates, directly influencing operational costs and the company's ability to innovate and adapt. Incorporating employee engagement metrics into forecasts provides insights into potential cost savings and areas where investment in training and development could spur growth.

Market Penetration and Social Media Engagement: Indicators of Market Dynamics

Understanding market penetration rates and social media engagement offers a window into the company's market position and brand health. These metrics provide early indicators of changes in consumer behavior or market demand, enabling more proactive adjustments to the financial forecast. For instance, a surge in social media engagement could signal an upcoming increase in demand, necessitating adjustments in inventory levels, marketing strategies, and financial projections.

Leveraging Non-Financial Data for Risk Management

Incorporating non-financial data into the forecasting process enhances the company's risk management capabilities. It enables a more nuanced understanding of potential risks and vulnerabilities, from market shifts and consumer trends to internal challenges related to workforce management and operational efficiency. By identifying these risks early, businesses can develop more robust strategies for mitigation, ensuring that the financial forecast remains realistic and achievable.

Technology as an Enabler

The effective integration of non-financial data into financial forecasting necessitates advanced analytics and data processing capabilities. Modern FP&A software solutions, equipped with AI and machine learning algorithms, can analyze vast datasets, identifying correlations and trends that may not be immediately apparent. These tools enable finance teams to seamlessly incorporate non-financial metrics into their forecasts, enhancing the depth and breadth of their analyses.

Case Study: A Retail Giant's Leap Forward

Consider the case of a leading retail giant that began incorporating customer satisfaction and employee engagement data into its forecasting model. By analyzing trends in these metrics, the company was able to predict shifts in customer demand more accurately and adjust its inventory and staffing levels accordingly. This strategic shift led to improved customer satisfaction, reduced inventory costs, and higher sales growth, underscoring the tangible benefits of integrating non-financial data into financial forecasts.

The incorporation of non-financial data into financial forecasting marks a pivotal shift towards a more holistic and dynamic approach to FP&A. It acknowledges the web of factors that influence a company's financial performance, extending beyond traditional financial metrics to encompass a broader array of determinants. By embracing this multifaceted approach, businesses can enhance the accuracy, relevance, and strategic value of their forecasts, positioning themselves for sustained success in a rapidly changing business environment.

Adjusting Forecasts for Seasonality and Market Trends

Seasonality refers to the predictable fluctuations in business activity that occur at regular intervals throughout the year, driven by factors such as holidays, weather changes, and consumer behavior patterns. These cyclical trends can significantly impact sales volumes, inventory requirements, and cash flow, making it imperative for financial forecasts to reflect these patterns accurately.

Adjusting forecasts for seasonality begins with a thorough analysis of historical data, identifying seasonal peaks and troughs in business activity. This analysis must extend beyond mere sales volumes, encompassing related variables such as production cycles, supply chain timings, and inventory levels. Advanced statistical models, such as time series analysis with seasonal decompositions, can then be employed to isolate the seasonal component of the data, providing a clearer understanding of its impact on financial performance.

Navigating Market Trends: The Pulse of Predictability

While seasonality deals with predictable patterns, adjusting forecasts for market trends involves interpreting the broader, often less predictable shifts in consumer preferences, technological advancements, and economic conditions. Staying attuned to these trends is crucial for maintaining the relevance and accuracy of financial forecasts.

The integration of market trend analysis into financial forecasting involves a continuous process of data collection and interpretation. This may include monitoring changes in consumer behaviors through social media analytics, keeping abreast of industry innovations, and analyzing economic indicators that may affect business operations. The key lies in identifying which trends are likely to have a lasting impact versus those that may be fleeting, using both qualitative insights and quantitative data to inform forecast adjustments.

The most effective forecasts are those that manage to integrate adjustments for both seasonality and market trends, recognizing the interplay between these two factors. For instance, a seasonal increase in demand might be amplified or mitigated by a prevailing market trend, such as a shift towards online shopping or sustainability concerns. Therefore, forecasts must be flexible, allowing for regular updates as new information becomes available.

Leveraging technology is paramount in adjusting forecasts for seasonality and market trends efficiently. Modern forecasting software can automate much of the data analysis process, applying machine learning algorithms to detect patterns and predict future trends. These tools can also facilitate scenario planning, allowing finance teams to explore various potential outcomes and prepare for different eventualities.

Case Study: Fashioning Success in Apparel Retail

Consider an apparel retailer facing significant seasonality in consumer demand, further complicated by rapidly changing fashion trends. By implementing a forecasting model that incorporated not only historical sales data but also social media trend analysis, the retailer was able to adjust its inventory procurement and marketing strategies seasonally and trend-wise. This approach led to improved stock turnover rates, higher customer satisfaction, and a noticeable increase in profitability, showcasing the value of a nuanced forecasting strategy.

Adjusting forecasts for seasonality and market trends is both an art and a science, requiring a deep understanding of one's business rhythms and the broader market context. Through careful analysis and the strategic use of technology, finance professionals can develop forecasts that are both resilient and responsive, turning potential vulnerabilities into sources of competitive advantage. This dynamic approach to forecasting not only enhances the accuracy of financial projections but also supports more informed decision-making across the organization, paving the way for sustained success in an ever-changing business environment.

CHAPTER 2:
FORECASTING
TECHNIQUES
AND TOOLS

Q uantitative forecasting techniques are grounded in the utilization of historical numerical data to forecast future events. Unlike their qualitative counterparts, which rely on expert opinions and market sentiments, quantitative methods apply mathematical models to discern patterns and relationships within historical data, thereby offering a more objective basis for forecasts.

Time series analysis represents a paramount quantitative technique, involving the examination of data points collected or recorded at successive equally spaced points in time. This method aims to identify the underlying patterns in data that recur over time, such as trends, seasonal variations, and cyclic movements. Among the most employed time series models is the Autoregressive Integrated Moving Average (ARIMA), which captures different aspects of temporal patterns and can be fine-tuned to accommodate various levels of complexity in data behavior.

Exponential Smoothing, another pivotal time series method, assigns exponentially decreasing weights to past observations, thereby prioritizing more recent data points. This technique is particularly useful for forecasts where the most recent trends are the most indicative of future outcomes, making it invaluable for rapidly changing markets.

Regression analysis serves as another cornerstone of quantitative forecasting, exploring the relationship between one dependent variable and one or more independent variables. This method is instrumental in identifying how the typical value of the dependent variable changes when any one of the independent variables is varied. In the context of FP&A, regression analysis can illuminate how factors such as market demand, price changes, and economic indicators influence a company's sales or expenses.

The advent of artificial intelligence (AI) and machine learning (ML) has significantly expanded the frontier of quantitative forecasting. These technologies employ complex algorithms to analyze vast datasets, learning from historical data to predict future outcomes with remarkable accuracy. AI and ML models can uncover subtle patterns and relationships within data that traditional statistical methods might overlook, offering deeper insights and foresights into financial planning.

Beyond direct forecasting, quantitative techniques facilitate scenario analysis, allowing finance teams to simulate different future scenarios based on varying assumptions. This application is particularly advantageous for stress-testing financial models against extreme market conditions, providing insights into potential vulnerabilities and resilience mechanisms.

Consider a technology company aiming to forecast its sales revenue for the upcoming quarter. By employing time series analysis, the company analyzes historical sales data, identifying seasonal spikes associated with product release cycles. Through regression analysis, it further examines how external factors such as economic trends and competitor actions have historically impacted its sales. Integrating these insights with AI-driven predictive models, the company can construct a nuanced sales forecast that not only reflects historical patterns but also adapts to external market dynamics.

Quantitative forecasting techniques offer a powerful toolkit for FP&A professionals, enabling the translation of raw historical data into actionable financial insights. Through the meticulous application of time series analysis, regression models, and AI-enhanced predictive tools, finance teams can develop robust forecasts that stand on a solid foundation of data-driven intelligence. As the financial landscape continues to evolve, the ability to adeptly apply these quantitative methods will be key to navigating future uncertainties and steering organizations toward strategic success.

Time Series Analysis: ARIMA, Exponential Smoothing

The ARIMA model stands as a beacon of predictability in the vast sea of financial data, adept at handling a variety of time series data with or without trends and seasonal patterns. ARIMA is a fusion of autoregressive (AR) and moving average (MA) models, integrated with differencing to stabilize the mean of the time series data. This integration allows ARIMA to effectively capture and forecast data points in a time series by considering the past values (autoregression) and the errors in previous predictions (moving average).

Diving into ARIMA's Components:

- Autoregression (AR): This aspect of the model captures the relationship between an observation and a specified number of lagged observations.

- Integrated (I): Differencing of raw observations to make the time series stationary, which is essential for the AR and MA components to work effectively.

- Moving Average (MA): This component models the error term as a combination of previous error terms.

The true strength of ARIMA lies in its adaptability; it can be tailored to fit the specific characteristics of any time series data, making it an invaluable tool for financial analysts forecasting revenue, stock prices, economic indicators, and more.

Exponential Smoothing: Weighing the Past with Precision

Exponential Smoothing, on the other hand, offers a more straightforward approach, focusing primarily on the most recent observations to predict future values. This method applies weights that decrease exponentially to past observations, thereby ensuring that more recent events have a more significant impact on the forecast than older events.

The simplest form of Exponential Smoothing, Single Exponential Smoothing, is highly effective for forecasts where no trend or seasonal pattern is evident. However, for more complex scenarios involving trends or seasonality, variations such as Double Exponential Smoothing (for trends) and Triple Exponential Smoothing, also known as Holt-Winters Method (for both trends and seasonality), are employed.

Exponential Smoothing in Action:

Imagine a retail company analyzing monthly sales to forecast the next quarter's revenue. Using Exponential Smoothing, the company can prioritize more recent monthly sales data, adjusting the smoothing constant to fine-tune the forecast's responsiveness to recent trends. This method becomes particularly beneficial in rapidly changing market conditions, allowing the company to swiftly adapt its financial strategy.

Integrating ARIMA and Exponential Smoothing in Financial Forecasting

When applied in concert, ARIMA and Exponential Smoothing encompass the breadth and depth of time series forecasting. For instance, a financial analyst at a multinational corporation might use ARIMA to forecast long-term economic indicators while applying Exponential Smoothing for short-term stock price predictions. This dual approach enables a comprehensive forecasting model that is both deep in its historical data analysis (ARIMA) and agile in its response to recent trends (Exponential Smoothing).

Time series analysis in financial forecasting is both vast and complex, yet ARIMA and Exponential Smoothing stand out as pillars of predictability and adaptability. By mastering these techniques, financial professionals can navigate the ebbs and flows of market trends and economic indicators, crafting forecasts that guide strategic decision-making with precision and insight. Whether predicting the future course of stock prices, revenue trends, or economic shifts, ARIMA and Exponential Smoothing serve as invaluable tools in the financial analyst's arsenal, enabling a data-driven approach to forecasting the future.

Regression Analysis for Forecasting

Central to regression analysis is its ability to model and analyze the relationships between a dependent variable (typically a financial metric of interest) and one or more independent variables (factors believed to influence the dependent variable). By mapping out these relationships, regression analysis provides a statistical framework for predicting the dependent variable's future values based on known values of the independent variables.

Types of Regression Analysis:

- Simple Linear Regression: Focuses on the relationship between a single independent variable and a dependent variable, fitting a straight line through the data points to model their relationship.

- Multiple Regression: Extends beyond simple linear regression by incorporating two or more independent variables. This approach is particularly useful for financial forecasting, where multiple factors can influence a financial outcome.

Application in Financial Forecasting:

Consider a company aiming to forecast next quarter's sales. Using multiple regression analysis, the company can analyze how various factors such as marketing spend, economic conditions, and competitor pricing affect its sales. By inputting the relevant data into a regression model, the company can predict sales with a degree of accuracy previously unattainable through simpler forecasting methods.

The Process of Regression Analysis:

1. Data Collection: Gathering historical financial data and potential influencing factors.

2. Model Selection: Choosing between simple or multiple regression based on the complexity of the relationships.

3. Estimation: Using statistical software to estimate the regression coefficients that best fit the data.

4. Validation: Testing the model's predictive power with a portion of the data not used in the estimation process.

5. Forecasting: Applying the model to predict future financial performance.

Regression Analysis in Action:

An investment firm, for instance, may use regression analysis to forecast the return on a portfolio of stocks based on economic indicators such as interest rates, inflation, and GDP growth. By understanding the relationship between these variables and stock returns, the firm can make informed investment decisions and adjust its strategies accordingly.

While regression analysis offers profound insights, it is not without challenges. Key considerations include ensuring data quality, selecting relevant independent variables, and being wary of overfitting the model to historical data, which can diminish its predictive accuracy in real-world scenarios.

Regression analysis stands as a cornerstone of financial forecasting, offering a nuanced understanding of the factors driving financial metrics. By leveraging this powerful analytical tool, finance professionals can enhance their forecasting accuracy, informing strategic decision-making and optimizing financial performance. As the financial landscape evolves, the application of regression analysis continues to expand, solidifying its role as an indispensable component of the financial analyst's toolkit. Through careful application and ongoing refinement, regression analysis enables a forward-looking perspective that is critical in navigating the complexities of today's financial environments.

The Use of Artificial Intelligence and Machine Learning in Forecasting

AI and ML technologies stand at the frontier of financial forecasting, offering unparalleled precision and insight. At their core, these technologies entail the development of algorithms that can learn from and make predictions on data. This capability is particularly transformative in the context of financial forecasting, where the sheer volume and complexity of data far exceed human analytical capacity.

The Mechanisms of AI and ML in Forecasting:

- Predictive Analytics: AI and ML excel in identifying patterns within vast datasets, enabling predictive analytics that forecast future financial trends with remarkable accuracy.

- Adaptive Learning: Unlike static models, ML algorithms

adapt over time, learning from new data to refine and enhance forecasting models. This dynamic adjustment is crucial in the rapidly changing financial landscape.

- Scenario Analysis: AI facilitates advanced scenario analysis, allowing organizations to explore and prepare for a wide range of financial outcomes based on varying conditions and assumptions.

Real-World Applications:

AI and ML are not mere theoretical concepts but are actively being applied in the finance sector with transformative effects. For instance, banks and investment firms now utilize ML models to predict stock market trends, assess credit risk, and optimize investment portfolios. Similarly, corporations employ these technologies to forecast revenue, manage cash flow, and streamline operational expenses.

The Process of Implementing AI and ML in Financial Forecasting:

1. Data Preparation: The foundation of any AI/ML model is data. High-quality, relevant data is gathered and preprocessed for analysis.

2. Model Selection: Based on the forecasting objectives, appropriate AI/ML models are selected. Options range from simple linear regression models to complex neural networks.

3. Training and Testing: The selected models are trained on a portion of the data, and their accuracy is then tested against another set. This iterative process continues until the model's

performance is optimized.

4. Deployment: Once validated, the model is deployed for real-time forecasting, providing actionable insights to guide financial decision-making.

Implementing AI and ML in forecasting is not without its challenges. These include data privacy concerns, the need for skilled personnel to manage and interpret AI/ML models, and the ongoing requirement for model adjustment and validation. However, by addressing these issues proactively, organizations can harness the transformative potential of AI and ML, achieving a level of forecasting precision and efficiency previously unimaginable.

The advent of AI and ML in financial forecasting heralds a new era of efficiency, accuracy, and strategic foresight. These technologies enable finance professionals to navigate the complexities of the financial environment with confidence, making informed decisions that drive organizational success. As AI and ML continue to evolve, their role in shaping the future of financial forecasting promises to be both profound and pervasive, underscoring the importance of embracing these technologies in today's data-driven world.

Qualitative Forecasting Methods

Qualitative forecasting, relies on expert opinions, market analysis, and the process of synthesizing intangible factors that influence financial outcomes. These methods are particularly valuable in capturing the dynamism of market sentiments, technological advancements, and consumer behavior trends, which are often elusive in quantitative models.

One of the cornerstones of qualitative forecasting is expert judgment. This involves leveraging the insights and experiences of individuals who possess profound knowledge in specific areas relevant to the financial forecast. The Delphi method, a systematic, interactive forecasting technique, refines this approach by gathering and distilling the opinions of a panel of experts over multiple rounds. Each round provides anonymous feedback, enabling experts to revise their views, gradually converging towards a consensus. The Delphi method is particularly effective in scenarios where a new market entry or the potential impact of a groundbreaking technology is being evaluated.

Market research stands as another pivotal qualitative forecasting tool. Unlike traditional data analysis, market research explores consumer behaviors, preferences, and attitudes through surveys, focus groups, and interviews. This direct pulse on current and potential customers offers invaluable insights into future market trends and the reception of new products or services. For FP&A professionals, integrating market research findings with financial projections ensures that forecasts are grounded in the realities of consumer demand.

Understanding the strategic moves of competitors is crucial for accurate financial forecasting. Competitor analysis provides a qualitative lens through which companies can anticipate potential market shifts, including new product launches, mergers, acquisitions, or changes in pricing strategies. By evaluating the strengths, weaknesses, opportunities, and threats (SWOT) associated with competitors, FP&A teams can craft more resilient and responsive financial plans.

The integration of qualitative forecasting methods into FP&A necessitates a balanced approach. While quantitative data offers a solid foundation, qualitative insights inject flexibility and responsiveness into financial forecasts. This blend allows companies to navigate the uncertainties of market conditions with greater agility and foresight.

For instance, a Vancouver-based tech startup, operating in the highly volatile field of renewable energy, may find quantitative data on past performance less indicative of future success. Here, qualitative methods like expert judgment and market research become invaluable, enabling the startup to anticipate market needs and align its product development accordingly.

Qualitative forecasting methods enrich the FP&A process, providing depth and context that numeric data alone cannot offer. By leveraging expert opinions, market research, and competitor analysis, finance professionals can formulate forecasts that are both insightful and adaptable. As the financial landscape continues to evolve, the integration of qualitative insights will remain a critical component in the toolkit of forward-thinking FP&A teams, guiding strategic decisions with a blend of precision and intuition.

Expert Judgment and the Delphi Method

The realms of expert judgment and the Delphi method emerge as quintessential facets within the financial forecasting domain. These methodologies, though steeped in qualitative analysis, offer a robust framework for navigating the unpredictable corridors of financial planning and analysis (FP&A). This segment elucidates leveraging expert judgment alongside the Delphi method, illustrating their symbiotic relationship in refining financial forecasts.

Expert judgment, as a forecasting technique, hinges on the insights garnered from individuals endowed with a deep understanding of specific markets, technologies, or trends. These experts draw upon their comprehensive experience, intuition, and knowledge to predict future financial outcomes. Unlike quantitative forecasting, which relies heavily on historical data, expert judgment leans into the nuanced understanding of potential market dynamics and the broader economic environment. It allows for a nuanced assessment of emerging trends, potential disruptions, and the subtle undercurrents that might influence financial landscapes.

The Delphi method, named after the ancient oracle of Delphi, is a systematic approach designed to harness the collective wisdom of a panel of experts. Through a series of rounds, experts provide forecasts and justifications anonymously. These responses are then aggregated and shared with the panel, prompting a re-evaluation of initial predictions in light of the group's insights. This iterative process continues until a consensus is reached or the divergence of opinions is adequately understood. The anonymity of the Delphi method helps mitigate the influence of dominant personalities, allowing for a more equitable and unbiased aggregation of expert opinions.

Incorporating expert judgment and the Delphi method into FP&A operations facilitates a more holistic approach to forecasting. For instance, when assessing the potential impact of a nascent technology on the market, quantitative data may be scant or non-existent. Here, the foresight derived from expert judgment becomes invaluable. By further employing the Delphi method, a company can distill these insights into a coherent forecast, refined through the lens of collective wisdom.

The integration of these methodologies enables FP&A professionals to chart a course through the uncertainty of market conditions with a higher degree of confidence. For example, in the dynamic landscape of digital currency, where traditional financial models struggle to predict long-term outcomes, the expert judgment of economists, combined with the iterative consensus-building of the Delphi method, can offer substantial foresight into future valuation and market acceptance.

Consider a scenario where an FP&A team at a multinational corporation is tasked with evaluating the financial implications of expanding into an emerging market. The volatile nature of this market, characterized by rapid policy changes and consumer preferences, makes quantitative analysis challenging. By assembling a panel of experts —ranging from local economists to cultural analysts—the team applies the Delphi method to refine its understanding. Through several rounds of deliberation, the experts converge on a set of projections that balance optimism with pragmatic caution, providing the FP&A team with a nuanced forecast to inform strategic decision-making.

Expert judgment and the Delphi method stand as pillars within the qualitative forecasting toolkit, offering depth, nuance, and a dynamic perspective to financial forecasting. By synthesizing the insights of seasoned experts through a structured, iterative process, FP&A teams can navigate the complexities of the financial landscape with enhanced precision and insight. As the business environment continues to evolve, the strategic deployment of these methodologies will remain indispensable in the quest for accurate, actionable financial forecasts.

Market Research as a Forecasting Tool

Market research, in its essence, is the systematic gathering, recording, and analyzing of data about issues relating to marketing products and services. The methodology encompasses both qualitative and quantitative research, providing a dual lens through which market dynamics can be viewed. Qualitative methods, such as focus groups and in-depth interviews, offer insights into consumer behavior, motivations, and preferences. Quantitative research, through surveys and analysis of statistical data, provides the empirical evidence needed to gauge market trends and consumer patterns.

The application of market research in financial forecasting is both an art and a science. It begins with the identification of market trends and consumer behaviors, which are then extrapolated to predict future market conditions. This predictive modeling is instrumental in developing strategies for product development, pricing, and distribution.

For instance, consider a scenario where a company aims to launch a new product line. Through market research, it identifies a growing trend towards sustainability among its target demographics. This insight becomes a cornerstone in forecasting demand for the new product, guiding the company in product design, positioning, and marketing strategies to align with consumer expectations towards sustainability.

Integrating Market Research into FP&A

The integration of market research into financial planning and analysis (FP&A) facilitates a grounded approach to forecasting.

It enables the synthesis of internal data with external market dynamics, offering a comprehensive view of potential financial outcomes. For FP&A professionals, market research sheds light on the external factors that could impact financial performance, including competitor activities, regulatory changes, and shifts in consumer behavior.

A practical application of this integration can be seen in budgeting processes. Market research informs revenue forecasts by providing insights into market size, growth rates, and market share opportunities. It also aids in risk assessment, enabling companies to identify potential challenges and opportunities in the marketplace, which could impact financial performance.

Case Study: Utilizing Market Research for Expansion Strategy

A retail company contemplating expansion into new geographic territories utilized market research to forecast potential success. Through a combination of demographic analysis, competitor analysis, and consumer behavior studies, the company gained a deep understanding of the new market. This research revealed a high demand for products aligned with local cultural preferences, not previously offered by competitors. Armed with these insights, the FP&A team developed financial models predicting the expansion's profitability, including anticipated revenue growth and market penetration rates. The forecasts derived from this market research were instrumental in securing board approval and investment for the expansion project.

Market research emerges not just as a tool for understanding the present but as a formidable instrument for predicting the future. It offers a foundation upon which robust financial forecasts can be built, taking into account the myriad factors that influence market dynamics. For FP&A professionals, the strategic application of market research in forecasting is indispensable. It not only enhances the accuracy of financial predictions but also informs strategic decision-making, ensuring that companies remain agile and responsive in the face of evolving market conditions.

Incorporating Competitor Analysis into Forecasts

Competitor analysis is the systematic investigation of rivals' strategies, strengths, weaknesses, and market positions. It serves as a strategic compass, guiding companies through the competitive landscape and enabling them to identify opportunities for differentiation and areas vulnerable to competition. In the context of financial forecasting, competitor analysis provides a panoramic view of the marketplace, offering insights that are crucial for making informed predictions about future financial trends and performance.

The incorporation of competitor analysis into financial forecasts enhances their accuracy and reliability. By understanding the competitive forces at play, FP&A professionals can better predict how changes in the market environment—such as a competitor launching a new product or altering its pricing strategy—will affect their company's financial performance. This insight allows for the adjustment of forecasts to reflect potential shifts in revenue, market share, and expenses.

Consider a scenario in which a competitor's investment in cutting-edge technology has the potential to disrupt the market. Through thorough competitor analysis, a company can forecast the impact of this technological advancement on its own operations and market position. This may lead to revising revenue projections downward or adjusting the marketing budget upwards to counter the competitive threat, thereby ensuring that the financial forecasts remain robust and reflective of market realities.

Methodologies for Incorporating Competitor Analysis into Forecasts

Incorporating competitor analysis into financial forecasts involves a multifaceted approach. It begins with gathering intelligence on competitors' financial health, market strategies, product offerings, and customer feedback. This intelligence can be derived from a variety of sources, including financial reports, industry conferences, market research firms, and customer surveys.

The next step is to analyze this data to discern patterns, trends, and strategic moves that could influence the market dynamics. Tools such as SWOT analysis (Strengths, Weaknesses, Opportunities, Threats) and Porter's Five Forces framework can be instrumental in this process, providing structured methodologies for evaluating competitive data and its potential impact on the company.

Case Study: Leveraging Competitor Analysis for Market Entry

A notable example of the power of incorporating competitor analysis into forecasts can be observed in the case of a technology firm evaluating entry into a new market segment. Through in-depth analysis of existing competitors in that segment, the firm identified a gap in the offerings where customer needs were not being fully met. This analysis included evaluating competitors' product features, pricing models, and customer service models. By integrating these insights into their financial forecasts, the FP&A team was able to project a strong demand for their new product, justify the required investment, and outline a competitive pricing strategy that leveraged the identified market gap. The forecasts not only supported the decision to enter the market but also provided a robust framework for tracking performance against expectations.

The integration of competitor analysis into financial forecasting is not merely a tactical move; it is a strategic imperative that enriches the forecasting process with a depth of market insight. It empowers FP&A professionals to anticipate competitive moves, adapt their strategies accordingly, and navigate their companies through the complexities of the marketplace with greater confidence and foresight. As markets continue to evolve at an unprecedented pace, the role of competitor analysis in forecasting will only magnify, becoming an indispensable tool in the arsenal of strategic planning.

Selecting the Right Tools for Forecasting

The landscape of forecasting tools spans a wide array of software and platforms, each with its unique capabilities, from traditional Excel-based models to sophisticated AI-driven analytical suites. The choice among these tools hinges on various factors including the complexity of the forecasting required, the volume of data processed, the need for real-time analytics, and the level of integration with other business systems.

An FP&A team must begin by cataloguing their specific

forecasting requirements—such as the frequency of forecasts (monthly, quarterly, rolling), the need for granular detail (product-level, department-level), and the scope of forecasts (cash flow, revenue, expenses). This preliminary assessment serves as a foundation for evaluating the suitability of forecasting tools against the company's needs.

Criteria for Tool Selection

1. Scalability: The ideal tool grows with your business, handling increased complexity and volume without a decline in performance.

2. Integration Capabilities: Seamless integration with existing ERP, CRM, and other data systems ensures that the tool can draw upon all relevant internal and external data sources, providing a holistic view for accurate forecasting.

3. User-friendliness: A tool that requires extensive training or specialised knowledge can be a barrier to widespread adoption. User-friendly interfaces and intuitive design facilitate broader engagement across departments.

4. Analytical Features: Look for advanced analytical capabilities, including scenario planning, sensitivity analysis, and predictive analytics, enabling deeper insights into future trends and potential risks.

5. Customization and Flexibility: The tool should allow for customization to accommodate unique business models, market conditions, and forecasting methodologies.

6. Cost-effectiveness: Evaluate the total cost of

HAYDEN VAN DER POST

ownership, including licensing, implementation, training, and maintenance. A cost-effective solution provides the right balance between features and affordability.

Case Study: Adopting an AI-Enhanced Forecasting Tool

A real-world illustration of selecting the right tool can be seen in the experience of a mid-sized retail chain facing rapid expansion. The company's existing Excel-based forecasting model was unable to keep pace with the growing complexity of its operations, leading to inaccuracies and missed opportunities. After a comprehensive evaluation process, the company chose a cloud-based forecasting tool enhanced with AI capabilities, known for its scalability and integration with their retail management system.

The new tool enabled the company to automate data collection from diverse sources, apply machine learning algorithms for predictive analysis, and easily simulate various business scenarios. The impact was immediate: forecasts became more accurate, strategic decisions were data-driven, and the company could dynamically adjust its financial strategies in real time, leading to a significant improvement in financial performance.

Selecting the right forecasting tools is a strategic endeavor that demands a thorough understanding of an organization's forecasting needs, a comprehensive evaluation of available options, and a keen eye for the tool's potential to drive strategic value. This process is not merely about upgrading technology; it's about empowering FP&A teams with the capabilities to foresee and shape the future trajectory of the business. As financial landscapes become increasingly complex and data-driven, the choice of forecasting tools will play a critical role in sustaining competitive advantage and driving business success.

Software Solutions for FP&A Forecasting

In financial planning and analysis (FP&A), the adoption of robust software solutions is not just a matter of technological upgrade but a strategic imperative. This segment meticulously examines the various software solutions pivotal for sculpting the future of FP&A forecasting. It delves into the core functionalities, inherent advantages, and potential limitations of these technologies, offering a compass to navigate through the myriad of options available in the market.

Exploring the Spectrum of FP&A Software Solutions

The spectrum of FP&A software solutions ranges from generalized platforms designed for broad business intelligence purposes to specialized tools crafted explicitly for financial forecasting. These solutions are engineered to tackle the multifaceted challenges in financial forecasting, including data aggregation from disparate sources, complex analytical computations, and the presentation of forecasts in a digestible format for stakeholders.

1. Generalized FP&A Platforms: These platforms offer a suite of tools encompassing budgeting, planning, forecasting, and reporting. Solutions like Oracle Hyperion, SAP BPC, and IBM Planning Analytics are renowned for their comprehensive capabilities, facilitating a unified approach to financial management. They excel in integrating financial data from across the enterprise, providing a singular truth source.

2. Specialized Forecasting Tools: Tailored to address specific

aspects of the forecasting process, these tools, such as Anaplan or Adaptive Insights, focus on leveraging advanced analytics, machine learning, and scenario modeling to enhance forecast accuracy. They offer flexibility and agility in updating forecasts, adapting to changes in real-time.

3. Business Intelligence (BI) Tools: BI tools like Tableau, Power BI, and Qlik Sense, although not exclusive to FP&A, play a crucial role in the forecasting process. They excel in data visualization and interactive dashboards, enabling finance professionals to derive actionable insights from complex datasets.

Core Functionalities to Look for in FP&A Software

- Data Integration and Management: Capabilities to seamlessly aggregate and manage data from various internal and external sources are fundamental. This ensures that the forecasting process is based on a comprehensive dataset, enhancing accuracy and reliability.

- Advanced Analytics and Modeling: forecasting lies in predictive analytics and modeling. Tools that offer sophisticated algorithms and the flexibility to construct custom models are invaluable. They enable finance teams to explore multiple scenarios and assess potential outcomes.

- Collaborative Workflows: Forecasting is inherently a collaborative process involving stakeholders from various departments. Software that facilitates collaborative workflows and integrates comments, assumptions, and adjustments in real-time can significantly streamline the forecasting process.

- Scalability and Customization: As organizations grow and

evolve, so do their forecasting needs. Solutions that are scalable and customizable allow businesses to adapt their forecasting processes without the need for frequent platform changes.

Choosing the Right Software: A Strategic Decision

Selecting the appropriate software for FP&A forecasting is a decision that goes beyond comparing features and prices. It requires a strategic evaluation of how well a solution aligns with the company's specific forecasting needs, integrates with existing systems, and supports the organization's long-term financial strategy.

Consideration must also be given to the vendor's reputation, the quality of customer support, and the community or ecosystem surrounding the product. A vibrant user community can be a rich resource for best practices, templates, and troubleshooting.

Implementing Software Solutions: A Roadmap to Success

The implementation of FP&A software is a transformative project that demands meticulous planning and execution. Key steps include:

- Defining Clear Objectives: Establishing clear goals for what the organization seeks to achieve with the new software is crucial. This guides the selection process and ensures that the chosen solution meets the identified needs.

- Stakeholder Engagement: Engaging stakeholders from across the organization ensures that the software accommodates the needs of all users and benefits the entire business.

- Pilot Testing: Conducting a pilot test with a select group of users can provide valuable insights into the software's performance and user experience before a full-scale rollout.

- Training and Support: Comprehensive training and ongoing support are essential to maximize the benefits of the new software. Users need to feel confident and proficient in leveraging the tool's capabilities.

Selecting and implementing the right software solution is a pivotal step towards achieving more accurate, efficient, and dynamic forecasting. It is a strategic investment that empowers finance teams to navigate through the uncertainties of the future with confidence, armed with insights and foresight to drive business growth and resilience. As the financial landscape continues to evolve, embracing the right software solutions in FP&A forecasting becomes not just an option but a necessity for maintaining a competitive edge.

Custom-built vs. Off-the-shelf Tools

Custom-built software solutions in FP&A are akin to crafting a bespoke suit. They are designed from the ground up to fit the specific contours of an organization's requirements, processes, and data ecosystems. These solutions offer a high degree of flexibility and can provide a competitive edge through unique features that are closely aligned with the company's strategic objectives.

- Advantages: The most compelling advantage is the tailor-made design, which ensures that every feature and functionality serves a precise purpose. Custom solutions can integrate seamlessly with existing systems, offering a unified platform that enhances data integrity and workflow efficiency. They also offer scalability and adaptability, evolving in tandem with the organization's growth and changing needs.

- Drawbacks: The bespoke nature of custom-built solutions comes with a higher price tag, both in terms of initial development costs and ongoing maintenance. The development timeline is also longer, requiring a significant investment of time from internal teams. Moreover, the organization becomes reliant on the original developers or an in-house team for updates, potentially leading to challenges in knowledge transfer and sustainability.

Off-the-shelf Software: Ready-to-wear Versatility

Off-the-shelf FP&A tools are pre-developed software solutions designed to meet the general needs of a wide range of businesses. These tools are ready for immediate deployment, offering a quick and cost-effective way to enhance forecasting capabilities.

- Advantages: The primary advantage lies in the immediacy and cost-effectiveness. Off-the-shelf solutions are less expensive upfront and can be deployed rapidly, allowing organizations to benefit from advanced forecasting capabilities without a protracted development phase. These solutions also come with vendor support, updates, and a community of users, providing a wealth of resources for troubleshooting and optimization.

- Drawbacks: The main limitation is the lack of customization. Off-the-shelf solutions may not perfectly align with an organization's unique processes or data structures, potentially leading to compromises in functionality. Additionally, while these tools are scalable, they may not offer the same level of flexibility as custom-built solutions, potentially requiring additional investments in supplementary tools or customizations to bridge gaps in functionality.

Guiding the Decision: Strategic Considerations

Choosing between custom-built and off-the-shelf FP&A tools is not a decision to be taken lightly. It requires a balanced consideration of several factors:

- Strategic Alignment: The choice should reflect the organization's strategic vision and forecasting objectives. Custom-built solutions may be warranted if unique functionality or integration capabilities are critical to achieving strategic goals.

- Cost-Benefit Analysis: A thorough analysis of the total cost of ownership, including development, maintenance, and opportunity costs, should inform the decision. The potential return on investment from enhanced forecasting capabilities must justify the costs involved.

- Flexibility and Scalability: The organization's growth trajectory and the potential evolution of its forecasting needs should be considered. The chosen solution should support scalability and adaptability to future requirements.

- Implementation Timeline: The urgency of the organization's forecasting enhancement needs should be weighed against the development timeline for custom solutions. Off-the-shelf tools offer a quicker path to deployment but may require compromises in fit and functionality.

The dichotomy between custom-built and off-the-shelf FP&A tools embodies a pivotal strategic decision for organizations aiming to enhance their forecasting prowess. By meticulously weighing the advantages and drawbacks of each option against their unique requirements and strategic objectives, organizations can chart a course towards a more informed, agile, and effective forecasting future. This decision not only influences the immediate efficiency and effectiveness of FP&A functions but also shapes the organization's ability to navigate the uncertainties of the financial landscape with confidence and precision.

Integrating Forecasting Tools with Other Business Systems

The power of FP&A lies not just in predicting future financial outcomes but in synthesizing a vast array of data across various business functions to inform those predictions. Integration ensures that forecasting tools don't operate in isolation but act as a nexus that brings together data from sales, marketing, operations, and human resources, among others. This holistic approach enables more accurate, timely, and actionable forecasts.

- Data Cohesion and Integrity: Integration facilitates the automatic flow of data across systems, eliminating manual data entry and the associated risks of errors and discrepancies. It ensures that the forecasting tools have access to real-time, consistent, and accurate data, enhancing the quality of the forecasts.

- Efficiency and Productivity: By automating data flows, integration streamlines processes, reduces the time spent on data consolidation, and allows the FP&A team to focus on analysis and strategy rather than data management.

- Agility and Responsiveness: In today's fast-paced business environment, the ability to rapidly adapt forecasts in response to internal changes or external market dynamics is crucial. Integration ensures that forecasting tools can immediately incorporate the latest data, facilitating swift decision-making.

Methodologies for Successful Integration

Integrating forecasting tools with other business systems requires careful planning, execution, and ongoing management. Here are key methodologies to ensure successful integration:

- Comprehensive Needs Assessment: Begin with a thorough assessment of the current and future data needs of the forecasting process. Understand which business systems hold relevant data and how this data impacts forecasting accuracy and relevance.

- Selection of Integration-Friendly Tools: Opt for forecasting and business systems that offer robust integration capabilities, including APIs and standard data exchange formats. Compatibility is key to reducing the complexity and cost of integration efforts.

- Data Governance Framework: Establish a data governance framework that defines data ownership, quality standards, and data sharing protocols. This framework is essential for maintaining the integrity and security of data across integrated systems.

- Phased Implementation Approach: Implement integration in phases, starting with the most critical data flows. This approach allows for the identification and resolution of issues with minimal impact on business operations.

- Continuous Monitoring and Optimization: Post-integration, continuously monitor the data flows and system performance to identify any issues or bottlenecks. Regularly review the integration architecture to optimize it for new business requirements or system updates.

Integrating forecasting tools with other business systems is a pivotal strategy for organizations striving for excellence in financial planning and analysis. This integration transcends technical execution, embodying a strategic alignment of business functions towards a unified goal of informed decision-making and strategic foresight. Through meticulous planning, careful selection of tools, and ongoing management, organizations can harness the full potential of integrated FP&A tools to navigate the complexities of the business landscape with agility and confidence. The journey towards integration may be complex, yet the rewards in terms of enhanced forecasting accuracy, operational efficiency, and strategic agility are profound, marking a significant step towards achieving a competitive advantage in the dynamic world of business.

CHAPTER 3: BUILDING A FORECASTING FRAMEWORK

F orecasting objectives serve as the guiding star for the entire forecasting process. They provide clarity on what the organization aims to achieve through its forecasting efforts, be it financial stability, resource optimization, risk mitigation, or guiding strategic decisions. Specificity in these objectives is crucial; vague goals lead to unfocused efforts that seldom yield actionable insights.

- Alignment with Strategic Goals: The primary objective of forecasting should be in harmony with the organization's strategic goals. Whether it's achieving a certain market share, revenue target, or cost reduction, the forecasting objectives should directly contribute to these broader goals.

- Realism and Achievability: Objectives need to be grounded in reality, taking into account the organization's capabilities, market conditions, and historical performance. Unrealistic goals set the stage for failure and disillusionment with the forecasting process.

- Measurability: Each objective should be quantifiable. Setting measurable targets enables the organization to track progress and make necessary adjustments.

Despite the apparent simplicity, setting forecasting objectives is often fraught with challenges:

- Complex Business Environments: In today's volatile market conditions, identifying objectives that are both ambitious and achievable can be daunting. The rapid pace of change makes it difficult to predict future conditions with certainty.

- Interdepartmental Alignments: Different departments may have divergent goals, making it challenging to establish a set of objectives that aligns with the overall strategic direction of the company.

- Data Limitations: The availability and quality of historical data can restrict the ability to set informed objectives. Incomplete or inaccurate data leads to misguided goals.

Strategies for Overcoming Challenges

- Broad Stakeholder Engagement: Involving a wide range of stakeholders in the objective-setting process ensures that multiple perspectives are considered, leading to objectives that are both comprehensive and aligned across departments.

- Scenario Planning: Engaging in scenario planning allows organizations to explore various future states and set objectives that are flexible and adaptable. This approach is particularly useful in uncertain or rapidly changing environments.

- Investing in Data Management: Enhancing the organization's capabilities in data collection, processing, and analysis can significantly improve the quality of information available for setting objectives.

- Continuous Review and Adaptation: Forecasting objectives should not be static. Regular reviews and adaptations in response to new information or changes in the business environment ensure that the objectives remain relevant and achievable.

Setting precise and aligned forecasting objectives is foundational to the success of any FP&A function. These objectives not only direct the forecasting process but also ensure that it is strategically focused and capable of driving informed decision-making. Overcoming the challenges in setting these objectives requires a deliberate approach, characterized by stakeholder engagement, flexibility, and a strong data foundation. With clear, realistic, and measurable objectives, organizations can harness the full power of forecasting to navigate the complexities of the business world, making informed decisions that drive strategic success.

Aligning with Strategic Business Goals

Strategic business goals define where an organization intends to go and how it plans to get there. These goals can range from expanding market share, driving innovation, enhancing customer satisfaction, to achieving sustainability targets. The clarity and specificity of these goals are paramount, as they lay the groundwork for alignment.

- Identifying Core Objectives: The first step is to clearly understand the organization's long-term objectives and the key drivers of its success. This involves profound discussions with senior leadership and a thorough analysis of the company's strategic plan.

- Breaking Down Goals: Once the overarching goals are identified, the next step involves breaking them down into smaller, actionable objectives. This makes it easier to see how forecasting can directly support each goal.

The Process of Alignment

Aligning forecasting with strategic business goals is not a one-time activity but a continuous process that evolves with the strategic direction of the organization.

- Developing a Collaborative Framework: The FP&A team must work closely with strategy and operations teams to ensure that their forecasting models incorporate the latest strategic insights and objectives. This collaborative approach ensures that forecasts reflect the strategic nuances of the organization's goals.

- Customizing Forecasting Models: To align with specific strategic goals, it may be necessary to customize forecasting models. This could mean adjusting the models to focus on particular business segments, geographies, or product lines that are central to the company's strategy.

- Scenario Analysis: Employing scenario analysis helps in

examining how different strategic choices, under varying market conditions, could affect the organization's future. This is crucial for aligning forecasts with the dynamic nature of strategic planning.

Challenges to Alignment

The journey towards perfect alignment is fraught with challenges, each requiring careful navigation.

- Evolving Strategies: Business strategies are not static; they evolve in response to internal and external pressures. The FP&A team must remain agile, updating forecasts to reflect these changes.

- Data Silos: Organizational data silos can hinder the flow of information between departments, making it difficult to align forecasts with strategic goals. Breaking down these silos through integrated data management systems is critical.

- Communication Gaps: Effective alignment requires seamless communication channels between the FP&A team and strategic decision-makers. Overcoming communication barriers is essential for ensuring that forecasts are in sync with strategic objectives.

Strategies for Effective Alignment

- Regular Strategy Reviews: Regular reviews of the strategic plan and its objectives ensure that the FP&A team's efforts remain aligned with the company's direction.

- Integrated Planning Processes: An integrated planning

process, where strategic planning and FP&A are tightly woven, ensures alignment across all levels of the organization.

- Leveraging Technology: Advanced analytics and forecasting tools can provide deeper insights and foster a more dynamic alignment with strategic goals.

Aligning forecasting with strategic business goals is a vital process that ensures FP&A efforts drive meaningful outcomes. Through a combination of understanding, collaboration, and continuous adjustment, organizations can ensure that their forecasting activities are not just numbers on a spreadsheet but are strategic assets that propel the company towards its desired future. This alignment not only enhances the strategic value of the FP&A function but also strengthens the organization's ability to navigate uncertainties, making informed decisions that uphold its strategic vision.

Tailoring Forecasts to Stakeholder Needs

The journey towards effective tailoring begins with a deep dive into understanding the unique needs and concerns of each stakeholder group.

- Segmenting Stakeholders: Categorizing stakeholders based on their interest and influence over the organization helps in prioritizing efforts. A dynamic matrix categorizing stakeholders into high interest-high influence, high interest-low influence, etc., can be a strategic tool in this endeavour.

- Engaging in Dialogue: Direct engagement with stakeholders through interviews, surveys, and meetings is invaluable. It uncovers the specific information they prioritize, the format they prefer, and the frequency at which they need updates.

- Analyzing Historical Interactions: Reviewing past interactions and feedback from stakeholders can provide insights into their preferences and expectations, guiding the customization of forecasts.

Customization Strategies

With a clear understanding of stakeholder needs, FP&A professionals can proceed to tailor forecasts in ways that maximize their utility and relevance.

- Adjusting the Level of Detail: Different stakeholders require different levels of detail. For example, while operational managers may need granular forecasts at the department level, board members might prefer high-level summaries. Tailoring the granularity of information to suit these needs is crucial.

- Varying the Forecast Horizon: The time horizon of forecasts can significantly impact their usefulness. Strategic investors may look for long-term projections, whereas operational teams might need short-term forecasts to manage day-to-day decisions.

- Scenario Planning: Offering multiple scenarios tailored to the strategic interests of different stakeholder groups can provide a comprehensive view of potential futures. This includes best-case, worst-case, and most likely scenarios, offering a spectrum of possibilities for consideration.

Leveraging Technology for Customization

Advanced technological tools play a pivotal role in enabling the customization of forecasts.

- Data Visualization Tools: Utilizing data visualization software to create interactive and customizable dashboards allows stakeholders to explore the data in ways that are most meaningful to them.

- Automated Reporting Systems: These systems can generate tailored reports for different stakeholder groups at predefined intervals, ensuring timely and relevant information delivery.

- Collaborative Forecasting Platforms: Platforms that allow for real-time collaboration can enable stakeholders to provide immediate feedback, which can be incorporated into the forecasts, enhancing their relevance and accuracy.

Challenges in Tailoring Forecasts

While the benefits of tailoring forecasts are clear, several challenges may arise.

- Resource Constraints: Customizing forecasts to meet the needs of all stakeholder groups can be resource-intensive. Prioritizing based on the strategic value of each stakeholder group can help mitigate this.

- Maintaining Consistency: Ensuring that customized forecasts remain consistent and do not present conflicting views of the future is essential. This requires a strong governance framework and robust data management practices.

- Overcoming Complexity: The complexity of managing multiple customized forecasts can be daunting. Streamlining processes through technology and clear protocols is crucial.

The ability to tailor forecasts to stakeholder needs significantly enhances the strategic value of the FP&A function. It ensures that forecasts serve as a bridge between the organization's strategic vision and the operational realities of different stakeholders. By embracing a structured approach to understanding and meeting these diverse needs, FP&A professionals can transform forecasts into strategic tools that drive informed decision-making across the organization. This alignment not only bolsters stakeholder confidence but also propels the organization closer to achieving its overarching goals, making the task of customization not just a tactical choice, but a strategic imperative.

Setting Up Measurable Targets

Measurable targets are designed to embody the strategic objectives of an organization in quantifiable terms. They serve multiple purposes:

- Guidance: They provide a clear direction for operational and strategic planning.

- Performance Measurement: They enable the evaluation of organizational performance against predefined benchmarks.

- Motivation: They serve as motivational tools for teams, aligning their efforts towards common goals.

The Process of Setting Measurable Targets

The process of setting measurable targets involves several critical steps:

- Strategic Alignment: Initially, it is imperative that targets are aligned with the organization's strategic goals. This alignment ensures that the efforts are directed towards the overarching objectives of the company.

- Benchmarking and Historical Analysis: Examining past performance and industry benchmarks provides a foundation for setting realistic and challenging targets. This step involves detailed data analysis and may leverage predictive analytics to inform target setting.

- Stakeholder Involvement: Engaging with stakeholders is crucial to setting targets that are not only challenging but also achievable and relevant. This involves discussions with department heads, executives, and sometimes, external stakeholders.

- SMART Criteria: Targets should adhere to the SMART criteria —Specific, Measurable, Achievable, Relevant, and Time-bound. This framework ensures that targets are well-defined and capable of being assessed objectively.

Incorporating Flexibility and Contingencies

While the importance of setting firm targets cannot be overstated, incorporating flexibility into these targets is crucial. Markets are dynamic, and unforeseen challenges can arise. Flexibility might involve setting ranges instead of absolute figures or incorporating regular review periods to adjust targets as necessary.

Leveraging Technology for Target Setting and Tracking

Modern FP&A relies heavily on sophisticated software and tools for setting and tracking measurable targets:

- Forecasting Software: Advanced forecasting software can aid in setting more accurate and realistic targets by analyzing vast datasets and identifying trends that inform future performance.

- Performance Tracking Dashboards: Dashboards provide real-time insights into performance against targets, enabling timely adjustments and interventions.

- Collaborative Platforms: These platforms enhance the setting and monitoring of targets by fostering communication and collaboration across departments.

Metrics to Consider

Setting up measurable targets involves the selection of appropriate metrics. These might include financial metrics like revenue growth, profit margins, and cash flow, or operational metrics like customer acquisition costs, employee productivity, and inventory turnover. The choice of metrics should reflect the strategic priorities of the organization and the specific objectives of different departments.

Challenges in Setting Measurable Targets

- Overambitious Targets: Setting targets that are overly ambitious can demotivate teams and lead to frustration.

- Underestimating Complexity: Failing to account for the complexity of achieving certain targets can result in resources being stretched too thin.

- Data Integrity: The effectiveness of targets depends on the quality of the data used to set them. Ensuring data integrity is paramount.

The establishment of measurable targets is a critical exercise that requires a careful balance between ambition and realism. It demands a deep understanding of the strategic objectives of an organization, a rigorous analysis of data, and an appreciation for the dynamics of the market. When executed effectively, measurable targets can propel an organization towards its strategic goals, ensuring that every effort contributes to the broader vision of success. In the landscape of FP&A, the ability to set, track, and adjust measurable targets distinguishes leading organizations from their competitors, driving them towards excellence and sustainable growth.

Creating a Forecasting Process

A forecasting process is its strategic underpinning. This foundational step ensures that the forecasting process is not an isolated exercise but is intrinsically linked to the strategic imperatives of the organization. It begins with a clear articulation of the organizational goals and the role of forecasting in achieving these objectives. Whether it's driving revenue growth, managing capital expenditure, or mitigating financial risks, the forecasting process must be tailored to serve these strategic ends.

Step-by-Step Development of the Forecasting Process

1. Data Collection and Management: The bedrock of any forecasting process is the data. This step involves identifying, collecting, and managing data from various sources, including historical performance data, industry benchmarks, and market analysis. The quality and integrity of data are paramount, necessitating stringent data management practices.

2. Methodological Selection: The next step involves selecting appropriate forecasting models and techniques. This selection is influenced by the nature of the data, the forecasting horizon, and the specific goals of the forecasting exercise. Techniques may range from quantitative methods, such as time series analysis and regression models, to qualitative methods, like expert judgment and scenario analysis.

3. Forecast Generation: With data and methodologies in place, the next phase is the generation of forecasts. This involves applying the chosen models to the data, adjusting for seasonality, trends, and cyclical patterns. Advanced forecasting software and tools play a crucial role in this step, offering sophisticated algorithms and computational power to process large datasets and generate accurate forecasts.

4. Validation and Adjustment: A critical, often overlooked step is the validation of forecasts. This involves comparing forecasts against actual outcomes to assess accuracy and making necessary adjustments to models and assumptions. Validation is an ongoing process, essential for refining the accuracy of forecasts over time.

5. Integration and Communication: The final step in the forecasting process is the integration of forecasts into the decision-making framework of the organization and communicating these insights to stakeholders. Effective communication is crucial, involving clear, concise, and actionable insights tailored to the needs of different stakeholders, from executive leadership to operational teams.

Incorporating Technology and Tools

The advent of advanced technologies has profoundly transformed the forecasting process. Artificial Intelligence (AI) and Machine Learning (ML) algorithms offer the capability to process and analyze vast amounts of data, identify patterns, and generate forecasts with a level of accuracy and efficiency unimaginable a few decades ago. The integration of these technologies into the forecasting process is not optional but a necessity in the contemporary data-driven landscape.

Cross-Functional Collaboration

A forecasting process does not operate in a silo. It requires the collaboration and input of various departments within the organization, from finance and operations to marketing and sales. This cross-functional engagement ensures that the forecasting process benefits from diverse perspectives and expertise, enhancing the relevance and accuracy of forecasts.

Challenges and Considerations

- Adapting to Change: One of the most significant challenges in creating a forecasting process is the dynamic nature of business environments. The process must be adaptable, capable of incorporating new data and adjusting to changing market conditions.

- Complexity Management: Balancing the complexity of forecasting models and techniques with the need for actionable insights can be challenging. Overly complex models may offer precision but at the cost of usability and interpretability.

Creating a forecasting process is a strategic endeavor that demands careful planning, a deep understanding of organizational goals, and a judicious selection of methodologies and technologies. It is a continuous cycle of data management, forecast generation, validation, and integration, underpinned by cross-functional collaboration and a steadfast commitment to strategic objectives. When meticulously executed, the forecasting process becomes a powerful tool in the arsenal of FP&A, driving informed decision-making and strategic agility.

Steps for Developing a Forecasting Model

The journey of constructing a forecasting model begins with a clear understanding of its purpose. This initial phase is crucial as it sets the direction and scope of the entire modeling process. It involves defining the objectives of the forecast, such as understanding revenue drivers, anticipating market trends, or assessing the impact of strategic decisions. By anchoring the model to specific goals, organizations can ensure relevance and focus in their forecasting efforts.

1. Data Exploration and Preparation

Data serves as the lifeblood of any forecasting model. This

stage involves an exhaustive exploration of available data sources, both internal and external to the organization. Internal data might include historical sales figures, customer interactions, and operational metrics, while external data could encompass market trends, economic indicators, and competitive intelligence.

- Cleaning and Normalization: Data often comes in disparate formats and quality levels. It is imperative to clean and normalize the data, addressing missing values, outliers, and inconsistencies to ensure accuracy and reliability in the forecasts.

- Feature Selection: Not all data points are relevant to every forecast. This step involves identifying and selecting the most predictive features that influence the forecast's objectives, a process that requires both statistical techniques and domain expertise.

2. Choosing the Right Forecasting Method

Forecasting methods can be broadly categorized into quantitative and qualitative approaches. The choice of method depends on various factors, including the nature of the data, the forecast horizon, and the level of detail required.

- Quantitative Methods: These include statistical models like ARIMA (AutoRegressive Integrated Moving Average) for time series forecasting and regression models for identifying relationships between variables. Machine learning techniques, such as neural networks and decision trees, offer sophisticated options for capturing complex patterns in large data sets.

- Qualitative Methods: When quantitative data is scarce

or the forecasting focus is on new products or markets, qualitative methods like the Delphi method or expert panels become invaluable. These methods leverage the insights and judgments of experts to generate forecasts.

3. Model Construction

With the data prepared and the forecasting method selected, the next step is constructing the model. This involves:

- Developing Hypotheses: Based on the data and the objective, hypotheses about potential outcomes are developed. These serve as the foundation for the model's structure.

- Algorithm Selection and Training: For quantitative models, this step involves selecting the appropriate algorithms and training them on the data. Training involves adjusting the model's parameters until it can accurately predict the desired outcome.

- Integration of Qualitative Insights: For models incorporating qualitative methods, this step involves synthesizing the insights from experts or market research into the model, often in the form of adjustments or factors.

4. Testing and Validation

Before a forecasting model can be deployed, it must be rigorously tested and validated to ensure its accuracy and robustness.

- Backtesting: By applying the model to historical data and comparing the forecasts with actual outcomes, analysts can assess the model's accuracy and make necessary adjustments.

- Sensitivity Analysis: This involves testing how changes in the model's inputs affect its outputs, which helps in understanding the model's reliability under various scenarios.

5. Implementation and Continuous Improvement

The final step is implementing the forecasting model within the organization's decision-making processes. This requires not only technical integration but also ensuring that stakeholders understand and trust the model's forecasts.

Continuous improvement is a hallmark of successful forecasting models. As new data becomes available and as the business and its environment evolve, the model should be regularly reviewed and refined. This iterative process ensures that the model remains aligned with the organization's strategic objectives and continues to provide valuable insights.

Developing a forecasting model is a meticulous and iterative process that requires a careful balance of statistical techniques, domain expertise, and strategic vision. By following these steps, organizations can create powerful tools that turn data into actionable insights, guiding them through the uncertainties of the future with confidence.

Collaboration Across Departments

The inception of effective collaboration begins with the

recognition that forecasting is not an isolated function of the finance department but a strategic tool that necessitates insights from across the organizational spectrum. Sales, marketing, operations, and human resources—all harbor valuable data and perspectives that can significantly enrich the forecasting model.

- Establishing Cross-Functional Teams: Creating teams that draw members from various departments ensures a holistic approach to forecasting. These teams can work on specific aspects of the forecast, contributing diverse data and insights that lead to a more comprehensive understanding of the factors at play.

- Communication Platforms and Tools: Leveraging technology to facilitate communication among cross-functional teams is crucial. Platforms that allow real-time collaboration and data sharing can dramatically enhance efficiency and coherence in developing forecasts.

Strategies for Enhancing Collaboration

Enhancing collaboration across departments requires deliberate strategies that align interests and facilitate seamless interaction.

- Shared Goals and Objectives: Ensuring that all departments understand how their inputs contribute to the organization's strategic goals can foster a sense of purpose and unity. This alignment encourages departments to share data and insights more openly and constructively.

- Regular Interdepartmental Meetings: Scheduled meetings, workshops, or seminars that bring together representatives from different departments can be instrumental in building relationships and understanding the forecasting needs and challenges from various perspectives.

- Recognition and Incentives: Recognizing and rewarding departments and individuals that contribute significantly to the forecasting efforts can motivate ongoing participation and support. Incentives can be aligned with the achievement of forecast accuracy, the contribution of innovative ideas, or the demonstration of exceptional collaborative spirit.

Overcoming Challenges in Collaboration

While the benefits of interdepartmental collaboration are manifold, organizations often encounter hurdles in its implementation.

- Cultural Barriers: Organizational silos and a lack of a collaborative culture can impede effective cross-departmental cooperation. Overcoming these barriers requires leadership commitment to fostering an open, inclusive, and cooperative organizational culture.

- Differing Priorities and Perspectives: Departments often operate with their own set of priorities and may have differing views on what constitutes relevant data for forecasting purposes. Bridging these differences requires clear communication, negotiation, and sometimes mediation to ensure that the collective goal of accurate and meaningful forecasting is not lost.

Implementing Best Practices

Certain best practices can significantly enhance the efficacy of interdepartmental collaboration in forecasting.

- Designated Liaisons: Appointing individuals from each department to act as liaisons can streamline communication and ensure that all departments have a voice in the forecasting process. These liaisons can gather and relay information, facilitate discussions, and serve as points of contact for their respective departments.

- Collaborative Forecasting Tools: Investing in forecasting tools that allow for input and access across departments can democratize the forecasting process. These tools can provide a platform for sharing data, assumptions, and scenarios, ensuring that the forecast is a collective effort reflective of the organization's comprehensive insights.

- Feedback and Continuous Improvement Loops: Establishing mechanisms for feedback on the forecasting process from all stakeholders can reveal insights into improving collaboration. Continuous improvement loops, where feedback is regularly solicited, reviewed, and acted upon, can drive the evolution of more effective collaborative practices over time.

Collaboration across departments is not merely a beneficial enhancement to the forecasting process; it is a critical component of its success. By breaking down silos and fostering a culture of shared goals and open communication, organizations can leverage the full spectrum of their collective knowledge and insights. This collaborative spirit, cultivated with intention and nurtured over time, transforms forecasting from a financial obligation into a strategic asset that propels the organization forward with clarity and confidence.

Regular Review and Adjustment of Forecasts

Forecasting, by its nature, is based on assumptions that hold true at the moment of their creation. However, as time progresses, these assumptions may no longer align with reality due to a myriad of factors such as economic shifts, competitive actions, technological advancements, or changes in consumer behavior. Regular reviews serve as checkpoints to reassess these assumptions and adjust forecasts accordingly.

- Scheduled Forecast Reviews: Instituting a regular schedule for forecast reviews is crucial. These reviews can be monthly, quarterly, or semi-annually, depending on the volatility of the industry and the speed at which the organization operates.

- Trigger Events for Ad-hoc Reviews: Besides scheduled reviews, it is also important to identify trigger events that necessitate an ad-hoc forecast review. Such events could include significant market shifts, mergers and acquisitions, regulatory changes, or unexpected competitive moves.

Adjustment Methodologies

The process of adjusting forecasts involves a blend of art and science, requiring analytical rigor alongside seasoned intuition.

- Scenario Analysis: Regularly revisiting and updating scenario analyses can provide a broader range of potential future outcomes, enabling more agile adjustments to forecasts. Incorporating new data and insights into these scenarios ensures they remain relevant.

- Sensitivity Analysis: Utilizing sensitivity analysis to understand how changes in key assumptions impact the forecast can guide adjustments. This analysis helps identify which variables have the most significant effect on the forecast outcome, prioritizing them for close monitoring.

- Rolling Forecasts: Transitioning to a rolling forecast model can enhance flexibility. Unlike static forecasts, rolling forecasts extend periodically, adding a new forecasting period (e.g., month, quarter) as the current period concludes, keeping the forecast perpetually fresh and reflective of the latest data.

The Role of Technology in Review and Adjustment

Advancements in technology have profoundly impacted the review and adjustment of forecasts, making the process more efficient and data-driven.

- Forecasting Software: Modern forecasting tools and software can automate much of the data collection and analysis process, providing real-time insights that inform forecast adjustments. These tools can also facilitate scenario and sensitivity analyses through intuitive interfaces.

- Artificial Intelligence and Machine Learning: AI and ML technologies can predict trends and patterns that might not be immediately apparent. Incorporating these technologies into the forecasting process can lead to more accurate adjustments by uncovering hidden insights in vast datasets.

Best Practices for Effective Review and Adjustment

To maximize the efficacy of forecast reviews and adjustments, several best practices should be observed.

- Documenting Assumptions: Clearly documenting the assumptions underlying each forecast at the time of its creation provides a benchmark against which to measure changes. This practice aids in understanding why adjustments are necessary and the impact of those adjustments.

- Engaging Cross-functional Teams: Involving representatives from various departments in the review process ensures a comprehensive perspective on factors that might necessitate forecast adjustments. This cross-functional engagement promotes a more accurate and holistic view of the organization's position.

- Feedback Loops: Establishing feedback loops that allow for the continual refinement of forecasting methodologies based on past accuracies and inaccuracies can significantly improve the quality of future forecasts.

The regular review and adjustment of forecasts are not merely administrative tasks but strategic imperatives that keep an organization's financial navigation aligned with the realities of a fluctuating business environment. By institutionalizing this process and leveraging technological advancements, organizations can enhance the accuracy of their forecasts, ensuring they are always steering the right course towards their financial objectives. This practice, rooted in diligence and foresight, transforms forecasting from a static snapshot into a dynamic, evolving vista of the organization's financial future.

Challenges in Forecasting

One of the paramount challenges in forecasting is the quality and availability of data. In an era where data is heralded as the new oil, the irony lies in the frequent encounters with either data droughts or floods. Data drought pertains to scenarios where critical financial data is scarce or outdated, making accurate forecasting a Herculean task. Conversely, a data flood involves being inundated with massive volumes of data, where the challenge is to sift through and identify what is relevant for forecasting purposes. For instance, a Vancouver-based technology startup, aiming to scale operations globally, found itself struggling to consolidate financial data from various international markets. The data, mired in inconsistencies due to differences in market regulations and economic conditions, posed a significant hurdle in creating a unified, accurate forecast.

Moreover, the inherent uncertainty of economic conditions magnifies the complexity of forecasting. Economic indicators such as inflation rates, currency fluctuations, and interest rates are perpetually in flux, influenced by a myriad of factors including geopolitical tensions, global pandemics, and technological advancements. Consider the impact of the unexpected Brexit vote or the unforeseen global pandemic on currency volatility. These events underscore the precariousness of economic forecasting and the need for FP&A professionals to constantly update their models in response to changing global conditions.

Another considerable challenge is differentiating forecasting from budgeting. While closely related, these two processes serve distinct purposes. Budgeting is about setting financial targets and allocating resources to meet those targets, often based on historical data. Forecasting, on the other hand, is a forward-looking process, predicting future financial outcomes based on current data and trends. The conflation of the two often leads to strategic missteps. A classic example would be a business that rigidly adheres to its budgeting figures without adjusting its forecast in response to a sudden market downturn, potentially missing out on critical adjustments to its expenditure and investment strategies.

The advent of sophisticated forecasting tools and techniques, while beneficial, also presents its own set of challenges. The selection and implementation of the right tools—be it traditional statistical methods, machine learning algorithms, or scenario planning software—require a deep understanding of not only the tools themselves but also the specific forecasting needs of the organization. A misalignment here can lead to wasted resources and suboptimal forecasts. For example, deploying a complex machine learning model in a scenario where simple exponential smoothing would suffice can unnecessarily complicate the forecasting process without any tangible benefit.

In overcoming these challenges, the role of human judgment and interdisciplinary collaboration cannot be overstated. While advanced tools and algorithms play a critical role, the nuanced understanding of market dynamics, regulatory environments, and organizational strategy by seasoned professionals ensures the relevance and applicability of forecasts. Emphasizing this point, a multinational corporation faced with divergent regulatory environments across its markets leveraged a combination of quantitative forecasting techniques and the expert judgment of its local finance teams to navigate the complexities effectively.

The challenges in forecasting are multifaceted, encompassing data quality and availability, economic uncertainty, the differentiation from budgeting, and the selection of appropriate forecasting tools and techniques. Addressing these challenges requires a blend of advanced analytical tools, strategic foresight, and the irreplaceable human element of judgment and experience. Through this multifaceted approach, organizations can navigate the turbulent waters of financial forecasting, steering towards a future marked by informed decision-making and strategic agility.

Data Quality and Availability Issues

In financial forecasting within FP&A, the bedrock upon which all analytical efforts are constructed is data. Yet, this foundation is frequently undermined by the dual adversaries of data quality and availability, presenting a formidable challenge to finance professionals worldwide. these issues cannot be overstated, as they directly influence the accuracy, reliability, and overall utility of financial forecasts.

Data quality issues often manifest in various forms, ranging from inaccuracies and inconsistencies to outright errors. These can stem from several sources, such as manual data entry errors, outdated systems that fail to capture data correctly, or discrepancies in data collected from different departments within an organization. For example, a retail giant operating across the globe might struggle with inconsistencies in sales data due to varying standards and practices in data recording across its international branches. Such discrepancies can skew forecasts, leading to strategic decisions based on flawed assumptions.

Furthermore, the issue of data silos within organizations exacerbates the challenge of data quality. Departments might operate their own data collection and management systems with little to no interoperability, leading to fragmented and sometimes contradictory datasets. The finance team of a manufacturing company, for instance, could find it challenging to reconcile inventory data from the warehouse management system with financial records, resulting in inaccuracies in cash flow forecasts.

On the other side of the spectrum lies the challenge of data availability. In an ideal world, FP&A professionals would have access to all the data they need, precisely when they need it. However, the reality is often a stark contrast, with critical data being either inaccessible, buried in inaccessible formats, or simply non-existent. This issue is particularly pronounced in rapidly evolving markets or industries undergoing significant regulatory changes, where historical data may offer little relevance to future conditions. An emerging fintech startup, for example, may find it difficult to forecast future growth accurately due to a lack of historical data in an entirely new market segment.

Even when data is available, it may not be in a usable format. The proliferation of big data technologies has led to a situation where organizations can collect vast amounts of data, but this data is often unstructured and requires significant processing before it can be utilized for forecasting purposes. A healthcare provider looking to forecast patient volumes may have ample data from electronic health records, social media, and other sources, but the diversity and unstructured nature of this data present a significant barrier to creating accurate forecasts.

To navigate these treacherous waters, FP&A professionals employ a variety of strategies. Data cleansing and validation procedures are put in place to ensure that data used for forecasting is as accurate and consistent as possible. Additionally, efforts to break down data silos through the integration of information systems across departments help to improve both the quality and availability of data. For instance, implementing an enterprise resource planning (ERP) system can facilitate the seamless flow of information between departments, enhancing the accuracy of forecasts.

Moreover, advanced analytics and machine learning algorithms are increasingly being utilized to extract insights from unstructured data, turning a potential obstacle into a valuable forecasting asset. These technologies can identify patterns and trends that would be impossible for humans to discern, thereby improving the predictive power of financial forecasts.

While data quality and availability issues pose significant challenges to financial forecasting in FP&A, they are not insurmountable. Through the strategic application of technology, improved data management practices, and a commitment to cross-departmental collaboration, organizations can overcome these challenges. By doing so, they ensure that their forecasting efforts are built upon a foundation of reliable, accessible data, enabling more informed decision-making and strategic planning.

Managing Uncertainties in Forecasting

The endeavor to manage uncertainties in forecasting is akin to charting a course through stormy seas. The unpredictability of market trends, economic fluctuations, and regulatory changes act as the gales that threaten to veer forecasts off course. Meanwhile, internal factors such as sales volatility, operational risks, and strategic shifts serve as the undercurrents, subtly but significantly influencing the organization's financial trajectory.

Consider the case of a burgeoning tech startup poised on the brink of expansion. Its forecasts are buffeted by the rapid pace of technological change, with emerging innovations potentially rendering existing product lines obsolete. At the same time, the volatility of the startup ecosystem, marked by fierce competition and shifting investor sentiment, adds layers of external uncertainty.

To steer through these uncertain waters, FP&A professionals employ several navigation tools. Scenario planning emerges as a critical strategy, enabling organizations to envisage multiple futures and prepare for them with agility. By constructing a range of scenarios, from the most optimistic to the most pessimistic, finance teams can test the resilience of their strategies against various outcomes. The tech startup, for instance, might develop scenarios ranging from the successful launch of a new product to the entrance of a disruptive competitor, each with tailored financial strategies.

Another pivotal tool in managing uncertainties is sensitivity analysis. This technique allows finance teams to identify which variables have the most significant impact on their forecasts and to what extent. By adjusting these key levers in their financial models, they can gauge the potential variations in outcomes. For a manufacturing company, the cost of raw materials and the efficiency of production processes might be such critical variables. Sensitivity analysis can help it understand how fluctuations in these areas could affect its financial health.

Risk management, an evergreen aspect of financial planning, plays a vital role in mitigating the adverse effects of uncertainties. Through the identification, assessment, and prioritization of risks, organizations can develop strategies to either avoid, transfer, mitigate, or accept these risks based on their risk appetite. A multinational corporation, for instance, faces currency exchange rate risks that can erode profit margins. By employing hedging strategies, it can manage the uncertainty associated with currency fluctuations.

Moreover, the adoption of rolling forecasts stands out as a dynamic approach to managing uncertainties. Unlike traditional annual budgets, rolling forecasts are continuously updated, providing a more flexible and responsive framework for adjusting to changes. This approach ensures that financial planning remains aligned with the current market reality, allowing for more accurate and timely decision-making.

In FP&A, technology acts as both a harbinger of uncertainty and a means to tame it. The integration of advanced analytics, artificial intelligence (AI), and machine learning (ML) into forecasting processes has opened new vistas for predictive accuracy. These technologies can process vast datasets, identify patterns, and forecast trends with a level of precision previously unattainable. For a retail giant, leveraging AI to forecast consumer behavior based on past purchasing data, social media trends, and economic indicators can significantly enhance the accuracy of its sales forecasts.

Managing uncertainties in forecasting is not about eliminating uncertainty— an impossible feat—but about navigating it with finesse and preparedness. By employing scenario planning, sensitivity analysis, risk management, and rolling forecasts, and by harnessing the power of technology, FP&A professionals can illuminate the path forward, turning uncertainties from formidable foes into navigable challenges. Through these strategies, organizations can not only survive the tempests of change but thrive in them, charting a course toward financial resilience and strategic success.

Overcoming Common Forecasting Biases

Forecasting, the art and science of predicting future financial outcomes, is a pivotal activity within financial planning and analysis (FP&A). However, it is not without its pitfalls. Among the most deceptive of these are cognitive biases—systematic patterns of deviation from norm or rationality in judgment. These biases can cloud the objectivity of forecasts, leading to skewed data interpretation and, ultimately, strategic missteps. Recognizing and mitigating these biases is crucial for enhancing the accuracy of financial forecasts and ensuring robust decision-making.

Anchoring Bias: One prevalent bias is the anchoring effect, where forecasters give disproportionate weight to initial information or data points as anchors and adjust insufficiently from these anchors when making subsequent judgments. For instance, if an FP&A team bases its sales growth projections on the previous year's exceptional results without considering a changing economic landscape, it may set unrealistic expectations for growth. This can be countered by rigorously examining initial assumptions and continuously validating them against a wide array of external data points and trends.

Confirmation Bias: Another common stumbling block is confirmation bias—the tendency to search for, interpret, and recall information in a way that confirms one's preconceptions, leading to statistical errors. An FP&A professional might, for example, focus on market data that supports their optimistic forecast for a new product launch while disregarding consumer research suggesting limited market acceptance. Combatting this bias requires a conscious effort to seek out and equally weigh both supporting and contradictory evidence when making forecasting decisions.

Overconfidence Bias: Overconfidence leads to an overestimation of one's own forecasting abilities and the accuracy of the information at hand. This can result in too narrow prediction intervals and an underestimation of risks. An effective strategy to mitigate overconfidence is to adopt range forecasts instead of point estimates, thereby acknowledging and incorporating uncertainty into predictions. Additionally, implementing a review process where forecasts are critically evaluated by independent parties can help in identifying and correcting overconfident projections.

Recency Bias: Recency bias occurs when forecasters place too much emphasis on the most recent events, underestimating the impact of earlier data. For example, a sudden spike in demand for a product might lead to overly optimistic long-term demand forecasts without considering historical sales cycles. To overcome this, FP&A teams should employ statistical models that appropriately weight historical data points and incorporate long-term trends into their forecasts.

Example of Mitigating Bias:

Consider a scenario involving a multinational corporation facing significant currency exchange risks. The FP&A team, influenced by recent stability in currency markets, might fall into the trap of recency bias, neglecting the historical volatility and potential for future fluctuations. By acknowledging this bias, the team can adjust their approach by incorporating a broader range of historical exchange rates and applying stochastic modeling techniques to simulate various future scenarios. This not only broadens their perspective but also equips them with a more nuanced and resilient forecasting model.

Incorporating Diverse Perspectives: One of the most effective ways to counteract biases is to incorporate diverse viewpoints and expertise in the forecasting process. Engaging team members from different backgrounds and departments can provide a wealth of perspectives that challenge prevailing assumptions and bring to light overlooked factors. For instance, consulting with the marketing team could offer insights into consumer trends that significantly impact sales forecasts, which might not be apparent from a purely financial analysis.

Overcoming common forecasting biases requires a multifaceted approach that includes acknowledging the presence of biases, employing statistical and modeling techniques to account for uncertainty, and fostering an environment that values diverse perspectives and critical evaluation. By systematically addressing these biases, FP&A professionals can significantly enhance the accuracy and reliability of their forecasts, thereby providing a firmer foundation for strategic decision-making. Through vigilant and unbiased forecasting, organizations can navigate the complexities of the business landscape with greater confidence and agility, driving towards a future marked by informed and effective financial planning.

CHAPTER 4:
SCENARIO AND CONTINGENCY PLANNING

F ramework for Scenario Development: scenario planning lies a framework that begins with the identification of driving forces—external conditions and trends that could significantly impact the organization's financial performance. These include economic indicators, technological advancements, regulatory changes, and market dynamics. By mapping these forces along axes of uncertainty and impact, FP&A professionals can prioritize those with the highest potential to affect financial outcomes and thus warrant deeper exploration in scenario development.

Incorporating External Variables: A robust scenario extends beyond the confines of internal data and performance metrics, weaving in a broad spectrum of external variables. For instance, a global pandemic's effect on supply chains and consumer behavior, or geopolitical tensions influencing market access and commodity prices, must be considered. Incorporating these variables requires a diligent scan of the macroeconomic environment and a keen eye for emerging trends that could pivot the course of the industry.

Example of Scenario Development: Imagine an FP&A team at a renewable energy company assessing the impact of regulatory changes on their financial outlook. The team could frame scenarios ranging from the introduction of favorable policies, like subsidies for green energy, to restrictive regulations that impose heavy tariffs on solar panel imports. Within these scenarios, financial projections—spanning revenue, costs, and cash flows—are recalibrated to reflect the varied potential regulatory landscapes. This exercise not only illuminates the financial implications of each scenario but also prepares the organization to pivot swiftly in response to unfolding regulatory changes.

Leveraging Technology for Enhanced Scenarios: The advent of advanced analytics and machine learning has dramatically enriched the scenario planning toolkit. These technologies enable FP&A teams to process vast datasets, identify patterns, and project future states with greater accuracy. Dynamic simulation models, powered by AI, can incorporate real-time data feeds, adjust to emerging trends on the fly, and provide a more granulated view of potential future states. For example, an AI model could simulate the financial impact of an abrupt change in consumer sentiment towards a product line, adjusting forecasts in real time as new market data becomes available.

Engaging Stakeholders in Scenario Planning: The utility of scenarios extends far beyond the confines of the finance department. Engaging a cross-functional team in scenario development—not only ensures a diversity of perspectives but also fosters organizational alignment on strategic priorities. A scenario workshop, for instance, can bring together leaders from operations, marketing, and product development to co-create scenarios that reflect a holistic view of the business landscape. This collaborative approach not only enriches the scenarios but also enhances buy-in and preparedness across the organization.

In crafting scenarios, the goal is not to predict the future with precision but to illuminate the spectrum of possibilities and prepare the organization to navigate them with agility. Each scenario serves as a narrative that tells a story of a potential future, enabling leaders to make informed decisions, allocate resources effectively, and steer the organization toward its strategic objectives, regardless of what the future holds. By developing robust scenarios, FP&A teams equip their organizations with a powerful tool to anticipate change, manage risk, and seize opportunities in a dynamic and uncertain world.

Frameworks for Scenario Development

In financial planning and analysis (FP&A), developing robust scenarios is pivotal for navigating the unpredictable waters of the global economy. This subsection zeroes in on the frameworks that underpin scenario development, offering a scaffold upon which FP&A professionals can construct scenarios that are not only illuminative but also actionable. By leveraging these frameworks, organizations can anticipate potential challenges and opportunities, ensuring they are well-prepared for whatever the future may hold.

Identifying Key Drivers and Uncertainties: The first step in any scenario development framework involves identifying the key drivers of change and associated uncertainties that could impact the organization's financial future. These drivers typically span economic, technological, regulatory, and social domains. For instance, an FP&A team might identify emerging technologies like blockchain as a key driver, with the associated uncertainty being the rate at which it will be adopted by the market. This step requires a keen understanding of the broader industry and global trends, often necessitating cross-departmental collaboration to pool expertise and insights.

Constructing Scenario Axes: Once the key drivers and uncertainties have been identified, the next step involves constructing scenario axes. This involves pairing two drivers that hold significant uncertainty and impact, positioning them on intersecting axes to create a matrix. Each quadrant of the matrix represents a distinct scenario. For example, an axis might juxtapose the rate of technological adoption against regulatory changes in the financial sector, creating four quadrants that explore various outcomes of these combined uncertainties.

Developing Scenario Narratives: With the scenario matrix as a guide, FP&A teams then flesh out detailed narratives for each scenario. These narratives describe possible futures in a coherent and comprehensive manner, incorporating the impact on key financial metrics such as revenue growth, cost structures, and cash flow. For instance, a narrative might detail how rapid adoption of blockchain technology, combined with favorable regulatory changes, could lead to significant cost savings and new revenue streams through the introduction of innovative financial products.

Example of a Scenario Framework Application: Consider a multinational corporation evaluating the impact of geopolitical tensions on its supply chain. Utilizing a scenario development framework, the FP&A team identifies two critical uncertainties: the severity of geopolitical tensions and the response of international markets. These form the axes of the scenario matrix. The resulting scenarios range from a 'business as usual' scenario with low tension and stable markets to a 'crisis' scenario with high tension and volatile markets. For each scenario, financial projections and strategic responses are mapped out, enabling the corporation to proactively adjust its supply chain strategy.

Incorporating Stakeholder Input: An effective scenario development framework also involves engaging stakeholders from across the organization and, when relevant, external experts. This collaborative approach ensures that the scenarios are grounded in a diverse set of perspectives, enhancing their relevance and applicability. Workshops and brainstorming sessions can be invaluable in this process, allowing stakeholders to contribute insights and challenge assumptions, thereby refining the scenarios.

Leveraging Technology for Dynamic Scenarios: Modern FP&A practices harness advanced analytics and simulation tools to bring scenarios to life. These tools allow for dynamic modeling of financial outcomes under different scenarios, incorporating real-time data and predictive analytics to adjust projections as new information becomes available. By integrating these technologies, the scenario development process becomes a continuous exercise in foresight, rather than a static analysis.

Frameworks for scenario development are critical tools in the FP&A arsenal, enabling organizations to navigate uncertainty with confidence. By systematically identifying key uncertainties, constructing scenario axes, developing detailed narratives, and leveraging both stakeholder input and technology, FP&A teams can create a robust foundation for strategic decision-making. Through these frameworks, the art of scenario planning becomes a structured, insightful process, guiding organizations towards strategic resilience and agility.

Incorporating External Variables (Economic, Political)

The anticipation and integration of external variables, particularly those of an economic and political nature, into financial forecasting and scenario development mark a sophisticated approach to financial planning and analysis (FP&A). This subsection delves into the methods and rationales behind the incorporation of these external factors, highlighting how they interplay with financial forecasts and the strategic planning process. Integrating these variables requires a nuanced understanding of global dynamics and their potential impact on an organization's financial health and strategic direction.

Understanding Economic Variables: Economic indicators are pivotal in shaping the financial landscape. These include inflation rates, interest rates, GDP growth, unemployment rates, and consumer spending habits. For instance, an increase in consumer spending can signal a robust economy, potentially leading to higher sales revenue for companies in the consumer goods sector. Conversely, high unemployment rates may indicate a downturn, prompting companies to brace for reduced consumer spending. FP&A professionals must stay abreast of these indicators, integrating them into forecasting models to ensure they reflect potential economic realities.

Navigating Political Factors: Political stability or instability can significantly affect market confidence and, consequently, financial forecasts. Regulatory changes, trade policies, fiscal policies, and geopolitical tensions are among the political variables that can have far-reaching effects on business operations. For example, the imposition of tariffs on imported goods can increase production costs and squeeze margins, necessitating adjustments in financial forecasts. Similarly, a change in fiscal policy, such as an increase in corporate tax rates, directly impacts the bottom line, requiring recalibration of profit forecasts.

Example of Integration in Scenario Planning: Consider a multinational corporation operating in multiple geopolitical hotspots. The FP&A team might develop scenarios that account for potential trade embargoes, sanctions, or changes in foreign policy following elections. By integrating these political variables, the company can explore the financial implications of each scenario, from disrupted supply chains to increased operational costs, and devise strategies to mitigate these risks.

Leveraging Data and Analytics: The integration of external variables into FP&A requires sophisticated data collection and analytics. Many organizations use advanced software tools to gather real-time data on economic and political developments, employing predictive analytics to assess their potential impact on financial performance. For example, machine learning algorithms can analyze patterns in economic data to forecast future trends, while sentiment analysis tools gauge the market's reaction to political events, providing valuable insights for scenario planning.

Collaboration for Comprehensive Analysis: The complexity of integrating economic and political variables into financial forecasting underscores the importance of collaboration. FP&A teams often work closely with external consultants, economists, and political analysts to understand the broader implications of these variables. Internally, cross-departmental collaboration allows for the pooling of expertise, ensuring that forecasts and scenario analyses are both robust and comprehensive.

Case Study: A tech company exploring expansion into emerging markets used a scenario analysis framework to assess the impact of political instability and economic volatility in target countries. By incorporating variables such as currency fluctuations, regulatory changes, and potential trade barriers, the company identified markets where the risk-reward ratio aligned with its strategic objectives. This proactive approach enabled the company to navigate uncertainties effectively, securing its position in key markets while mitigating financial risk.

the thoughtful integration of external economic and political variables into FP&A practices enables organizations to anticipate and respond to potential challenges and opportunities. By leveraging data analytics, fostering collaboration, and employing comprehensive scenario planning, FP&A professionals can craft forecasts and strategies that are both resilient and adaptable in the face of global uncertainties.

Stress-testing Financial Models

In financial planning and analysis (FP&A), the durability and reliability of financial models under various scenarios is paramount. Stress-testing, an advanced analytical method, serves as a crucible, subjecting financial models to extreme conditions to evaluate their resilience. This subsection unravels the essence of stress-testing financial models, delineating its significance, methodologies, and real-world applications, thereby offering a deep dive into its strategic importance in financial forecasting.

The Essence of Stress-Testing: stress-testing involves simulating the impact of various adverse scenarios on a company's financial health. These scenarios may include economic recessions, sudden market downturns, geopolitical crises, or catastrophic events. The objective is to identify vulnerabilities within the financial model that could lead to liquidity crunches, solvency issues, or breaches in financial covenants. By anticipating these risk factors, companies can devise strategies to fortify their financial standing against potential shocks.

Methodological Approach: Stress-testing a financial model requires a methodical approach, beginning with the identification of specific scenarios relevant to the company's operational landscape. This is followed by quantifying the potential impact of these scenarios on key financial metrics such as cash flow, profitability, and debt levels. Advanced statistical techniques and simulation tools are employed to model outcomes under these adverse conditions, providing a probabilistic range of results rather than a single deterministic outcome.

Example of Application: Consider a real estate development firm assessing the robustness of its financial model against interest rate hikes. The FP&A team constructs a scenario where interest rates rise sharply by 200 basis points within a year. They simulate the impact on the firm's debt servicing costs, project financing capabilities, and overall profitability. The stress test reveals a significant strain on cash flows, prompting the company to reconsider its leverage strategy and explore locking in current rates through hedging.

Incorporating Macro-Economic Indicators: A pivotal aspect of stress-testing is the inclusion of macro-economic indicators to ensure the scenarios are grounded in plausible economic conditions. This involves integrating data on GDP growth rates, unemployment rates, inflation, and other relevant economic metrics into the stress-testing framework. By doing so, FP&A professionals can ensure that the stress scenarios reflect potential real-world economic trajectories, enhancing the model's predictive accuracy and reliability.

Collaborative Dynamics: Effective stress-testing is not a siloed activity but involves collaboration across various departments within the organization. Input from operations, sales, marketing, and risk management teams is crucial in identifying potential risk factors and understanding the operational implications of stress scenarios. This cross-functional engagement enriches the stress-testing process, ensuring that the financial models are robust and encompass a comprehensive view of potential challenges.

Case Study: A multinational corporation in the energy sector deployed stress-testing to evaluate its exposure to oil price shocks. By simulating scenarios with oil prices plummeting to historic lows, the FP&A team assessed the impact on revenue, cost structures, and investment plans. The stress test uncovered a high vulnerability to price volatility, leading the company to adjust its hedging strategy and diversify its energy portfolio to mitigate risk.

Concluding Insights: Stress-testing financial models is an indispensable process in FP&A, equipping decision-makers with the insights needed to navigate through turbulent times. Rigorously evaluating financial models against extreme but plausible scenarios, companies can identify and address vulnerabilities, ensuring financial resilience. This process, when executed with diligence and foresight, becomes a strategic tool for safeguarding the company's financial health and securing its long-term success in an unpredictable world.

Linking Scenarios to Strategy

The process of translating the outcomes of stress tests and scenario analyses into actionable strategic decisions stands as a critical juncture. This subsection delves into the nuanced methodology of linking scenarios to strategy, illuminating how organizations can harness these insights to steer through the complexities of the business landscape with agility and foresight.

Strategic Alignment: The initial step in this process involves the alignment of scenario outcomes with the overarching strategic objectives of the organization. This necessitates a thorough examination of how different stress scenarios impact the strategic goals, whether it be growth, market expansion, sustainability, or risk mitigation. Strategic alignment ensures that the insights derived from scenario analyses are not viewed in isolation but as integral components of the strategic planning process.

Example of Strategic Integration: A technology startup, operating in the highly volatile realm of renewable energy, utilizes scenario analysis to anticipate potential shifts in government policy and global energy prices. The stress-testing results indicate a vulnerability to policy shifts that could render certain technologies obsolete. In response, the company's strategic adjustment involves diversifying its technology portfolio and ramping up investment in R&D, ensuring resilience against policy-induced market disruptions.

Decision Trees and Scenario Planning: To systematically link scenarios to strategy, organizations often employ decision trees and scenario planning tools. These tools enable decision-makers to visualize the branching pathways of decisions and outcomes based on different scenarios. By mapping out these pathways, companies can identify critical decision points and develop contingent strategies that are activated when certain conditions are met.

Leveraging Predictive Analytics: The integration of predictive analytics into scenario planning offers a powerful tool for linking scenarios to strategy. Predictive models can forecast the probability of specific scenarios occurring, allowing companies to prioritize strategic responses based on the likelihood and potential impact of different outcomes. This approach enables organizations to allocate resources more efficiently, focusing on scenarios with the highest strategic significance.

Case Study - Retail Chain Expansion: A retail chain considering expansion into emerging markets conducts a comprehensive scenario analysis, focusing on economic growth rates, consumer spending patterns, and geopolitical stability. The analysis reveals significant risks associated with geopolitical instability in certain regions. As a strategic response, the chain develops a phased expansion strategy, initially targeting more stable markets and establishing contingency plans for rapid exit from markets showing signs of instability.

Feedback Loops and Continuous Monitoring: Effective linking of scenarios to strategy requires the establishment of feedback loops and continuous monitoring mechanisms. As real-world conditions evolve, the assumptions underpinning the scenario analyses must be revisited and revised. This iterative process ensures that the strategic responses remain aligned with the current external environment, allowing organizations to adapt swiftly to unforeseen changes.

Embedding Flexibility in Strategic Planning: The ultimate goal of linking scenarios to strategy is to embed flexibility and agility within the strategic planning process. By considering a wide range of potential futures, organizations can develop adaptable strategies that can be fine-tuned or radically shifted in response to emerging threats and opportunities. This approach transforms scenario planning from a static exercise into a dynamic framework for strategic decision-making.

Concluding Perspective: The process of linking scenarios to strategic decision-making is a vital component of modern FP&A practices. It bridges the gap between theoretical risk assessment and practical strategic action, empowering organizations to navigate the uncertainties of the business world with confidence and strategic acumen. By embedding scenario-based thinking into the fabric of strategic planning, companies can anticipate changes, mitigate risks, and seize opportunities, driving sustainable growth and long-term success in an ever-changing global landscape.

Strategic Implications of Different Scenarios

Navigating through the labyrinth of financial forecasting requires a keen understanding of how varied scenarios can unfold and their consequent strategic implications. This segment delves into the core of assessing different scenarios, dissecting their potential impacts on an organization's strategic trajectory. By examining the ramifications of varied futures, leaders can craft strategies that are not only resilient but also opportunistic, capitalizing on the foresights rendered by thorough scenario analysis.

Scenario Analysis as a Strategic Lens: Scenario analysis acts as a prism, refracting the multitude of possible futures into actionable insights. It equips leaders with the foresight to anticipate and navigate through potential challenges and opportunities. For instance, consider the case of an international e-commerce giant assessing the impact of global trade policy changes. By simulating scenarios ranging from free trade agreements to protectionist policies, the company can foresee potential changes in supply chain costs and customer tariffs, allowing for preemptive strategic adjustments to maintain competitive pricing and profit margins.

Example of Dynamic Strategy Adaptation: In pharmaceuticals, a leading company might use scenario analysis to explore the impacts of varying drug approval rates by regulatory bodies. A scenario where regulatory processes accelerate could open pathways to faster market entry and increased R&D investment, whereas a scenario of stricter regulations might necessitate a pivot towards enhancing the robustness of clinical trials and reallocating resources towards lobbying and compliance activities.

Strategic Risk Management: Different scenarios bring to light the spectrum of risks an organization might face. Strategic risk management involves identifying these risks within each scenario and devising strategies to mitigate them. For example, a multinational manufacturing firm may face risks of supply chain disruptions due to geopolitical tensions. By creating scenarios that encapsulate various degrees of geopolitical risk, the firm can develop contingency plans, such as diversifying its supplier base or investing in local production capabilities, thereby minimizing potential disruptions.

Opportunity Exploration Through Scenario Analysis: Beyond risk mitigation, scenario analysis serves as a tool for identifying and seizing opportunities that different futures might present. A technology startup, for instance, might explore scenarios related to the adoption rates of a new technology. In scenarios predicting rapid adoption, the startup might aggressively invest in scaling operations and expanding market presence. Conversely, scenarios indicating slow adoption could lead to strategies focusing on niche markets or pivoting to adjacent technologies.

Case Study - Financial Services Adaptation: Consider a financial services firm evaluating the implications of emerging fintech innovations. Scenario analysis could reveal opportunities for strategic partnerships or acquisitions in scenarios where fintech gains substantial market share. Alternatively, scenarios predicting regulatory challenges for new fintech entrants might encourage the firm to invest in developing its own digital platforms, leveraging its regulatory expertise and existing customer base.

Incorporating Stakeholder Perspectives: Effective scenario planning requires considering the perspectives of various stakeholders, including customers, employees, investors, and regulators. For example, scenarios that anticipate shifts in consumer preferences towards sustainable products can lead to strategic shifts in product development, marketing, and supply chain operations, aligning with stakeholder values and expectations.

Embedding Agility in Strategic Planning: The strategic implications of different scenarios underscore the importance of agility in organizational planning. By preparing for a range of outcomes, organizations can pivot their strategies in response to actual developments, maintaining strategic alignment with evolving market and environmental conditions. This agility facilitates a proactive rather than reactive stance to change, positioning organizations to capitalize on opportunities and mitigate emerging threats effectively.

Concluding Perspective: The strategic implications of different scenarios form the bedrock of informed decision-making in an uncertain world. Through rigorous scenario analysis, organizations can illuminate the paths ahead, crafting strategies that are both robust in the face of challenges and agile in capitalizing on opportunities. This dual focus on resilience and opportunism enables organizations to not only survive but thrive, regardless of the twists and turns the future may hold.

Adjusting Business Strategies Based on Forecasts

The Art of Strategic Flexibility: adjusting business strategies lies the principle of strategic flexibility. This concept is exemplified by a tech giant that, foreseeing a shift towards cloud computing, reallocates investments from hardware-centric projects to cloud services. This proactive realignment not only capitalizes on emerging trends but also mitigates risks associated with declining demand for traditional products.

Example of Market Entry Timing: Consider a consumer goods company forecasting an economic recovery in a key market. By advancing the launch of a new product line to coincide with this upturn, the company maximizes its market entry impact. Conversely, forecasts indicating an economic downturn might prompt a delay in the launch, avoiding the erosion of consumer purchasing power.

Supply Chain Adaptation: A pivotal area where forecasts drive strategy is in supply chain management. A global retailer, through predictive analytics, might anticipate a significant spike in demand for certain products. In response, it could enhance its inventory levels and optimize distribution logistics to meet this demand surge efficiently. This adjustment ensures customer satisfaction and capitalizes on sales opportunities while minimizing the risk of overstock.

Financial Strategy Revision: Financial forecasts play a crucial role in shaping investment, financing, and dividend policies. For instance, a corporation forecasting increased cash flow might decide to ramp up its investment in research and development or return value to shareholders through increased dividends. Alternatively, forecasts of tighter cash flows could lead to more conservative approaches, such as cost-cutting measures and a focus on core business operations to maintain financial stability.

Case Study - Strategic Shift in the Automotive Industry: An automotive company, through forecasting, identifies a growing consumer preference for electric vehicles (EVs) over traditional internal combustion engine vehicles. In response, the company accelerates its EV development programs, reallocates marketing budgets to highlight its commitment to sustainability, and adjusts its production lines to increase EV output. This strategic shift not only positions the company as a leader in the emerging EV market but also aligns its operations with future market demands.

Incorporating External Factors: Successful strategy adjustment based on forecasts also involves considering external factors, such as regulatory changes or geopolitical events. For example, a multinational corporation, anticipating stricter environmental regulations, might invest in cleaner technologies and processes ahead of time, ensuring compliance and securing a competitive advantage as regulations come into effect.

Engaging with Stakeholders: Effective adjustment of business strategies requires transparent communication with stakeholders. By sharing insights from forecasts and involving stakeholders in strategic discussions, companies can foster trust, align expectations, and ensure cohesive action towards common goals.

Cultivating a Culture of Agility: Ultimately, adjusting business strategies based on forecasts demands a culture of agility within the organization. This involves continuous learning, openness to change, and the empowerment of teams to make data-driven decisions. By embedding these qualities into the organizational fabric, companies can navigate the uncertainties of the business world with confidence and dexterity.

Concluding Insight: The dynamic process of adjusting business strategies in light of forecasted trends underscores the importance of agility and foresight in today's business environment. Through calculated adjustments and strategic realignments, organizations can not only defend but also enhance their market position, ensuring long-term success in an unpredictable world. This approach turns forecasting into a powerful tool for strategic planning, enabling businesses to stay ahead of the curve and turn potential challenges into opportunities for growth and innovation.

Contingency Planning

Foundational Principles of Contingency Planning: Contingency planning starts with the identification and assessment of potential risks that could disrupt business operations. This proactive analysis is exemplified by a global shipping company which, recognizing the threat of maritime piracy in international waters, devises alternative shipping routes and security protocols to ensure the safe and timely delivery of goods.

Example of Supply Chain Disruption: A real-life scenario underscores the significance of contingency planning in supply chain management. During the 2011 Tōhoku earthquake and tsunami in Japan, automotive manufacturers worldwide faced critical shortages of parts. Those with effective contingency plans quickly activated alternative suppliers, minimizing production delays. In contrast, manufacturers without such plans experienced significant operational disruptions.

Technological Failure Mitigation: In an era where technology underpins business operations, planning for IT failures is paramount. A financial institution regularly conducts disaster recovery drills, simulating cyber-attacks or system failures. These exercises ensure that backup systems and protocols are in place, enabling swift recovery with minimal impact on client services and compliance obligations.

Financial Contingencies: Financial contingency planning is vital for weathering economic uncertainties. For instance, a retail chain, anticipating a potential economic downturn, might establish a liquidity reserve. This reserve acts as a financial buffer, allowing the company to navigate through reduced consumer spending without resorting to drastic cost-cutting measures that could impair long-term growth.

Case Study - Navigating Regulatory Changes: The pharmaceutical industry, known for its stringent regulatory environment, offers insights into contingency planning for regulatory changes. A biotech company, anticipating possible shifts in health care policy, engages in scenario planning exercises. These exercises explore strategic responses to various regulatory landscapes, ensuring the company remains agile and compliant amidst regulatory volatility.

Integrating External and Internal Factors: Effective contingency planning requires a holistic view that integrates both external threats, such as natural disasters and market volatility, and internal vulnerabilities, including key personnel dependencies and operational bottlenecks. A comprehensive approach involves regular risk assessments, fostering a culture of risk awareness across all levels of the organization.

Stakeholder Engagement and Communication: Transparent communication with stakeholders is crucial in contingency planning. By informing investors, employees, and customers about preparedness measures, businesses can build trust and demonstrate a commitment to operational integrity. Moreover, engaging stakeholders in the planning process can uncover valuable insights and foster a collective sense of responsibility towards business continuity.

The Agility Factor: At the core of successful contingency planning lies organizational agility. This entails the flexibility to pivot strategies swiftly, the capacity for rapid decision-making, and the empowerment of teams to act decisively under pressure. Cultivating these attributes transforms contingency planning from a defensive mechanism into a strategic advantage, enabling businesses to turn challenges into opportunities for innovation and growth.

Contingency planning is not merely a response strategy but an integral component of prudent business management. It embodies the foresight to anticipate change, the wisdom to prepare meticulously, and the agility to act promptly. In an unpredictable business environment, contingency planning equips companies with the resilience to not just survive but thrive, turning potential disruptions into narratives of endurance and strategic ingenuity. Through diligent preparation and adaptive strategies, businesses can navigate the complexities of the modern world, safeguarding their legacy and charting a course toward sustainable success.

Identifying Key Risk Triggers

Understanding Risk Triggers: A key risk trigger is an event or condition that, if it occurs, has the potential to cause significant harm to a company's operations, financial performance, or reputation. These triggers can be as varied as a sudden market downturn, geopolitical tensions, technological failures, or natural disasters. The first step in identifying these triggers involves a thorough risk assessment process, where potential vulnerabilities are mapped out across all facets of the business.

Example of Market Volatility: Consider the scenario of a UK-based technology firm with significant operations in emerging markets. Given the susceptibility of emerging markets to political instability, a sudden change in political climate could severely impact the firm's operations. By monitoring political developments and establishing a link between specific events and potential impact, the firm can identify key risk triggers and develop preemptive strategies to mitigate these risks.

Cybersecurity Threats: In today's digital age, cybersecurity emerges as a critical area where risk triggers must be vigilantly identified. For instance, a multinational corporation might employ threat intelligence platforms to monitor for signs of impending cyber-attacks, such as unusual traffic patterns or attempts to breach network security. By identifying these triggers early, the company can activate its cyber defense protocols, minimizing the risk of data breaches and related financial and reputational damage.

Supply Chain Disruptions: The global nature of supply chains exposes businesses to a multitude of risk triggers. A notable example is a consumer goods manufacturer that relies on a single supplier for a critical component. The sudden bankruptcy of this supplier would constitute a key risk trigger. Proactively identifying such dependencies and establishing alternative sources or stockpiling essential supplies can significantly reduce vulnerability to supply chain disruptions.

Financial Risk Indicators: Financial health is paramount for any business, making it essential to identify triggers that could signal financial distress. For a retail chain, a key financial risk trigger could be a consistent decline in same-store sales over several quarters. Recognizing this early allows the company to investigate underlying causes and implement corrective measures before the situation escalates into a severe financial crisis.

Regulatory Compliance: For industries such as

pharmaceuticals and finance, regulatory changes can be a significant risk trigger. An investment bank, for instance, stays abreast of impending financial regulations through a dedicated compliance team. This team's role is to forecast how new laws could impact operations and to devise strategies to comply proactively, thereby averting potential legal and financial penalties.

Implementing Monitoring Systems: Identifying key risk triggers is an ongoing process that requires continuous monitoring. Many companies invest in sophisticated monitoring systems that use data analytics and artificial intelligence to predict potential risks based on historical and real-time data. These systems can provide early warnings, allowing businesses to respond to threats before they materialize.

Fostering a Risk-Aware Culture: Beyond systems and processes, cultivating a risk-aware culture within the organization plays a crucial role in identifying risk triggers. Encouraging employees to report potential risks and providing them with the necessary training to recognize these triggers can significantly enhance a company's ability to anticipate and mitigate threats.

Identifying key risk triggers is a vital component of a comprehensive risk management strategy. By understanding potential vulnerabilities, monitoring for signs of impending threats, and cultivating a proactive, risk-aware culture, companies can protect themselves against significant losses. This process not only guards against immediate threats but also strengthens the organization's overall resilience, enabling it to navigate the complexities of the modern business environment with confidence and strategic foresight.

Preparing Contingency Plans

The Essence of Contingency Planning: contingency planning is about readiness—readying an organization to respond swiftly and effectively to unforeseen challenges. It involves identifying potential risks, as discussed in the previous section on risk triggers, and then crafting detailed plans to address those risks should they become reality. This process demands a blend of strategic foresight, operational flexibility, and resilience.

Key Components of Contingency Plans: Effective contingency plans are comprehensive, yet flexible, encompassing several key components:

- Risk Assessment: Thoroughly understanding the potential risks and their impact on operations.

- Response Strategies: Designing specific actions to mitigate the impact of identified risks.

- Resource Allocation: Determining the resources required to implement response strategies and how they will be mobilized.

- Communication Plans: Establishing clear lines of communication for disseminating information internally and externally.

- Recovery Plans: Outlining steps to return to normal operations or to a new state of normalcy post-crisis.

Example of a Retail Giant: Consider a global retail giant facing the risk of natural disasters in regions where its key warehouses are located. The company's contingency plan includes relocating inventory across a network of warehouses to mitigate the risk of supply chain disruption. Detailed scenarios cover various types of natural disasters, with pre-defined actions to safeguard employees, secure assets, and ensure business continuity.

Financial Services Firm: A financial services firm, recognizing the risk of cyber-attacks, develops a contingency plan centered around data security and client trust. This plan includes real-time monitoring for suspicious activities, predefined steps for isolating breaches, and communication protocols to manage client concerns transparently. The firm conducts regular drills, simulating cyber-attacks to test and refine their contingency responses.

Manufacturing Sector: A manufacturing company, dependent on a volatile raw material supply, prepares for potential shortages by developing relationships with alternative suppliers in diverse geographies. Their contingency plan details the activation process for alternative sourcing, including financial considerations, quality checks, and logistical arrangements to ensure production lines remain uninterrupted.

Implementing the Plans: Once developed, the real test of a contingency plan's effectiveness lies in its implementation. This involves:

- Training: Ensuring that all stakeholders understand their roles and responsibilities within the plan.

- Testing: Conducting regular drills and simulations to test the robustness of the plan and to identify areas for improvement.

- Review and Update: Keeping the plan current by regularly reviewing and updating it to reflect changing risk landscapes and operational realities.

A Culture of Preparedness: An underlying principle in effective contingency planning is fostering a culture of preparedness within the organization. This means encouraging vigilance, promoting open communication about potential risks, and instilling confidence in the team's ability to manage crises.

Preparing contingency plans is a strategic imperative that equips organizations to face uncertainties with confidence. By systematically identifying risks, crafting detailed response strategies, and ensuring readiness through training and testing, companies can navigate crises with minimal disruption. In doing so, they not only safeguard their operational and financial stability but also uphold their commitments to stakeholders, thereby strengthening trust and resilience in the face of adversity.

Embedding Flexibility in Forecasts

The Imperative for Flexibility: Rigid forecasts, much like brittle steel, are prone to fracture under the pressure of rapid change. Flexibility in forecasting, therefore, emerges as a bulwark against the unpredictability of the business environment. It enables organizations to adjust their strategies proactively, optimizing outcomes in the face of uncertainty.

Strategies for Flexible Forecasting:

- Rolling Forecasts: Unlike traditional annual forecasts, rolling forecasts provide a continuously updated view of the financial horizon, typically over a 12 to 18-month period. This approach allows for regular adjustments based on the latest data, ensuring that the forecast remains relevant and actionable.

- Scenario Planning: By mapping out a range of possible futures—each with its own set of assumptions and outcomes—scenario planning allows companies to prepare for diverse eventualities. This not only broadens the strategic vision but also equips decision-makers with the insights needed to navigate multiple futures.

- Sensitivity Analysis: This involves testing how changes in key assumptions—such as cost inputs, sales volumes, or interest rates—affect the forecast. By identifying which variables have the most significant impact, organizations can focus their attention and resources on monitoring and managing these critical factors.

Example of a Tech Start-up: A burgeoning tech start-up, operating in the volatile realm of renewable energy, employs flexible forecasting to navigate the sector's uncertainties. By utilizing a rolling forecast model, the start-up regularly updates its projections based on the latest industry trends, regulatory changes, and technological advancements. This agility enables it to secure funding and pivot its R&D focus in alignment with emerging opportunities.

Pharmaceutical Industry Case: In the pharmaceutical industry, where product development timelines span years, a major player uses scenario planning to anticipate shifts in regulatory landscapes across different regions. This flexible forecasting approach allows it to adjust its market entry strategies, ensuring timely compliance and maximizing the global reach of its innovative treatments.

Implementing Flexibility in Forecasts:

- Technology Enablement: Advanced forecasting software and analytical tools play a crucial role in enabling flexibility. These technologies facilitate real-time data analysis, scenario simulations, and sensitivity testing, making it easier for companies to adjust their forecasts on the fly.

- Cross-functional Collaboration: Flexibility in forecasting thrives on diverse perspectives. Engaging cross-functional teams in the forecasting process ensures that a wide array of insights and considerations inform the forecast, enhancing its adaptability.

- Continuous Learning and Adaptation: Embedding a culture of continuous learning and adaptation ensures that the organization remains agile. Regularly reviewing forecast accuracy, learning from discrepancies, and refining methodologies contribute to a more flexible and resilient forecasting process.

Embedding flexibility in forecasts is not merely about adjusting numbers; it's about institutionalizing agility within the fabric of financial planning. By employing rolling forecasts, scenario planning, and sensitivity analysis, organizations can navigate the uncertainties of the business landscape with confidence. This adaptive approach not only safeguards financial health but also fosters a culture of proactive, strategic decision-making. In the end, the most successful organizations will be those that view their forecasts not as static predictions, but as dynamic, adaptable tools for navigating the future.

CHAPTER 5:
INTEGRATING ESG
INTO FINANCIAL
FORECASTING

Tracing its origins back to the early 2000s, ESG reporting initially emerged as a niche interest among a small cohort of socially responsible investors. Fast forward to the present, and it has become a pivotal element of corporate discourse, a lens through which companies are evaluated not just on their financial health but on their wider impact on the world.

In Vancouver, for instance, a city renowned for its green initiatives and sustainable urban development, local businesses have led by example, embedding ESG principles into their operations and reporting. These case studies serve not only as a testament to the feasibility of such integration but also as beacons for companies worldwide deliberating over the ESG pivot.

Why ESG Reporting Has Gained Momentum

The ascendancy of ESG reporting can be attributed to a confluence of factors. Firstly, the undeniable reality of climate change and its far-reaching effects on economies has propelled environmental stewardship to the forefront of corporate responsibility. Secondly, social issues, ranging from labor practices to diversity and inclusion, have garnered unprecedented attention, catalyzing a demand for more socially responsible business practices. Lastly, governance—the G in ESG—has seen a heightened focus on transparency, ethics, and accountability, partly fueled by high-profile scandals that have eroded public trust in corporate institutions.

The Financial Implications of ESG

Far from being a cost center, ESG initiatives have demonstrated significant financial merits. Companies leading in ESG reporting often enjoy enhanced brand loyalty, risk mitigation, and access to capital, as an increasing number of investors incorporate ESG criteria into their decision-making processes. Moreover, ESG leadership can translate into competitive advantage, attracting talent, and fostering innovation.

In FP&A, the integration of ESG factors into forecasting and reporting is not without its challenges. Traditional financial models and forecasts, historically focused on quantifiable financial metrics, must now accommodate the qualitative nuances of ESG data. This necessitates a recalibration of forecasting models to capture the subtleties of ESG impacts on financial performance and risk assessment.

Tools and Techniques for ESG Forecasting

The integration of ESG considerations into financial forecasting involves a blend of quantitative and qualitative analyses. On the quantitative side, metrics such as carbon footprint, energy efficiency, and employee turnover rates offer tangible data points that can be correlated with financial outcomes. Qualitatively, stakeholder surveys, reputation indices, and governance scores provide insights into the less tangible aspects of ESG performance.

Advanced forecasting techniques, leveraging artificial intelligence and machine learning, are emerging as powerful tools for synthesizing these diverse data streams, offering predictive insights that inform strategic decision-making. These technologies enable dynamic scenario planning, allowing finance teams to model various ESG trajectories and their potential impacts on the business.

As we stand on the cusp of a new era in financial reporting, where ESG considerations are woven into the fabric of corporate reporting, the role of FP&A professionals has never been more pivotal. Embracing ESG reporting is not merely a compliance exercise but a strategic imperative that aligns companies with the broader societal shifts towards sustainability and responsible business practices.

the rise of ESG reporting marks a significant evolution in the field of FP&A, presenting both challenges and opportunities. As companies navigate this landscape, they will not only contribute to a more sustainable and equitable world but also uncover new avenues for growth and innovation. The journey of integrating ESG into financial forecasting is complex, but the rewards—for the planet, for society, and for the bottom line—are unmistakable.

Environmental Considerations and Financial Performance

At the forefront of the ESG triad, environmental considerations have become a lightning rod for investors and companies alike. The financial implications of environmental stewardship—or lack thereof—are profound. Companies that proactively manage their environmental impact, such as reducing carbon emissions and enhancing sustainability practices, often see a reduction in operational costs through energy efficiency and waste minimization. Furthermore, these practices mitigate regulatory and reputational risks, protecting and potentially increasing the company's market value.

For instance, a Vancouver-based renewable energy company, by virtue of its innovative approach to minimizing environmental impact, not only benefited from tax incentives but also experienced a surge in investor interest, underscoring the tangible financial benefits of environmental consciousness.

Social Capital: A Hidden Financial Lever

The 'Social' component of ESG emphasizes the importance of managing relationships with employees, suppliers, customers, and communities. Companies that excel in social responsibility often enjoy enhanced employee morale and productivity, stronger customer loyalty, and a reduced risk of litigation. These factors collectively contribute to stable revenue streams and can significantly influence a company's financial health.

A compelling example can be seen in companies that have

prioritized diversity and inclusion, resulting in a more innovative and resilient workforce. Such strategic social investments not only foster a positive corporate culture but also drive financial performance through innovative products and services that cater to a broader market.

Governance: The Bedrock of Sustainable Financial Growth

Governance, the third pillar of ESG, focuses on a company's leadership, executive pay, audits, internal controls, and shareholder rights. Strong corporate governance can lead to better decision-making, fostering a culture of accountability and transparency that attracts investors. A well-governed company is often perceived as less risky, which can lead to a lower cost of capital and higher valuation.

The financial implications of governance are evident in the premium investors are willing to pay for companies with robust governance structures. These companies tend to outperform their peers in the long run, as effective governance mechanisms safeguard against mismanagement and fraud, ensuring sustainable financial growth.

Quantifying the Financial Impact of ESG

The task of integrating ESG into financial forecasting is challenging, given the qualitative nature of many ESG factors. However, empirical evidence increasingly supports the notion that ESG factors are correlated with financial performance. Companies with high ESG scores often exhibit stronger financial metrics, including higher return on equity, lower cost of debt, and overall outperformance in the stock market.

Advanced analytical tools and methodologies are being

developed to quantify the financial impact of ESG factors more accurately. These tools leverage data analytics, artificial intelligence, and machine learning to parse through vast amounts of ESG data, identifying patterns and correlations that inform investment decisions and financial forecasts.

In Vancouver's dynamic market, for instance, startups focusing on clean technology and sustainable urban development have not only attracted substantial investment but have also demonstrated resilience and growth in volatile economic conditions. This confluence of innovation, sustainability, and financial performance exemplifies the integral role of ESG considerations in shaping the future of finance.

The integration of ESG factors into financial analysis and forecasting is not merely a trend but a fundamental shift in how companies are evaluated and valued. As the financial impact of ESG becomes increasingly quantifiable, it is imperative for financial professionals to develop a nuanced understanding of ESG dynamics. By doing so, they can guide their organizations towards sustainable growth, leveraging ESG as a strategic asset in the competitive landscape of tomorrow's financial markets.

A Global Surge in ESG Regulations

Across the globe, regulatory bodies have been intensifying their focus on ESG reporting and disclosures. From the European Union's Non-Financial Reporting Directive (NFRD) to the Securities and Exchange Commission (SEC) in the United States proposing enhanced climate-related disclosures, the regulatory landscape is rapidly evolving. These regulations require companies to provide detailed and reliable data on their ESG practices, pushing the integration of ESG factors from a voluntary to a mandatory element in financial reporting.

For example, the Task Force on Climate-related Financial Disclosures (TCFD) has set forth a framework prompting companies to evaluate and disclose the financial impact of climate-related risks and opportunities. Such regulations compel financial planners and analysts to incorporate ESG risk assessments and sustainability metrics into their forecasting models, going beyond traditional financial indicators.

Implications for Financial Forecasting

The regulatory emphasis on ESG disclosures has significant implications for financial forecasting. Firstly, it demands a broader data set for analysis, necessitating the inclusion of non-financial metrics such as carbon emissions data, social impact indicators, and governance scores. This expansion of data parameters challenges traditional forecasting models and requires a reevaluation of risk assessment methodologies to incorporate ESG-related risks.

Secondly, the dynamic nature of the regulatory environment means that forecasts need to be adaptable and responsive to changes in compliance requirements. For instance, a heightened regulatory focus on carbon emissions could lead to increased operational costs for certain industries, a factor that must be accounted for in long-term financial forecasts.

Moreover, the regulatory trends towards greater transparency and accountability in ESG practices encourage a proactive approach to sustainability initiatives. Financial forecasts must, therefore, not only account for the costs associated with these initiatives but also anticipate the potential benefits, such as improved brand reputation, access to green financing, and increased competitive advantage.

Navigating the Regulatory Maze

For CFOs and finance professionals, staying abreast of the ever-changing regulatory landscape is paramount. Implementing robust ESG data management and reporting systems is crucial to meet compliance requirements and enhance forecasting accuracy. Furthermore, engaging with regulatory developments and participating in industry discussions can provide valuable insights into future trends and regulatory expectations.

An illustrative case is found in the energy sector, where companies are increasingly leveraging renewable energy sources in response to regulatory pressures. This strategic pivot not only aligns with regulatory demands but also positions these companies favorably in market forecasts, anticipating a shift in consumer preferences towards sustainability.

Strategic Forecasting in a Regulated World

To navigate this regulated environment, companies must adopt a strategic approach to forecasting that integrates ESG considerations at its core. This involves developing flexible forecasting models that can easily adapt to regulatory changes, investing in ESG data analytics capabilities, and fostering a culture of sustainability and compliance across the organization.

As financial forecasting becomes intertwined with ESG

THE CFO GUIDE TO FORECASTING IN FP&A

compliance and performance, the role of finance professionals is expanding. They are now pivotal in steering their organizations towards a sustainable future, underpinned by robust, regulation-compliant financial strategies.

The tightening ESG regulatory landscape presents both challenges and opportunities for financial forecasting. By embracing these regulations as a catalyst for innovation, companies can refine their forecasting practices, enhance their sustainability credentials, and secure a competitive edge in the evolving financial markets.

The Mechanics of ESG Scoring

ESG scoring involves evaluating companies based on their environmental impact, social responsibility, and governance practices. These scores are derived from a plethora of data points, including carbon emissions, labor practices, board diversity, and anti-corruption measures, among others. Agencies specializing in ESG assessments employ sophisticated models to analyze this data, providing scores that offer investors insight into the sustainable and ethical nature of a company's operations.

For instance, a high ESG score indicates that a company is not only mitigating risks related to climate change, social justice, or corporate governance but is also capitalizing on opportunities in these areas. Conversely, a low ESG score might signal potential vulnerabilities or a lack of preparedness in addressing these critical issues.

Why ESG Scores Matter to Investors

The relevance of ESG scores to investors stems from the

137

growing recognition that sustainable and ethical practices can significantly influence a company's financial performance and risk profile. A study by MSCI, for instance, has highlighted that companies with high ESG scores tend to exhibit lower volatility and fewer instances of significant drawdowns than their lower-scoring counterparts. This stability is particularly appealing to investors seeking to mitigate risk and capitalize on long-term value creation.

Furthermore, ESG scores provide a lens through which investors can assess a company's future readiness and resilience. Companies that score well on ESG metrics are often those that are proactive in adapting to changing environmental regulations, fostering inclusive and equitable workplaces, and implementing robust governance structures. These practices not only reduce regulatory and reputational risks but also position these companies to thrive in a transitioning global economy.

Incorporating ESG Scores into Investment Strategies

Investors are leveraging ESG scores in various ways to inform their investment strategies. Some adopt a screening approach, excluding companies with low ESG scores from their portfolios to minimize risk exposure. Others employ a best-in-class strategy, selecting the highest-scoring companies within a sector or industry to capitalize on their leadership in sustainability practices.

Moreover, ESG scoring is influencing thematic investing, where investors focus on opportunities aligned with specific sustainability themes, such as renewable energy or water conservation. ESG scores provide a crucial data point in identifying companies that are not only leaders in their industries but are also driving positive environmental and social change.

The Future of ESG Investing

As the financial markets continue to evolve, the relevance of ESG scoring is set to increase, driven by regulatory pressures, shifting consumer preferences, and the growing recognition of sustainability risks. This evolution underscores the need for companies to integrate ESG principles into their core operations and for investors to consider ESG scores as a vital component of their investment analysis.

In navigating this landscape, investors are not just passive observers but active participants shaping the future of sustainable finance. By prioritizing ESG scoring in their investment decisions, they are catalyzing a shift towards a more sustainable and equitable global economy.

The integration of ESG factors into financial forecasting and investment strategies marks a significant stride towards aligning financial success with social and environmental stewardship. As this trend continues to gain momentum, ESG scoring will undoubtedly play a pivotal role in defining the investment paradigms of the future, heralding an era where finance serves not only as a tool for wealth creation but also as a catalyst for global sustainability and ethical governance.

The evolution of Environmental, Social, and Governance (ESG) considerations from peripheral to central elements of financial forecasting underscores a profound shift in the corporate world. This transition reflects a growing consensus about the material impact of ESG factors on a company's long-term viability and profitability. Here, we delve into the methodologies and implications of incorporating ESG factors into financial forecasts, illustrating how this integration reshapes forecasting models and investment strategies.

Methodologies for ESG Integration

Incorporating ESG factors into financial forecasts involves a meticulous process of identifying and quantifying how environmental, social, and governance issues directly affect financial metrics such as revenue, expenses, assets, and liabilities. This process often requires analysts to venture beyond conventional financial data, sourcing information from ESG rating agencies, sustainability reports, and even social media sentiment analysis.

For example, an analyst might adjust the expected future revenue growth of a company downward if it scores poorly on environmental practices, anticipating potential fines, regulatory hurdles, or a consumer boycott. Similarly, strong governance factors, such as effective board oversight and transparent accounting practices, could lead to a lower risk premium being applied to the company's cash flows, reflecting a higher degree of confidence in its financial projections.

Quantifying the Impact

The quantification of ESG impacts is perhaps the most challenging aspect of integrating these factors into forecasts. Analysts often employ scenario analysis to understand the potential variance in financial outcomes under different ESG conditions. This might include a "best case" scenario where proactive ESG practices lead to enhanced brand loyalty and a "worst case" scenario where ESG negligence results in significant financial and reputational damage.

Another approach is the use of sensitivity analysis, which examines how changes in specific ESG metrics—such as carbon footprint reduction or improvements in employee satisfaction—could influence key financial indicators. This approach not only highlights the financial relevance of ESG factors but also aids in prioritizing ESG initiatives based on their potential impact on the bottom line.

ESG and Risk Management

Incorporating ESG factors into forecasts is also integral to modern risk management practices. ESG risks—ranging from stranded assets due to regulatory changes in the energy sector to reputational damage from poor labor practices—pose significant threats to financial performance. By embedding ESG considerations into their forecasts, companies and investors can identify and mitigate these risks more effectively.

For instance, a forecast that includes detailed analysis of potential regulatory changes affecting carbon-intensive assets can guide strategic divestments and capital allocation decisions, protecting the company from future value erosion. Similarly, understanding the financial implications of social risks can prompt companies to enhance their operational practices, reducing the likelihood of costly lawsuits or boycotts.

ESG as a Driver of Value Creation

Beyond risk mitigation, integrating ESG factors into financial forecasts illuminates pathways for value creation. Companies that excel in ESG practices often benefit from lower capital costs, enhanced employee productivity, and access to new markets. These benefits, quantified and projected in financial forecasts, can reveal significant opportunities for sustainable growth.

Moreover, as investors increasingly favor companies with strong ESG profiles, these forecasts can serve as a strategic tool for attracting investment. By demonstrating the financial merits of their ESG initiatives, companies can differentiate themselves in a crowded market, appealing to a growing segment of socially conscious investors.

The incorporation of ESG factors into financial forecasting represents a convergence of ethical stewardship and financial prudence. It demands a broadening of the analytical lens, incorporating a diverse array of data points and scenarios. Yet, the benefits of this approach are profound, offering enhanced risk management, opportunities for value creation, and alignment with the shifting expectations of investors, consumers, and society at large.

As the significance of ESG considerations continues to rise, the ability to effectively integrate these factors into financial forecasts will become a distinguishing competency for companies and analysts alike. This integration not only reflects a commitment to sustainable and ethical operations but also signals a deeper understanding of the complex interplay between societal trends and financial performance.

Framework for Financial Impact Assessment

The assessment of the financial impact of ESG initiatives begins with the establishment of a robust framework that links ESG actions directly to financial outcomes. This framework encompasses various components, including cost savings, revenue enhancement, risk mitigation, and capital acquisition costs.

1. Cost Savings: ESG initiatives often lead to significant cost reductions through energy efficiency, waste minimization, and sustainable supply chain practices. For instance, a switch to renewable energy sources can reduce long-term energy expenses, while efficient water use and waste management can lower operational costs.

2. Revenue Enhancement: Companies that proactively engage in ESG initiatives can differentiate their products and services, access new markets, and improve customer loyalty. For example, developing sustainable products can attract environmentally conscious consumers, potentially increasing market share and pricing power.

3. Risk Mitigation: ESG initiatives play a crucial role in mitigating risks associated with regulatory compliance, reputational damage, and operational inefficiencies. By proactively addressing ESG concerns, companies can avoid costly penalties, lawsuits, and boycotts that might arise from non-compliance or societal backlash.

4. Capital Acquisition Costs: A strong ESG profile can enhance a company's attractiveness to investors, leading to lower cost of capital. Investors increasingly consider ESG factors as integral to risk assessment, with companies that score well on ESG metrics often benefiting from easier access to capital and more favorable borrowing terms.

Quantitative and Qualitative Assessment Methods

To quantify the financial impact of ESG initiatives, companies employ a mix of quantitative and qualitative methods. Quantitative analyses might include calculating the return on investment (ROI) for sustainable infrastructure projects or the cost savings resulting from reduced energy consumption. Advanced statistical models and scenario analysis can help forecast the long-term financial implications of ESG strategies, incorporating variables such as potential regulatory changes, market trends, and consumer behavior shifts.

Qualitative assessments, on the other hand, involve evaluating the strategic benefits of ESG initiatives that might be harder to quantify, such as improvements in brand reputation, employee morale, and customer satisfaction. These assessments often draw on stakeholder surveys, market research, and competitive analysis to gauge the potential impact on market positioning and corporate image.

An essential aspect of assessing the financial impact of ESG initiatives is considering the diverse perspectives of various stakeholders, including investors, customers, employees, regulators, and the community. Engaging with stakeholders can provide valuable insights into the perceived value of ESG efforts and highlight areas of concern or opportunity. This stakeholder-centric approach ensures that the assessment of ESG initiatives is aligned with broader corporate objectives and societal expectations.

While assessing the financial impact of ESG initiatives offers numerous benefits, it also presents challenges, including the availability and reliability of ESG data, the evolving nature of ESG reporting standards, and the difficulty of attributing financial outcomes directly to specific initiatives. However, these challenges also represent opportunities for innovation in data collection, analysis, and reporting. As methodologies for ESG assessment continue to evolve, companies have the opportunity to lead in transparency, accountability, and strategic integration of ESG into financial planning.

The assessment of the financial impact of ESG initiatives is a complex yet critical component of contemporary financial forecasting. By developing a nuanced understanding of the cost-benefit dynamics of ESG actions, companies can make informed decisions that align environmental and social responsibility with financial objectives. In doing so, they not only contribute to a more sustainable and equitable global economy but also enhance their competitive advantage, financial resilience, and long-term value creation potential.

The Essence of ESG-Inclusive Scenario Analysis

Scenario analysis, a tool traditionally used to forecast financial outcomes under different sets of assumptions, gains a new dimension when intertwined with ESG considerations. This approach involves creating varied future scenarios that not only reflect potential financial performances but also gauge the impact of environmental policies, social changes, and governance practices on business operations and strategy.

1. Environmental Scenarios: These scenarios explore the ramifications of environmental factors such as climate change, resource scarcity, and energy transition on business models. For example, a scenario might examine the financial implications of stringent carbon regulations for a manufacturing firm, considering potential shifts in operational costs, compliance expenditures, and investment in green technologies.

2. Social Scenarios: Social scenarios contemplate the effects of changing demographics, consumer preferences, and social policies on market dynamics and workforce management. An example could involve assessing the impact of evolving consumer demands for ethical products on sales revenue and brand loyalty.

3. Governance Scenarios: Governance scenarios focus on the consequences of changes in corporate governance structures, regulatory environments, and ethical standards. A scenario might analyze the financial outcomes of enhanced corporate transparency and ethical practices, including potential benefits such as increased investor confidence and reduced legal risks.

Integrating ESG into Financial Forecasting: The Methodology

The methodology for incorporating ESG considerations into scenario analysis involves several key steps:

1. Identification of ESG Factors: The initial phase involves pinpointing the ESG factors most relevant to the organization's industry, geography, and operational context. This requires thorough research and stakeholder engagement to understand external and internal ESG risks and opportunities.

2. Development of ESG Scenarios: Based on the identified ESG factors, develop a range of plausible future scenarios that describe how these factors could evolve over time and affect the organization. Each scenario should be comprehensive, considering the interplay between ESG factors and financial outcomes.

3. Quantitative and Qualitative Analysis: For each scenario, conduct both quantitative analyses, such as financial modeling and risk assessment, and qualitative evaluations to appraise the broader strategic implications. This dual approach ensures a holistic understanding of potential impacts.

4. Stress Testing and Sensitivity Analysis: Apply stress testing to evaluate the resilience of the organization's financial performance under each ESG scenario. Sensitivity analysis can help determine which ESG factors have the most significant impact on financial outcomes.

5. Strategic Recommendations: Based on the scenario analysis, formulate strategic recommendations that guide the organization in mitigating ESG risks, capitalizing on opportunities, and aligning business practices with sustainability goals. This might include initiatives such as diversifying energy sources, enhancing supply chain sustainability, or investing in employee well-being programs.

Incorporating ESG considerations into scenario analysis presents challenges, such as the uncertainty associated with long-term ESG trends and the complexity of quantifying social and environmental impacts. Nevertheless, by adopting a forward-looking perspective and leveraging robust data analytics, organizations can navigate these challenges effectively. The strategic insights gained from ESG-inclusive scenario analysis empower decision-makers to steer their companies toward sustainable growth, resilience, and societal contribution.

scenario analysis with ESG considerations is not merely an

exercise in compliance or risk avoidance; it is a strategic imperative that enables organizations to envision and prepare for a future where financial success is inseparable from environmental stewardship and social responsibility. Through this advanced approach to forecasting, finance leaders can illuminate the path toward a more sustainable and equitable world, ensuring their organizations thrive amid the complexities of the 21st century.

The New Paradigm of ESG Investment

ESG investment involves the inclusion of ESG criteria in the decision-making process for investments, transcending the traditional focus on financial returns to encompass ethical considerations, sustainability, and societal impact. This paradigm shift reflects a growing recognition among investors that ESG factors are significant drivers of risk and return.

1. Risk Mitigation: ESG investing enables investors to identify non-financial risks that could impact the financial performance of investments. For instance, companies with poor environmental practices may face regulatory fines, reputational damage, and operational disruptions, which can adversely affect their stock prices.

2. Value Creation: Companies that excel in ESG practices often experience enhanced brand loyalty, operational efficiencies, and innovation capacities, leading to superior long-term financial performance. Investors are increasingly viewing strong ESG performance as indicative of good management and competitive advantage.

3. Investor Demand: The surge in demand for sustainable investment products from institutional and retail investors

alike has spurred the development of a broad range of ESG-focused financial instruments, including mutual funds, exchange-traded funds (ETFs), and green bonds.

Financing Implications: The Rise of Green Bonds and ESG Loans

The financing landscape is also evolving with the integration of ESG considerations, particularly through the growth of green bonds and ESG-linked loans:

1. Green Bonds: Green bonds are fixed-income securities designed to raise capital specifically for projects with environmental benefits, such as renewable energy, energy efficiency, and sustainable water management. These bonds often offer issuers access to a wider pool of investors and potentially lower borrowing costs due to the increasing appetite for sustainable investment options.

2. ESG-Linked Loans: ESG-linked loans tie the terms of the loan, particularly the interest rate, to the borrower's performance on predefined ESG criteria. This innovative financing mechanism incentivizes companies to improve their ESG performance by directly linking financial costs to sustainability achievements.

Strategic Considerations for Integrating ESG into Investment and Financing

To navigate the ESG investment and financing landscape effectively, investors and companies must consider several strategic factors:

1. ESG Materiality: Not all ESG issues are equally relevant to every industry or company. Identifying which ESG factors are material—most likely to impact financial performance—is crucial for focused analysis and decision-making.

2. Quality of ESG Data: The reliability and comparability of ESG data remain challenges, necessitating rigorous due diligence and the use of multiple data sources to assess ESG performance accurately.

3. Regulatory Environment: The evolving regulatory framework around ESG disclosure and sustainable finance, varying significantly by region, requires careful navigation. Companies and investors must stay abreast of regulatory developments to ensure compliance and capitalize on opportunities.

4. Stakeholder Engagement: Engaging with stakeholders, including investors, customers, and employees, on ESG issues can provide valuable insights, enhance transparency, and build trust.

the integration of ESG considerations into investment and financing decisions represents a profound shift towards sustainable finance. By embracing ESG investment and innovative financing mechanisms like green bonds and ESG-linked loans, investors and companies can not only contribute to a more sustainable and equitable world but also uncover new opportunities for value creation and risk mitigation in an increasingly complex marketplace. This strategic alignment of financial objectives with sustainability goals sets the stage for a resilient and forward-looking financial sector.

Navigating Data Complexity and Quality

One of the most significant challenges in ESG integration is the issue of data: its complexity, quality, and availability. ESG data are diverse, ranging from quantitative metrics, such as carbon emissions, to qualitative assessments, like corporate governance practices. This diversity poses standardization and comparability challenges.

1. Data Standardization: Unlike financial data, which follows well-established reporting standards, ESG data lacks uniformity, making apples-to-apples comparisons difficult. This hampers the ability of analysts to effectively incorporate ESG considerations into financial forecasts.

2. Data Quality and Reliability: The accuracy and reliability of ESG data can vary significantly. Companies might report favorable ESG activities while omitting less flattering information, a practice known as "greenwashing." This necessitates a critical evaluation of reported data and often requires third-party verification to ensure reliability.

Opportunity for Innovation in Data Analytics

The challenges of ESG data also open up substantial opportunities for innovation. There is a growing demand for sophisticated analytical tools that can aggregate, standardize, and analyze disparate ESG data types. This has led to the emergence of startups and established financial service companies developing new methodologies and technologies, including artificial intelligence and blockchain, to enhance the ESG data analytics landscape.

Regulatory and Reporting Challenges

The regulatory environment around ESG reporting and integration is rapidly evolving, with significant variations across jurisdictions. This presents both a challenge and an opportunity:

1. Navigating Regulatory Complexity: Companies and investors must stay informed of the latest regulatory changes in ESG reporting requirements in their operating regions. This necessitates a proactive approach to compliance and strategy adaptation.

2. Leveraging Regulatory Frameworks: At the same time, new regulations can provide a clear framework for ESG integration and reporting, offering a roadmap for companies and investors. This can facilitate more straightforward integration of ESG factors into financial forecasting and investment strategies.

Stakeholder Engagement and Expectations

The rise of ESG has significantly shifted stakeholder expectations. Investors, customers, and employees are increasingly demanding transparency and accountability in ESG practices. This shift presents both a reputational risk and a strategic opportunity.

1. Managing Expectations: Companies must manage stakeholder expectations effectively, balancing the demand for ESG integration with the practical challenges of implementation. Failure to meet stakeholder expectations can lead to reputational damage and financial consequences.

2. Engagement as an Opportunity: Proactive engagement with stakeholders on ESG issues can be a significant opportunity. It can enhance brand loyalty, attract investment, and drive innovation. Stakeholder feedback can provide valuable insights into potential ESG risks and opportunities, informing more accurate and comprehensive financial forecasts.

The integration of ESG factors into financial forecasting is a complex journey fraught with challenges, from data complexity and regulatory hurdles to managing shifting stakeholder expectations. However, within these challenges lie significant opportunities for innovation, strategic differentiation, and value creation. By embracing the complexities of ESG integration, companies and investors can pioneer new frontiers in sustainable finance, driving both financial performance and positive societal impact.

The Multifaceted ESG Data Ecosystem

ESG data integration lies the challenge of traversing a landscape teeming with diverse data types and sources. The ESG data ecosystem is a tapestry woven from a myriad of threads—each representing different environmental impacts, social responsibilities, and governance practices. From greenhouse gas emissions and water usage to labor standards and board diversity, the breadth of data points is staggering. This diversity, while offering a comprehensive view of a company's ESG performance, also presents a formidable challenge in data collection, analysis, and interpretation.

Overcoming Data Standardization Hurdles

A pivotal challenge confronting finance professionals in navigating the ESG data landscape is the lack of standardization. Unlike financial information, which benefits from decades of standardization efforts, ESG metrics are often reported in varying formats, without a universally accepted set of standards. This heterogeneity complicates the process of comparing ESG metrics across companies, industries, and regions.

Progress is being made, however, as organizations like the Sustainability Accounting Standards Board (SASB) and the Global Reporting Initiative (GRI) work towards harmonizing ESG reporting standards. Financial analysts are increasingly leveraging these frameworks to guide their ESG data integration efforts, mitigating the challenges posed by data diversity.

Harnessing Technology for Enhanced Data Analytics

Technology plays a pivotal role in navigating the ESG data landscape. Advanced data analytics tools, powered by artificial intelligence (AI) and machine learning, are emerging as indispensable allies in the quest to harness the power of ESG data. These technologies offer the capability to sift through vast amounts of unstructured data, identify patterns, and extract actionable insights—transforming raw ESG data into a strategic asset for financial forecasting.

Furthermore, blockchain technology is beginning to find applications in ensuring the authenticity and traceability of ESG data, addressing concerns about data reliability and integrity. These technological advancements are not only enhancing the efficiency and accuracy of ESG data analysis but are also paving the way for innovative financial products and strategies centered around sustainability.

Navigating the Evolving Regulatory and Investor Landscape

The regulatory environment for ESG reporting is in a state of flux, with new frameworks and requirements emerging globally. This evolving regulatory landscape, while challenging, provides a clear impetus for companies to enhance their ESG data reporting and integration practices. Moreover, as investor demand for ESG information continues to grow, adept navigation of the ESG data landscape becomes a competitive advantage, enabling companies to attract capital and achieve market differentiation.

Strategies for Successful ESG Data Navigation

To effectively navigate the ESG data landscape, finance professionals should adopt a multi-pronged strategy:

1. Leverage Established Frameworks: Utilize existing ESG reporting frameworks as a guide to standardize data collection and reporting processes.

2. Invest in Technology: Embrace technological solutions for data analytics, ensuring the ability to process and analyze ESG data efficiently.

3. Stay Informed: Keep abreast of regulatory changes and investor expectations regarding ESG reporting to ensure compliance and alignment with market demands.

4. Engage Stakeholders: Foster dialogues with stakeholders

to understand their ESG information needs, tailoring data collection and reporting practices accordingly.

The ESG data landscape, with its inherent complexities and evolving nature, presents a challenging yet rewarding frontier for financial forecasting. Through strategic engagement with this landscape, leveraging technological advancements, and adhering to emerging standards, finance professionals can unlock the transformative potential of ESG data—propelling financial analysis into a new era of sustainability and insight.

ESG as a Catalyst for Innovation

The pursuit of ESG excellence often spurs innovation, driving companies to develop new products, services, and processes that reduce environmental impact, enhance social contribution, and uphold exemplary governance standards. For instance, a Vancouver-based tech firm recently made headlines by launching a revolutionary software that leverages AI to optimize energy consumption in commercial buildings, significantly reducing their carbon footprint. This innovation not only addresses the 'Environmental' component of ESG but also positions the company at the forefront of the green technology market, illustrating how ESG-focused innovation can open up new business avenues and revenue streams.

Enhancing Brand Reputation and Customer Loyalty

In an era where consumers are increasingly making purchasing decisions based on corporate responsibility, ESG credentials serve as a powerful tool for enhancing brand reputation. Companies that are perceived as responsible citizens often enjoy heightened customer loyalty and an expanded customer base. By transparently communicating their ESG initiatives and achievements, businesses can forge stronger connections with their customers, distinguishing themselves in a crowded marketplace. For example, a clothing retailer that commits to fair labor practices and sustainable materials is likely to resonate strongly with a growing demographic of ethically conscious consumers, thereby securing a competitive advantage.

Attracting and Retaining Top Talent

A strong ESG proposition is also a magnet for top talent. Today's workforce, especially the millennial and Gen Z segments, is increasingly looking to align with organizations that share their values. By demonstrating a firm commitment to ESG principles, companies can attract high-caliber employees who are motivated not just by financial rewards but by the opportunity to contribute to meaningful change. This can lead to enhanced employee satisfaction, lower turnover rates, and, ultimately, a more dynamic and innovative organizational culture.

Navigating Regulatory Landscapes and Minimizing Risks

As regulatory frameworks around environmental protection, social responsibility, and corporate governance become more stringent, a robust ESG strategy can help companies Navigate these complexities with greater ease, minimizing regulatory risks. Moreover, by proactively addressing ESG issues, companies can anticipate and mitigate potential social and environmental risks that could disrupt their operations and damage their reputation. This proactive risk management not only safeguards the company's operational continuity but also reassures investors and stakeholders of its long-term viability.

Unlocking Access to Capital

The growing emphasis on sustainable and responsible investment has led to a surge in ESG-focused funds. Investors are increasingly channeling capital towards companies that demonstrate strong ESG performance, recognizing the link between ESG excellence and financial resilience. By integrating ESG principles into their core strategy, companies can unlock access to a wider pool of investment, benefiting from lower capital costs and enhanced investment attractiveness.

Strategies for Harnessing ESG for Competitive Advantage

1. Innovate with Purpose: Identify how ESG principles can drive innovation within your business model, leading to the development of sustainable products and services.

2. Build Transparency: Cultivate trust with your stakeholders through transparent reporting and communication of your ESG efforts and achievements.

3. Foster an Ethical Culture: Embed ESG values into your corporate culture, attracting talent and building a workforce that is engaged and committed to your company's mission.

4. Engage Proactively with Regulators: Stay ahead of the regulatory curve by actively engaging with policymakers and contributing to the development of pragmatic regulatory frameworks.

5. Leverage Financial Instruments: Explore ESG-linked financial instruments and bonds to finance your sustainability initiatives and demonstrate your commitment to ESG principles.

Leveraging ESG for competitive advantage is not merely a compliance exercise but a strategic imperative. In the dynamic landscape of global business, where consumer preferences, regulatory pressures, and societal expectations are constantly evolving, ESG offers a framework for sustainable growth, innovation, and resilience. By embracing ESG, companies can not only navigate the challenges of the modern marketplace but also lead the charge towards a more sustainable and equitable future.

Understanding the Spectrum of Stakeholder Expectations

Stakeholders encompass a broad array of entities and individuals, including but not limited to investors, customers, employees, regulators, and the community at large. Each group has distinct ESG expectations, reflecting their unique interests and values. Investors may prioritize governance practices and environmental sustainability as indicators of long-term value creation, while customers are increasingly inclined towards supporting businesses that demonstrate social responsibility and environmental stewardship. Employees seek workplaces that are not only inclusive and ethical but also actively engaged in making a positive societal impact.

Investor Demand for Transparency and Performance

Investors are elevating the bar for ESG transparency and

performance, viewing robust ESG practices as indicative of a company's risk management efficacy and long-term resilience. They expect detailed disclosures on ESG strategies, goals, and outcomes, alongside evidence of how these initiatives contribute to financial performance. For instance, a transparent ESG report that includes data-driven results of reduced carbon emissions or improved workforce diversity can significantly enhance investor confidence.

The modern consumer looks beyond the product or service to the ethos of the company behind it. Environmental sustainability, ethical sourcing, and social equity are no longer optional but essential facets of a company's value proposition. Companies can meet these expectations by embedding ESG principles into their product development, operations, and marketing strategies, thereby turning ESG compliance into a competitive differentiator.

The contemporary workforce is increasingly motivated by purpose and impact. Employees expect their employers to uphold high ethical standards, provide equitable and inclusive working environments, and engage in meaningful social contributions. Companies that actively involve their employees in ESG initiatives often experience heightened morale, loyalty, and productivity, turning their workforce into powerful ambassadors of their ESG commitment.

With the regulatory landscape around ESG continuously evolving, compliance is a moving target. However, forward-thinking companies are choosing to exceed mere compliance, anticipating future regulations and integrating best practices into their operations ahead of mandates. This proactive approach not only minimizes the risk of non-compliance but also positions the company as a leader in corporate responsibility, often influencing the direction of future regulations.

The community within which a company operates is both a stakeholder and a partner. Meeting community expectations involves not just minimizing negative impacts but actively contributing to societal well-being. Initiatives can range from local environmental conservation efforts to programs supporting local businesses and education. Genuine community engagement fosters goodwill, strengthens brand loyalty, and can lead to collaborative solutions to shared challenges.

Strategies for Meeting Stakeholder Expectations on ESG

1. Comprehensive Stakeholder Analysis: Regularly assess and map stakeholder expectations regarding ESG to understand their priorities and concerns. This analysis should inform ESG strategy development and execution.

2. Integrated Reporting: Adopt a transparent approach to ESG reporting, integrating ESG metrics and achievements into annual reports and other communications to provide a holistic view of company performance and impact.

3. Stakeholder Engagement: Establish regular dialogues with stakeholders through forums, surveys, and meetings to gather feedback, share progress, and co-create ESG solutions. This engagement should be an ongoing process rather than a one-time event.

4. Operational Integration: Embed ESG considerations into every facet of the business, from supply chain management and innovation to employee training and community relations. This ensures that ESG principles are not siloed but

are a pervasive part of the corporate culture and operations.

5. Continuous Improvement: View ESG as a journey, not a destination. Set ambitious yet achievable goals, measure progress meticulously, and be prepared to recalibrate strategies in response to changing stakeholder expectations and global sustainability challenges.

Meeting stakeholder expectations on ESG is a complex but rewarding endeavor that requires a strategic, informed, and proactive approach. By understanding the diverse expectations of their stakeholders and integrating ESG principles deeply into their corporate ethos and operations, companies can not only meet these expectations but also drive innovation, enhance resilience, and secure a competitive advantage in an increasingly conscientious market. In doing so, they not only contribute to their own success but also to the broader goal of sustainable development.

CHAPTER 6: LEVERAGING TECHNOLOGY FOR ADVANCED FORECASTING

A I and ML stand at the forefront of technological innovation in FP&A. These technologies are increasingly being integrated into forecasting systems, enabling the analysis of vast datasets with unparalleled precision. AI algorithms can identify patterns and trends that might elude human analysts, providing a more nuanced understanding of financial forecasts. Moreover, machine learning models continuously improve, refining their predictions as they process more data. This dynamic capability allows for forecasts that adapt to changing market conditions in real-time, offering a significant edge in strategic planning.

Predictive analytics harnesses statistical algorithms and machine learning techniques to forecast future events based on historical data. It goes beyond traditional forecasting methods by assessing the probability of future outcomes and their potential implications. In FP&A, predictive analytics can be applied to various domains, such as cash flow projections, revenue forecasts, and risk assessment, allowing companies to make informed decisions with a higher degree of confidence.

The adoption of cloud computing in FP&A systems has revolutionized data accessibility and collaboration. Cloud-based forecasting tools offer the flexibility to access financial models and data analytics from anywhere, at any time, facilitating a more agile response to market changes. Additionally, the cloud enables seamless integration of data sources, ensuring that forecasts are based on the most comprehensive and up-to-date information available.

While blockchain is often associated with cryptocurrencies, its applications in FP&A are gaining traction. Blockchain can enhance the transparency and security of financial transactions, creating an immutable ledger of all operations. This capability is particularly valuable in scenarios involving multiple stakeholders or complex supply chains, where it can provide a single source of truth for financial data. Moreover, blockchain's smart contracts can automate financial agreements based on predefined conditions, streamlining operations and reducing the potential for errors.

As forecasting technologies become more sophisticated, the importance of effective data visualization grows. Advanced visualization tools transform complex data sets into intuitive, interactive dashboards and reports, making it easier for stakeholders to grasp key insights at a glance. This not only enhances the decision-making process but also democratizes access to financial forecasts, enabling a broader range of stakeholders to engage with and contribute to strategic discussions.

The Internet of Things is starting to play a role in FP&A by providing real-time data from a network of connected devices. This real-time data can be leveraged for more accurate and timely forecasts, particularly in industries reliant on physical inventory, supply chains, or operational efficiency. IoT can offer granular insights into asset utilization, production rates, and operational bottlenecks, feeding into more precise financial models.

The latest trends in forecasting technology are transforming FP&A from a reactive, historical analysis function into a proactive, forward-looking strategic asset. By leveraging AI and ML, predictive analytics, cloud computing, blockchain technology, advanced data visualization, and IoT, finance professionals can enhance the accuracy, efficiency, and strategic value of their forecasts. As these technologies continue to evolve, the capability to anticipate and navigate the financial future with confidence will increasingly differentiate successful organizations from their competitors. The integration of these technological advancements into FP&A practices not only optimizes financial forecasting but also propels businesses towards a more innovative, data-driven future.

The Intersection of AI and FP&A

AI's role in FP&A transcends traditional data analysis, introducing sophisticated algorithms capable of predictive analytics, natural language processing, and pattern recognition. These capabilities enable finance teams to not only dissect past performance but also to forecast future financial outcomes with a high degree of accuracy. AI-driven tools can sift through massive datasets, identifying correlations and trends that might be imperceptible through conventional analysis.

AI's transformational impact on FP&A is machine learning—a branch of AI that improves its performance and accuracy over time without being explicitly programmed to do so. ML algorithms learn from historical financial data, evolving and adapting to new information. This continuous learning process equips FP&A professionals with forecasting models that become progressively more accurate, providing a reliable basis for strategic decision-making.

Deep Learning for Deeper Insights

An advanced subset of machine learning, deep learning, utilizes artificial neural networks to analyze data. In the context of FP&A, deep learning algorithms can process and interpret the complexities of financial data at a depth previously unattainable. This includes unstructured data such as market news, social media sentiment, and economic reports, allowing for a holistic view of factors influencing financial forecasts.

AI and ML significantly enhance the efficiency of financial forecasting processes by automating routine tasks, such as data collection and initial analysis. This automation frees up finance professionals to focus on higher-level strategic analysis and decision-making. Furthermore, AI can optimize forecasting models in real-time, adjusting predictions based on emerging data and trends, ensuring that forecasts remain relevant and actionable.

AI and ML excel in their ability to simulate various financial scenarios, assessing a wide range of outcomes based on different assumptions and variables. This capability is invaluable for risk management, as it allows FP&A teams to evaluate the financial implications of potential risks and devise strategies to mitigate them. AI-powered scenario analysis supports dynamic decision-making, enabling organizations to navigate uncertainties with confidence.

Despite the transformative potential of AI and ML in FP&A, finance professionals must navigate challenges such as data quality, privacy concerns, and the need for specialized skills to develop and manage AI models. The integration of AI into FP&A also requires a strategic approach, aligning technological capabilities with business objectives to maximize the value of AI-driven forecasting.

The advancements in AI and machine learning are revolutionizing the field of FP&A, offering unprecedented opportunities for enhancing the accuracy, efficiency, and strategic value of financial forecasts. As these technologies continue to evolve, their integration into FP&A practices will not only redefine the role of finance professionals but also empower organizations to achieve a competitive advantage through data-driven insights and decision-making. Embracing AI and ML represents a forward leap toward a future where financial forecasting is not only about predicting the future but actively shaping it.

Defining Predictive Analytics

Predictive analytics employs statistical algorithms and machine learning techniques to identify the likelihood of future outcomes based on historical data. It is the science of mining data, analyzing it through various models, and making predictions about unknown future events. In FP&A, this translates to an enhanced ability to forecast financial trends, revenues, and expenditures with a higher degree of precision.

Applications in FP&A

1. Revenue Forecasting: By analyzing patterns in sales data, economic indicators, and market trends, predictive analytics enables FP&A professionals to forecast future revenue streams. This aids in making informed decisions regarding budget allocations, investment opportunities, and risk management.

2. Expenditure Analysis: Predictive analytics can foresee fluctuations in operational costs and expenses, helping organizations to optimize their spending and improve profit margins. It takes into account variables such as inflation rates, supply chain logistics, and labor market conditions.

3. Cash Flow Management: Through the predictive analysis of receivables, payables, and liquidity requirements, organizations can better manage their cash flow, ensuring sufficient liquidity for operations while optimizing investment returns.

4. Risk Assessment: Identifying potential financial risks before they materialize is another area where predictive analytics shines. By examining historical data and current market conditions, FP&A teams can predict credit risks, market volatility, and other financial threats, implementing strategies to mitigate these risks ahead of time.

The efficacy of predictive analytics in FP&A hinges on the quality and breadth of data available. This encompasses not only internal financial records but also external data sources such as market trends, competitor performance, and global economic indicators. The integration of diverse data sets enriches the predictive model, offering a more nuanced and comprehensive forecast.

Leveraging predictive analytics necessitates the adoption of advanced software and platforms that can handle complex data sets and perform analyses. Tools equipped with AI and machine learning capabilities are at the forefront, capable of continuously refining their predictive models based on new data and outcomes. This adaptive learning process is crucial for maintaining the accuracy and relevancy of forecasts in a rapidly changing financial landscape.

While predictive analytics holds tremendous potential, FP&A professionals must navigate several challenges, including data privacy concerns, the complexity of integrating new technologies, and the need for specialized skills to interpret predictive models. Moreover, predictive analytics should be viewed as a complement to human expertise, where the technology provides valuable insights, but strategic decisions are guided by the seasoned judgment of finance professionals.

The application of predictive analytics in FP&A represents a significant shift towards data-driven financial management. It affords organizations the foresight to navigate market complexities, anticipate financial trends, and make strategic decisions that align with long-term objectives. As predictive analytics continues to evolve, its role in shaping the future of FP&A will undoubtedly expand, offering new avenues for growth, efficiency, and competitive advantage.

Understanding Blockchain Technology

blockchain is a distributed ledger technology that maintains a continuously growing list of records, called blocks, which are securely linked together using cryptography. Each block contains a cryptographic hash of the previous block, a timestamp, and transaction data, thereby creating a chain of blocks that is resistant to data modification. This characteristic of blockchain not only ensures the integrity of financial data but also facilitates transparency and auditability in financial transactions.

Applications in FP&A

1. Smart Contracts for Automated Compliance: Blockchain technology enables the execution of smart contracts, which are self-executing contracts with the terms of the agreement between buyer and seller being directly written into lines of code. In FP&A, smart contracts can automate compliance with financial regulations and policies, reducing the time and resources spent on manual compliance checks.

2. Enhanced Transaction Security: The cryptographic security measures inherent in blockchain technology offer enhanced protection against fraud and unauthorized transactions. By securely recording each financial transaction on a blockchain, FP&A departments can ensure the authenticity and integrity of their financial data.

3. Streamlined Reconciliation Processes: In traditional FP&A practices, financial reconciliation can be a labor-intensive process involving the comparison of transaction records from multiple sources. Blockchain technology, with its distributed ledger, allows for real-time verification and reconciliation of financial transactions across different departments and entities, thereby streamlining the reconciliation process and reducing errors.

4. Improved Intercompany Transactions: For multinational corporations, managing intercompany transactions can be complex due to different currencies, tax laws, and financial systems. Blockchain technology facilitates smoother intercompany transactions by providing a unified platform that records transactions in a transparent and immutable manner, simplifying the settlement process and reducing transaction costs.

5. Decentralized Financial Planning: Blockchain enables a decentralized approach to financial planning and analysis, where financial data and models can be shared securely across different segments of an organization without a central point of control. This not only enhances collaboration between departments but also ensures that financial planning is based on comprehensive and up-to-date information.

The integration of blockchain technology into FP&A processes has the potential to significantly reduce operational costs, improve the accuracy of financial forecasts, and enhance the overall efficiency of financial operations. Moreover, the inherent transparency and traceability offered by blockchain can improve stakeholder confidence in the company's financial practices.

Despite its potential, the adoption of blockchain in FP&A faces challenges, including the need for a robust technological infrastructure, the complexity of integrating blockchain with existing financial systems, and the requirement for specialized skills to develop and manage blockchain applications. However, as these challenges are gradually addressed, and as more finance professionals become knowledgeable about blockchain technology, its adoption within FP&A is expected to accelerate, paving the way for a more secure, efficient, and transparent financial future.

Blockchain technology holds the promise of transforming FP&A by redefining how financial data is recorded, processed, and shared. Its impact extends beyond mere efficiency gains, offering a new paradigm for financial integrity, collaboration, and strategic decision-making. As we move forward, embracing blockchain within FP&A will be instrumental in navigating the complexities of the modern financial landscape.

Future-Proofing Your Forecasting Process

Before commencing the evaluation process, it is crucial for CFOs to gain a comprehensive understanding of the current technological landscape. This entails staying informed about the latest developments in AI, ML, blockchain, predictive analytics, and other relevant technologies. It also requires an awareness of how these technologies have been successfully implemented in similar contexts, providing a benchmark for what can be achieved.

Identifying Organizational Needs

A pivotal step in evaluating technology options is the precise identification of the organization's requirements. This involves a thorough analysis of existing FP&A processes to pinpoint inefficiencies, data silos, or areas where accuracy could be improved. By understanding these needs, CFOs can focus their search on technologies that offer the most relevant solutions.

Compatibility with Existing Systems

One of the significant challenges in integrating new technologies is ensuring compatibility with existing systems and workflows. It is essential to assess whether potential technological solutions can seamlessly interface with current software and databases or if substantial modifications will be needed. This evaluation should also consider the scalability of the technology to accommodate future growth and changing business requirements.

Cost-Benefit Analysis

Implementing new technologies often requires a substantial investment. Therefore, conducting a detailed cost-benefit analysis is vital to determine the potential return on investment. This analysis should account for both direct costs, such as purchase and implementation expenses, and indirect costs, like training and potential downtime during the transition. The benefits, meanwhile, should be quantified in terms of efficiency gains, accuracy improvements, and the potential for enhanced strategic decision-making.

Vendor Assessment

Choosing the right technology provider is as critical as selecting the technology itself. CFOs should evaluate vendors based on their track record, customer support, and commitment to continuous improvement. It is also wise to consider the vendor's stability and the likelihood they will remain a long-term partner. Engaging with other users to gather feedback on their experiences with the vendor and the technology can provide invaluable insights.

Security and Compliance Considerations

In today's digital age, data security and regulatory compliance are paramount concerns. Any new technology must meet the highest standards of data protection and be capable of complying with relevant financial regulations. This necessitates a rigorous assessment of the technology's security features and the vendor's ability to respond to evolving compliance requirements.

Pilot Testing

Before making a final decision, conducting a pilot test of the technology within a controlled environment can offer a practical evaluation of its effectiveness. Pilot testing allows CFOs to identify any unforeseen issues and assess the technology's impact on processes and outcomes. This step is crucial for validating the initial assessment and ensuring that the selected technology aligns with the organization's objectives.

Evaluating technology options for FP&A integration is a multifaceted process that requires careful consideration of numerous factors. By systematically analyzing organizational needs, assessing compatibility, conducting cost-benefit analyses, evaluating vendors, considering security and compliance, and undertaking pilot testing, CFOs can make informed decisions that significantly contribute to the resilience and competitiveness of their organizations. This strategic approach ensures that the chosen technologies not only meet current requirements but also position the organization to adeptly navigate future financial landscapes.

Strategic Planning and Project Management

A robust strategic plan, complemented by strong project management, lays the foundation for successful implementation. This involves setting clear objectives, defining milestones, and establishing a realistic timeline. Effective project management ensures that the plan stays on track, with regular reviews to adjust for any unforeseen issues. Assigning a dedicated project manager or team, skilled in both finance and technology, can bridge the gap between the FP&A department and IT, facilitating smoother communication and problem-solving.

Stakeholder Engagement and Change Management

One of the most significant challenges in implementing new technology is managing the human aspect. Resistance to change is natural, and without proper management, it can derail the adoption process. Early and continuous engagement with stakeholders across all levels of the organization is essential. This includes clear communication about the reasons for the change, the benefits it will bring, and the impact on individual roles. Providing training and support helps ease the transition, building competence and confidence in using the new system.

Technical Integration and Data Migration

Integrating new technology with existing systems and migrating data is a complex task that requires careful planning and execution. Technical compatibility issues can lead to delays or, in worst-case scenarios, loss of data. Engaging with IT experts and the technology vendor early in the process can help identify potential technical issues before they become problems. Running parallel systems for a short period can also ensure that the new system operates as expected while providing a fallback option if issues arise.

Testing and Quality Assurance

Rigorous testing is critical to identify and fix any bugs or issues before the full-scale launch. This includes unit testing, system testing, and user acceptance testing. Involving end-users in the testing phase not only helps in identifying issues from a user perspective but also aids in building their familiarity and comfort with the system. Continuous quality assurance processes should be established to monitor the system's performance and address any issues promptly as they arise after implementation.

Scalability and Future-Proofing

Even after a successful implementation, it is vital to consider the long-term perspective. The selected technology should be scalable and adaptable to future business growth and changes in the financial landscape. Regular reviews of the system's performance and flexibility in adapting to new requirements are essential to ensure that the investment continues to deliver value.

Measuring Success and ROI

To gauge the success of the implementation, predefined metrics and KPIs should be established and monitored. These could include improvements in forecast accuracy, efficiency gains, or cost savings. Demonstrating a clear return on investment (ROI) is crucial to validate the decision to implement new technology and support future investments in innovation.

Overcoming the challenges of implementing new FP&A technology requires a holistic approach that encompasses strategic planning, stakeholder engagement, technical integration, rigorous testing, and continuous improvement. Addressing these areas effectively not only ensures a smoother transition but also maximizes the benefits of the new technology, ultimately enhancing the organization's financial forecasting capabilities. By anticipating potential challenges and proactively developing strategies to mitigate them, CFOs can guide their organizations through the complexities of technological transformation, securing a competitive edge in the evolving landscape of finance.

Identifying Skills Gaps

The first step in a comprehensive training and upskilling initiative is to assess the current skill sets within the finance team and identify gaps that new technologies might exacerbate. This assessment should not only focus on technical abilities but also on analytical thinking, data interpretation skills, and the ability to translate complex financial data into actionable business insights. Surveys, interviews, and performance reviews can provide valuable insights into where the team stands and where it needs to go.

One size does not fit all when it comes to training. Each member of the finance team might have different learning needs based on their background, experience, and current role. Developing customized learning pathways allows for targeted skill development, ensuring that each team member receives the training they need to excel. These pathways can include a mix of in-house training sessions, online courses, workshops, and certifications, focusing on areas such as data analytics, AI applications in finance, and scenario planning.

Sometimes the best resources for training and upskilling are not found within the organization but through partnerships with technology vendors, academic institutions, and professional training organizations. These partners can provide specialized training programs that are directly relevant to the tools and technologies the finance team will be using. Furthermore, expert-led workshops and seminars can offer insights into industry best practices and emerging trends, keeping the team ahead of the curve.

Theoretical knowledge is vital, but the real learning happens through practical application. Incorporating hands-on training sessions where team members can interact with new technologies, simulate forecasting scenarios, and analyze real-world data sets can significantly enhance the learning experience. These sessions not only improve technical skills but also build confidence in using these technologies in daily operations.

Training and upskilling should not be viewed as a one-time initiative but as an ongoing process. The financial landscape and the technologies that drive it are constantly evolving, and so must the skills of those who navigate it. Encouraging a culture of continuous learning, where seeking out new knowledge and staying abreast of industry developments is valued and rewarded, ensures that the finance team remains adaptable and innovative.

As with any strategic initiative, it's essential to monitor the progress of training and upskilling efforts. Regular feedback sessions, performance assessments, and skill audits can help identify areas where further training is needed. Training programs should be dynamic, adapting to the changing needs of the team and the organization, as well as advancements in technology.

The implementation of advanced FP&A technologies brings with it the necessity to ensure that finance teams have the skills and knowledge to leverage these tools effectively. Through careful planning, customized training programs, practical experience, and a commitment to ongoing learning, organizations can ensure their finance teams are well-equipped to lead the charge in making data-driven decisions and driving strategic growth. Training and upskilling are not just about keeping pace with technology—they are about empowering finance professionals to become strategic partners in the future success of their organizations.

Trends Shaping the Future of FP&A

The relentless pace of technological innovation stands as the primary architect of the future FP&A blueprint. AI and ML are not merely tools for automating repetitive tasks but are evolving into sophisticated advisors, capable of providing deep insights and foresight into financial trends. The adoption of blockchain technology promises to introduce unprecedented levels of transparency and efficiency in transactions and reporting. Moreover, the rise of big data analytics enables the processing and interpretation of vast datasets to uncover hidden patterns, risks, and opportunities.

Yet, technology is just one facet. The globalization of markets demands that FP&A practices transcend borders, accommodating diverse regulatory landscapes and economic conditions. Sustainability and ethical considerations are becoming central to corporate strategies, with ESG (Environmental, Social, and Governance) factors being intricately woven into financial forecasting and reporting.

Challenges on the Horizon

With great power comes great responsibility, and the advanced capabilities of emerging technologies bring their set of challenges. Data privacy and security emerge as paramount concerns, with finance teams navigating a minefield of regulations such as GDPR and CCPA. The risk of reliance on algorithms and data models also looms large, with the potential for systemic biases and errors that could lead to flawed forecasts or decision-making.

Another significant challenge is the digital skills gap within existing finance teams. As technology evolves, so too must the skillsets of those who wield it. Upskilling and reskilling initiatives become crucial, not just for operational competency but for strategic advantage.

Opportunities for Innovation and Leadership

The future also holds boundless opportunities for those ready to embrace change. The integration of AI and ML into FP&A processes opens up new avenues for predictive forecasting, scenario planning, and real-time decision-making. Finance teams can transition from their traditional roles to become strategic advisors, using data-driven insights to guide business strategies and innovation.

Furthermore, the increased emphasis on sustainability and ESG factors offers a chance to redefine corporate values and impact positively on society and the environment. By aligning financial strategies with sustainable practices, organizations can not only enhance their brand reputation but also unlock new markets and opportunities for growth.

Preparing for What Lies Ahead

To navigate this future landscape successfully, finance teams and CFOs must foster a culture of continuous learning and adaptability. Investing in technology and data analytics capabilities, while also focusing on soft skills such as strategic thinking and effective communication, will be key. Collaboration across departments and with external partners will become increasingly important, as will the ability to synthesize complex data into actionable insights.

The future of FP&A is a journey into uncharted territories, marked by rapid technological advancements, evolving global markets, and shifting societal expectations. By staying agile, embracing innovation, and focusing on strategic value creation, finance teams can not only navigate these changes but lead their organizations to new heights of success. The future outlook for FP&A is not without its challenges, but for those prepared to face them head-on, it is replete with opportunities to redefine the essence of financial forecasting and analysis in the digital age.

Strategic Integration of Technology

The modern CFO finds themselves at the intersection of finance and technology, propelling the strategic integration of advanced tools and systems across the organization. This role extends beyond mere approval of IT budgets to a deep, hands-on involvement in selecting and deploying technologies that enhance financial forecasting, operational efficiency, and strategic decision-making. CFOs are now pivotal agents in driving the adoption of AI, ML, blockchain, and data analytics, ensuring these technologies align with the company's broader financial and strategic goals.

Navigating the Technological Landscape

A crucial aspect of the CFO's evolving role is the ability to navigate the ever-expanding technological landscape. This involves not only identifying the most relevant technologies but also understanding their potential impact on the organization's financial health and competitive edge. CFOs must assess the ROI of new tech investments, considering not just the cost savings or efficiency gains but also the potential for innovation and transformation. This strategic assessment requires a blend of financial acumen and technological literacy, domains that the contemporary CFO must master.

Cultivating a Technology-forward Culture

Another facet of technology adoption spearheaded by CFOs is fostering a culture that embraces change and innovation. This entails championing the cause of digital transformation across all levels of the organization, from the boardroom to the operational teams. CFOs play a crucial role in breaking down resistance to change, advocating for a shift in mindset that views technology as an enabler of business success. By leading by example, CFOs can cultivate an environment where continuous learning, experimentation, and adaptation are valued and encouraged.

The CFO as a Strategic Advisor

The technological empowerment of the CFO role enhances their capacity to serve as strategic advisors to the CEO and the board. With deep insights derived from advanced analytics and forecasting tools, CFOs can offer more informed perspectives on market trends, competitive dynamics, and strategic opportunities. This advisory capacity is elevated by their understanding of technological capabilities, allowing them to guide the organization towards innovative solutions and strategic investments that drive growth and sustainability.

While the shift towards technology adoption presents numerous opportunities, it also comes with its challenges. CFOs must navigate issues such as cybersecurity risks, data privacy regulations, and the integration of new technologies with existing systems. Furthermore, the digital skills gap within finance teams poses a significant challenge, necessitating focused efforts on training and development to equip teams with the necessary skills for the digital age.

The role of the CFO in technology adoption is emblematic of the broader transformation occurring within the business world. As organizations grapple with rapid technological advancements and shifting market demands, the CFO's ability to integrate technology into financial and strategic frameworks becomes increasingly critical. This evolution positions the CFO not merely as a guardian of financial integrity but as a visionary leader driving technological innovation and strategic growth. In embracing this expanded role, CFOs can steer their organizations towards resilience, adaptability, and sustained success in the digital era.

CHAPTER 7:
BUILDING AN
EFFECTIVE
COMMUNICATION
STRATEGY

U nderstanding your audience is the segmentation of stakeholders into clearly defined groups. These include internal stakeholders such as senior management, department heads, and team members, as well as external stakeholders like investors, regulatory bodies, and customers. Each group possesses unique concerns, priorities, and levels of financial literacy, necessitating a tailored approach to communication.

For senior management, the focus should be on providing strategic overviews and actionable insights. They are primarily interested in how financial forecasts impact the organization's strategic goals and long-term viability. Therefore, distilling complex data into concise, high-level summaries that outline potential risks and opportunities is paramount.

Department heads seek to understand the operational implications of financial forecasts. The communication here should link financial outcomes to departmental objectives, emphasizing how forecasted financial trends may necessitate adjustments in departmental strategies or resource allocation.

Investors require transparency and a clear articulation of how forecasts align with the organization's growth and profitability objectives. Building trust through honest and straightforward communication about potential financial outcomes, including risks, is essential. Utilizing data visualization can aid in making complex financial projections more accessible and understandable.

Communicating with regulatory bodies demands a focus on compliance, accuracy, and clarity. The financial forecasts should be presented in a manner that aligns with regulatory standards and expectations, ensuring that all required disclosures and assumptions are transparently communicated.

For team members, the goal is to foster engagement and a deeper understanding of the organization's financial direction. Simplifying financial jargon and linking the impact of forecasts to individual roles and contributions can enhance alignment and motivation.

Once stakeholders are segmented, the next step is tailoring the message. This involves:

1. Choosing the Right Language: Adjusting the complexity of the language to match the financial literacy of each segment.

2. Highlighting Relevant Information: Emphasizing information that is pertinent to the interests and concerns of each stakeholder group.

3. Engaging Storytelling Techniques: Transforming data into compelling narratives that elucidate the strategic implications of financial forecasts.

Channels of Communication

Selecting the appropriate channels of communication is critical. While senior management may prefer formal presentations or detailed reports, team members might benefit more from interactive workshops or infographics that elucidate key financial concepts and forecasts.

Feedback Loops

Establishing mechanisms for feedback is crucial to understanding whether your audience comprehends the communicated forecasts and their implications. Feedback loops, whether through formal surveys, Q&A sessions, or informal conversations, provide insights into areas where further clarification may be necessary.

Understanding your audience in financial forecasting is not just about disseminating information; it's about creating a dialogue where complex financial data is translated into actionable insights for every stakeholder. By segmenting the audience, tailoring the message, choosing the appropriate communication channels, and establishing feedback loops, FP&A professionals can ensure their forecasts are not only heard but understood, thus driving informed decision-making across the organization. This approach not only enhances the strategic value of the FP&A function but also strengthens the organization's financial acumen and resilience in the face of future challenges.

The preliminary step in tailoring messages involves a deep dive into understanding the preferences and expectations of different stakeholder groups. This entails a comprehensive analysis of their roles, concerns, and the decision-making contexts they operate within. Whether it's the granularity of data desired by the CFO, the strategic implications relevant to board members, or the operational impacts pertinent to department heads, recognizing these nuances is crucial.

Customized Content for Each Group

1. Board Members and Investors: Communication with this group should emphasize the strategic implications of financial forecasts, including growth prospects, risk management strategies, and potential returns on investment. The narrative should be forward-looking, focusing on long-term value creation and resilience building.

2. Executive Team: This group requires a blend of strategic and operational insights derived from financial forecasts. The messaging should elucidate how financial trends align with or diverge from the organizational strategy and the ensuing implications for operational execution.

3. Department Heads: Here, the communication should drill down into the specific impacts of financial forecasts on departmental budgets, resource allocation, and project planning. The goal is to provide actionable insights that department heads can use to adjust their strategies or

operations in alignment with the broader organizational financial health.

4. Operational Teams: For operational teams, the message needs to be simplified and direct, highlighting how financial forecasts affect their day-to-day work, objectives, and performance metrics. This group benefits from visuals and examples that link financial outcomes to operational realities.

5. External Stakeholders (Customers, Suppliers, Regulatory Bodies): External stakeholders require tailored messages that focus on the stability and growth prospects of the organization, compliance with financial regulations, and ethical considerations. The communication should build confidence in the organization's financial management and strategic direction.

Leveraging Diverse Communication Channels

Effective tailoring also involves choosing the right channels to convey messages to different stakeholders. For example, while an in-depth report might be appropriate for internal strategists, a webinar or an engaging infographic could be more effective for broader external audiences.

An essential component of tailoring messages is the solicitation and incorporation of feedback from stakeholders. This iterative process ensures that the communication strategy remains aligned with stakeholder needs and preferences, thereby enhancing the effectiveness of future messages.

Tailoring messages for different stakeholders is not just about adjusting the content; it's about framing financial forecasts in a way that resonates with the specific interests, concerns, and decision-making contexts of each group. By meticulously customizing the delivery and presentation of financial information, FP&A professionals can drive deeper engagement, foster informed decision-making, and ultimately, steer the organization towards its strategic goals. This approach not only demonstrates respect for the diverse perspectives within the stakeholder community but also underscores the strategic value of the FP&A function as a vital connector across the organization's ecosystem.

Simplification without Dilution

The first step towards effective communication with non-experts is the simplification of technical details. This does not imply watering down the information but rather distilling it to its essence. It involves identifying the core message or insight that needs to be communicated and presenting it in the most straightforward manner possible. For instance, instead of discussing the specifics of an ARIMA model used in forecasting, focus on what the model predicts about future revenue trends and why this is relevant for the listener.

Use of Analogies and Metaphors

Analogies and metaphors are powerful tools for bridging the gap between complex financial concepts and the everyday experiences of non-expert audiences. By linking a technical detail to a well-understood concept, you can illuminate its significance in a relatable way. For example, comparing the concept of rolling forecasts to navigating a road trip with adjustable routes can help demystify this approach to financial planning.

Visual Aids and Storytelling

Visual aids such as graphs, charts, and infographics can transform abstract numbers into tangible insights. They are particularly effective in conveying trends, relationships, and comparisons in financial data. Coupling visual aids with storytelling techniques further enhances their impact. Narrating the story behind the numbers—such as how a particular trend is influencing departmental budgets or project timelines—can make the information more memorable and engaging for non-expert audiences.

Interactive Presentations

Interactive presentations that allow for real-time manipulation of data can be instrumental in communicating with non-experts. Tools that enable the audience to visualize how changes in one variable affect others can make abstract concepts concrete. For instance, using a simple slider to show the impact of different growth rates on future revenue can make the implications of forecasts more accessible.

Feedback Loops

Establishing feedback loops is crucial when communicating technical details to non-experts. Encouraging questions and providing clarifications in layman's terms ensures that the message is accurately received and understood. It also offers an opportunity to gauge the effectiveness of your communication and refine your approach accordingly.

Communicating technical details to non-experts is less about simplifying information and more about making it accessible, relevant, and engaging. By focusing on core insights, employing analogies, leveraging visual aids and storytelling, utilizing interactive presentations, and fostering feedback loops, FP&A professionals can ensure their financial forecasts are comprehensible and actionable. This approach not only empowers stakeholders to participate in informed decision-making but also elevates the strategic role of the finance function within the organization. Through these methods, the bridge between the complex world of financial forecasting and the operational realities of the organization is not just built but reinforced, facilitating a shared understanding and collaborative effort towards achieving the organizational goals.

Foundations of Trust

Transparency and honesty lay the groundwork for trust between FP&A professionals and their stakeholders, which include employees, investors, regulatory bodies, and the public. Trust, once established, facilitates smoother decision-making processes, encourages investment, and fosters a positive corporate image. Conversely, a lack of transparency can lead to suspicion, decreased stakeholder engagement, and, in severe cases, legal and reputational repercussions.

Strategies for Enhancing Transparency

1. Comprehensive Disclosure: Ensure that financial reports and forecasts include all relevant information, both positive and negative. This includes not only what is required by regulations but also any additional insights that could influence stakeholder decisions. For instance, openly discussing potential risks to future revenue streams can prepare investors for possible market fluctuations.

2. Clarity in Reporting: Financial documents should be free of jargon and accessible to individuals without a finance background. This involves not only simplifying language but also explaining the significance of financial metrics and how they relate to the organization's broader goals.

3. Proactive Communication: Do not wait for stakeholders to ask questions or for problems to arise. Regularly update all relevant parties on financial performance, potential challenges, and strategies being employed to address them. This proactive approach not only demonstrates transparency but also shows a commitment to honesty and accountability.

Building a Culture of Integrity

Creating an environment where honesty is the norm starts with leadership. Leaders must model the values of transparency and honesty in their actions and communications. Furthermore, organizations should:

- Integrate these values into their mission statements and operational guidelines.

- Recognize and reward behaviors that exemplify transparency and honesty.

- Implement systems for anonymous feedback and whistleblowing, ensuring employees can report unethical behavior without fear of retaliation.

Practical Applications and Real-world Examples

Overcoming Challenges

While the benefits of transparency and honesty are clear, implementing these principles can present challenges. These include managing stakeholder reactions to unfavorable news and balancing the need for openness with competitive considerations. Strategies to navigate these challenges include phased disclosures, where information is released in stages, and employing scenario analysis to prepare stakeholders for various outcomes.

Emphasizing transparency and honesty in financial communications is not merely a matter of ethical compliance but a strategic imperative that can significantly impact an organization's success and resilience. By fostering trust through clear, proactive, and truthful reporting, FP&A professionals can contribute to building a stable and positive relationship with all stakeholders, thereby securing a competitive edge in the complex landscape of modern finance. The cumulative effect of these efforts elevates the organization's reputation, facilitates smoother operations, and ultimately drives sustainable growth.

Elevating Understanding through Visualization

1. Choosing the Right Visualization Tools: The first step in effective financial communication is selecting the appropriate visualization tools. Options range from simple bar and line charts for trend analysis to heat maps for highlighting variances and scatter plots for revealing correlations. The choice depends on the data's nature and the message to be conveyed. For instance, a CFO aiming to illustrate the company's revenue growth across different regions might opt

for a geo-map.

2. Interactive Dashboards: The evolution of FP&A software has ushered in the era of interactive dashboards. These platforms allow users to drill down from high-level overviews to granular data points. For example, an interactive dashboard could enable stakeholders to explore quarterly sales figures down to individual transactions by region or product line. This depth of interaction promotes a deeper understanding and engagement with the data.

Best Practices in Financial Reporting

1. Consistency and Comparability: For financial reports to be effective, they must maintain consistency in format and metrics. This consistency aids in comparability, allowing stakeholders to track performance over time easily. Furthermore, aligning reports with industry standards and benchmarks can provide valuable context, helping stakeholders gauge the company's performance against peers.

2. Narrative Reporting: Beyond the figures, incorporating narrative elements into financial reports can significantly enhance their impact. This involves explaining the 'why' behind the numbers, offering insights into what drove the results, and outlining future implications. A narrative approach makes reports more accessible and engaging, facilitating strategic dialogue among non-financial stakeholders.

Leveraging Technology for Enhanced Reporting

1. Automated Reporting Tools: Automation in financial reporting not only streamlines the process but also reduces

the risk of human error. Tools like ERP (Enterprise Resource Planning) and CPM (Corporate Performance Management) software can automatically generate standard reports, freeing up time for financial analysts to focus on more strategic tasks.

2. Integration with Business Intelligence (BI) Systems: Integrating financial reporting systems with BI tools can provide a more holistic view of organizational performance. This integration allows for the pulling in of non-financial data—such as operational metrics and market trends—into financial reports, offering a comprehensive overview that supports informed decision-making.

Incorporating Feedback for Continuous Improvement

An often-overlooked aspect of financial reporting is the incorporation of stakeholder feedback. Regularly soliciting and acting upon feedback ensures that reports remain relevant, understandable, and valuable to all stakeholders. This iterative process fosters a culture of continuous improvement in financial communication.

In an era where data drives decisions, the role of visualization and reporting techniques in FP&A cannot be overstated. By embracing the latest tools and practices, finance professionals can transcend traditional reporting paradigms, turning complex financial data into compelling narratives that drive strategic action. This transition from numbers on a page to interactive, insight-driven storytelling marks a significant evolution in the field of finance, one that promises to enhance transparency, foster engagement, and facilitate more informed decision-making across all levels of an organization.

Ensuring Accuracy and Transparency

1. Rigorous Data Validation Processes: trustworthy financial reporting lies the unfaltering commitment to data accuracy. Implementing comprehensive data validation checks, including reconciliation procedures and variance analysis, ensures that the reported figures are reliable and free from error. For instance, employing automated reconciliation tools can significantly reduce discrepancies between ledgers and sub-ledgers, ensuring a solid foundation for reporting.

2. Transparent Disclosure Practices: Transparency in financial reporting goes beyond mere compliance with regulations. It involves providing stakeholders with a clear understanding of the financial statements, including the methodologies used in financial estimations and the assumptions underlying the forecasts. Adopting a policy of full disclosure, where all material information is communicated openly, builds trust with investors, regulators, and other stakeholders.

Adapting to Regulatory Changes and Standards

1. Staying Abreast of Regulatory Updates: The regulatory landscape for financial reporting is continuously evolving. Organizations must remain vigilant in updating their reporting practices to align with the latest International Financial Reporting Standards (IFRS) or Generally Accepted Accounting Principles (GAAP), depending on their jurisdiction. This could involve periodic training for the finance team or consulting with external auditors to ensure compliance.

2. Implementing Sustainability Reporting: With the growing emphasis on Environmental, Social, and Governance (ESG) factors, incorporating sustainability reporting into the

financial reporting framework has become indispensable. This practice not only aligns with regulatory trends but also meets the increasing demand for corporate responsibility from consumers and investors. Integrating ESG metrics with financial performance indicators offers a holistic view of the organization's sustainability efforts and their financial implications.

Leveraging Technology to Enhance Reporting Efficiency

1. Adoption of Cloud-Based Reporting Solutions: The shift towards cloud-based financial reporting tools offers unparalleled benefits in terms of accessibility, scalability, and security. These platforms facilitate real-time data analysis and reporting, enabling finance teams to generate timely and accurate reports. Moreover, cloud solutions often come with built-in compliance checks, reducing the burden of regulatory adherence.

2. Utilizing Advanced Analytics for Forward-Looking Insights: Moving beyond historical reporting, best practices now involve leveraging predictive analytics and scenario analysis to provide forward-looking insights. This approach enables organizations to anticipate future trends, assess potential risks, and prepare strategies accordingly. Advanced analytics tools can sift through vast datasets to identify patterns and predict outcomes, enriching the financial reports with strategic foresight.

Fostering Stakeholder Engagement through Interactive Reporting

1. Development of User-Friendly Dashboards: An integral aspect of modern financial reporting is the creation of

interactive dashboards that present complex financial data in an intuitive and engaging manner. These dashboards should offer customizable views to suit the diverse informational needs of different stakeholders, from executive leadership to department heads.

2. Incorporating Narrative Elements: To augment the impact of financial reports, incorporating narrative elements that contextualize the data is crucial. This involves not just presenting the numbers, but also telling the story behind them—highlighting key achievements, explaining variances, and setting the stage for future goals. This narrative approach transforms financial reporting from a statutory obligation into a compelling narrative of the organization's journey.

Embarking on the path to best practices in financial reporting is not merely about adherence to standards and regulations; it is about embracing a culture of transparency, accuracy, and continuous improvement. By integrating rigorous data validation, staying updated with regulatory changes, leveraging technology, and engaging stakeholders through narrative reporting, organizations can elevate their financial reporting to not only meet but exceed expectations. This commitment to excellence in financial reporting is foundational to guiding strategic decision-making and securing the organization's long-term success and sustainability.

In the rapidly evolving domain of financial planning and analysis (FP&A), the ability to convey complex financial data in a comprehensible and impactful manner is paramount. This is where the proficient use of data visualization tools steps in as a cornerstone for enhancing the effectiveness of financial reports. The following discourse meticulously explores the strategies and nuances of employing data visualization tools to revolutionize financial reporting, thereby transforming raw data into actionable insights.

Selecting the Right Visualization Tools

1. Assessment of Features and Functionalities: The initial step in harnessing the power of data visualization involves the careful selection of tools that align with the organization's reporting needs. Criteria for selection include the tool's capability for real-time data integration, support for various data formats, and the diversity of visualization options such as charts, graphs, and heat maps. For example, tools like Tableau or Microsoft Power BI offer extensive customization options and connectivity with multiple data sources, enabling FP&A professionals to tailor reports to specific analytical requirements.

2. Scalability and User Accessibility: Consideration of the tool's scalability is crucial to accommodate growing data and user base. Additionally, the chosen visualization tool should offer a user-friendly interface that empowers both finance professionals and non-expert stakeholders to navigate and interpret the data effortlessly. The aim is to democratize data access, ensuring that all relevant parties can derive insights without the need for extensive technical know-how.

Designing Effective Visualizations

1. Adhering to Visualization Best Practices: The efficacy of a financial report significantly depends on the clarity and simplicity of its visualizations. Adherence to best practices such as minimizing clutter, using consistent color schemes, and selecting the appropriate chart types for particular data sets, is vital. For instance, time series data can be best

represented through line charts to depict trends over time, while pie charts might elucidate the composition of revenue streams.

2. Contextualization and Storytelling: Beyond mere graphical representation, effective visualization involves embedding data within a narrative context. This includes providing annotations, explanations, and highlights that guide the viewer through the data's story. By crafting a narrative around the numbers, FP&A professionals can present compelling cases for strategic decisions, investment opportunities, or risk mitigation measures.

Integrating Interactive Elements

1. Interactive Dashboards and Drill-Down Features: Modern data visualization tools offer interactive capabilities that allow users to explore data at varying levels of granularity. Implementing interactive dashboards where users can drill down from aggregate figures to transaction-level details, or filter data according to specific dimensions, significantly enhances the utility and engagement of financial reports. This interactivity enables stakeholders to perform ad-hoc analyses and gain deeper insights into the underlying drivers of financial performance.

2. Real-Time Data Feeds and Updates: Leverage visualization tools that support real-time data integration to provide up-to-the-minute financial insights. This capability is especially critical in dynamic business environments where timely information can influence decision-making processes. Real-time dashboards ensure that stakeholders have access to the most current data, facilitating agile responses to market trends and operational challenges.

Fostering Collaboration and Feedback

1. Shared Access and Collaborative Annotations: Effective utilization of visualization tools extends to fostering a collaborative environment. Features that allow multiple users to access, comment on, and annotate reports can spark discussions and collective analysis. This collaborative approach not only enriches the interpretation of data but also encourages a culture of transparency and shared understanding within the organization.

2. Training and Capacity Building: To maximize the benefits of data visualization tools, investing in training and capacity building for the FP&A team and other stakeholders is essential. Tailored training sessions can enhance familiarity with the tools' features, promote best practices in visualization design, and stimulate innovative reporting solutions.

The adept use of data visualization tools in financial reporting is not merely an exercise in aesthetics; it is a strategic imperative that enhances comprehension, facilitates insightful analysis, and drives informed decision-making. Through careful tool selection, thoughtful design, interactivity, and collaboration, FP&A professionals can elevate the impact of financial reports, turning them into powerful catalysts for strategic action and organizational growth. As the financial landscape continues to evolve, the ability to effectively communicate complex data through visualization will remain a critical skill set for finance teams worldwide.

Foundations of Interactive Reporting

1. Bridging Data Silos: The core of robust interactive reporting lies in the integration of disparate data sources into a unified analytics platform. This consolidation enables a holistic view of financial performance, weaving together strands from sales, operations, marketing, and external market data. Tools such as QlikView or SAP Business Objects have been pioneers in facilitating such integration, offering FP&A teams the ability to draw comprehensive insights.

2. Customization and Personalization: Unlike traditional reports, interactive reporting allows users to tailor views and analyses to their specific needs. Through customization, CFOs might focus on high-level strategic insights, while department heads drill down into operational metrics. This personalization enhances relevance and drives actionable insights across all levels of the organization.

Dynamics of Dashboards

1. Real-Time Operational Insights: Dashboards elevate the decision-making process by providing real-time visibility into operational metrics. Through the use of live dashboards, finance teams can monitor cash flow, revenue streams, and expense trends as they happen, enabling rapid adjustments to strategy in response to emerging challenges or opportunities.

2. Scenario Modeling and Forecasting: Advanced dashboards include functionalities for scenario modeling and forecasting, allowing FP&A professionals to test various assumptions and predict their financial outcomes. This capability is crucial for strategic planning, risk management, and capital allocation, as it provides a sandbox for exploring financial futures.

Implementing Interactive Features

1. User-Driven Data Exploration: interactive reporting is the concept of user-driven exploration. Features such as "drag-and-drop" interfaces, expandable data hierarchies, and filterable attributes empower users to ask questions and receive immediate answers. This exploratory approach encourages deeper engagement with the data and fosters a culture of curiosity and analytical thinking.

2. Annotations and Collaborative Analysis: Interactive reports and dashboards support annotations and comments, turning them into collaborative tools for team analysis. This feature is especially beneficial during review meetings or when seeking input from multiple stakeholders, as it captures collective intelligence and facilitates informed decision-making.

1. Data Governance and Quality: As the backbone of interactive reporting, data must be accurate, consistent, and timely. Implementing strict data governance policies and quality checks is imperative to ensure the integrity of reports and dashboards. Regular audits and user feedback loops can help maintain high standards of data quality.

2. User Training and Adoption: The sophistication of interactive tools can sometimes be a double-edged sword. Comprehensive training programs and ongoing support are essential to help users navigate complex interfaces and utilize advanced features effectively. Early adoption and championing by leadership can also drive widespread acceptance and utilization.

Interactive reporting and dashboards represent a paradigm

shift in FP&A, moving from static, backward-looking reports to dynamic, forward-looking insights. By integrating data from across the organization, offering customization, and enabling real-time, interactive exploration, these tools provide unprecedented agility and depth of analysis. However, the potential of these tools is fully realized only when supported by robust data governance, quality control, and an organizational culture that values data-driven decision-making. As we continue to navigate the complexities of the modern business landscape, the role of interactive reporting and dashboards in shaping strategic financial decisions will undoubtedly continue to grow.

Feedback and Continuous Improvement

effective FP&A lies the ability to not only generate accurate forecasts but to also reflect upon and analyze the outcomes of previous forecasts. This process begins with the systematic collection of feedback from a diverse array of stakeholders including, but not limited to, department heads, financial analysts, and strategic decision-makers. The goal here is to glean insights into the accuracy of forecasts, the utility of the financial data presented, and the perceptions of stakeholders regarding the clarity and relevance of the information provided.

Feedback serves as a compass, guiding FP&A professionals in adjusting their sails to the ever-changing winds of market dynamics, organizational shifts, and external economic factors. It is through this feedback that the finance team can identify discrepancies between forecasted and actual results, uncovering underlying assumptions that may no longer hold true.

The journey toward forecasting excellence is cyclical, not linear. A robust continuous improvement cycle in FP&A encompasses several key steps: Reflect, Analyze, Plan, and Act (RAPA). This cycle begins with reflection on the feedback received, followed by a deep analysis to understand the root causes of discrepancies and areas for enhancement. Planning involves setting actionable goals for improvement, be it through refining forecasting models, adopting new technologies, or enhancing data collection methodologies. Action, the final step, puts these plans into motion, closing the loop and setting the stage for the next cycle of feedback and refinement.

The incorporation of advanced technologies such as artificial intelligence (AI) and machine learning plays a pivotal role in this cycle. AI-driven models can significantly enhance the accuracy of forecasts by identifying complex patterns in historical data that human analysts might overlook. Moreover, machine learning algorithms learn from each forecasting cycle, automatically adjusting to improve future predictions based on past feedback and outcomes.

Consider the example of a Vancouver-based technology firm that embarked on a journey to revamp its forecasting process. Initially plagued by forecasts that frequently missed the mark, the firm instituted a structured feedback mechanism that involved all key stakeholders in the forecasting process. This feedback was systematically collected and analyzed after each quarterly forecast, leading to actionable insights that were promptly implemented.

One critical change was the transition to a more dynamic forecasting model that leveraged machine learning to adjust forecasts in real-time based on incoming financial data.

This shift not only improved the accuracy of the forecasts but also increased stakeholder trust in the FP&A function. The continuous improvement cycle became a catalyst for transformation, turning the firm's FP&A department from a back-office function into a strategic powerhouse that guided decision-making at the highest levels.

The path to FP&A excellence is forged through the relentless pursuit of feedback and a commitment to continuous improvement. By instilling these principles into the very fabric of the FP&A function, organizations can ensure that their forecasting processes remain agile, responsive, and aligned with the strategic objectives of the business. The journey is ongoing, a perpetual cycle of learning and adaptation that propels the organization forward into the future of finance.

Gathering Feedback on Forecasts and Reports

The architecture of effective feedback collection is built on the premise of accessibility and ease. Financial teams must establish multifaceted channels that encourage open communication and make the feedback process as seamless as possible. These channels might include digital surveys, structured interviews, focus groups, and interactive review sessions. Each serves a unique purpose, from gathering quantitative ratings on forecast accuracy to qualitative insights on report comprehensibility and utility.

Digital surveys, for example, can be strategically deployed following the dissemination of quarterly financial reports. Leveraging platforms that allow for anonymity can significantly increase participation rates and honesty in responses. In contrast, focus groups and interviews provide the depth and nuance that surveys might miss, offering a space for stakeholders to express concerns, suggestions, and interpretations in a more conversational setting.

The true value of feedback lies not in its collection but in its integration into the forecasting and reporting process. It entails a meticulous review of feedback data to discern patterns, anomalies, and actionable insights. For instance, consistent comments on the complexity of financial reports may signal a need for simplification or enhanced data visualization efforts. Similarly, discrepancies between forecasted and actual figures could indicate specific areas where forecasting models need refinement.

Integrating feedback effectively requires the FP&A team to adopt a mindset of humility and openness to change. It often involves cross-departmental collaboration to understand the operational or market-driven reasons behind forecasting inaccuracies or report misinterpretations. This collaborative review process ensures that feedback leads to meaningful adjustments, whether in the assumptions used in models, the presentation of data, or the frequency and channels of communication.

The advancement in data analytics and AI offers powerful tools for analyzing feedback on a granular level. Text analytics and sentiment analysis can process open-ended survey responses and focus group transcripts to identify common themes and sentiments. Machine learning algorithms can help correlate feedback with specific forecasting outcomes, uncovering deeper insights into the efficacy of different forecasting techniques or the clarity of reports.

Drawing from Vancouver's vibrant tech scene, a SaaS company

implemented an AI-driven feedback analysis tool to dissect stakeholder feedback on its FP&A reports. This tool enabled the company to quickly identify that while their forecasts were generally accurate, the reports were often perceived as too dense and jargon-heavy, making it difficult for non-finance stakeholders to extract actionable insights. In response, the FP&A team initiated a series of workshops focused on data storytelling and visualization, significantly increasing report accessibility and stakeholder satisfaction.

The practice of gathering and integrating feedback should not be viewed as a one-off exercise but as a continuous loop that fuels the evolution of FP&A practices. It is a strategic imperative that aligns financial forecasting and reporting more closely with the dynamic needs of the business and its stakeholders. Engaging regularly with feedback mechanisms ensures that the FP&A function remains agile, responsive, and deeply integrated into the strategic fabric of the organization.

Prioritizing feedback as a core component of the FP&A process, finance teams can drive greater accuracy in forecasts, enhance the strategic value of reports, and ultimately contribute more significantly to informed decision-making and organizational success.

Implementing a Continuous Improvement Cycle in FP&A Forecasts and Reports

The notion of continuous improvement lies at the very heart of financial planning and analysis (FP&A). It is a relentless pursuit of perfection, acknowledging that the financial landscapes businesses navigate are ever-evolving. Implementing a continuous improvement cycle within FP&A is not merely about enhancing the technical aspects of forecasting and reporting; it's about cultivating an organizational culture that breathes adaptability, learning, and growth. In this dance of numbers, models, and predictions, every feedback loop, every piece of data, becomes a stepping stone towards refinement and excellence.

The first step in embedding a continuous improvement cycle within FP&A activities is to establish a clear, structured process that encompasses the entire forecasting and reporting lifecycle. This involves setting benchmark standards for accuracy, comprehensiveness, and clarity against which every forecast and report can be measured. However, the foundation of this process is not static; it must be flexible enough to evolve with changing business needs and external environments.

For example, a critical part of this foundation could involve adopting a modular approach to financial models, where components can be independently updated without disrupting the integrity of the entire model. This allows for quicker adjustments in response to feedback or new information, facilitating a more dynamic improvement process.

The continuous improvement cycle in FP&A can be distilled into four pivotal actions: Review, Analyze, Act, and Monitor.

1. Review: Regularly scheduled reviews of forecasts and reports are crucial. These reviews should not only assess the accuracy of past forecasts but also evaluate the effectiveness of the communication of financial insights. Incorporating diverse perspectives, including those from non-finance departments, can reveal insights into how financial data impacts decision-making across the organization.

2. Analyze: This stage involves a deep dive into the feedback collected, identifying root causes of inaccuracies or areas for enhancement in reporting. Advanced analytics and AI can play a significant role here, offering quantitative and qualitative analyses of vast datasets of feedback and performance metrics.

3. Act: Armed with insights from the analysis, the FP&A team must then implement targeted actions. This could range from adjusting forecasting models, refining data collection methods, to reimagining the presentation of financial reports. Each action should be aligned with the goal of enhancing the clarity, accuracy, and strategic value of financial forecasts and reports.

4. Monitor: The effectiveness of implemented changes must be monitored closely. This involves setting up key performance indicators (KPIs) that specifically measure the impact of improvements on forecast accuracy and stakeholder engagement with reports. Monitoring provides the data necessary to loop back to the review stage, ensuring the cycle of continuous improvement remains in motion.

For a continuous improvement cycle to truly take root, it must be deeply embedded into the FP&A culture. Leadership plays a crucial role in this, modeling an openness to learning and change. Creating spaces for open dialogue, encouraging experimentation, and recognizing achievements in improving forecasting and reporting processes are all practices that nurture a culture of continuous improvement.

Training and development are also key components. By investing in ongoing education for the FP&A team in areas such as advanced analytics, data visualization, and soft skills like communication, organizations can equip their teams with the tools and knowledge they need to drive continuous improvement.

Moreover, embracing technologies that facilitate agility and learning, such as cloud-based FP&A platforms, AI, and machine learning algorithms, can provide the infrastructure that supports an environment of continuous growth and adaptation.

Implementing a continuous improvement cycle within FP&A is a strategic imperative that extends beyond mere process optimization. It is about fostering an organizational ethos that values precision, clarity, and strategic insight in financial forecasting and reporting. Through structured reviews, meticulous analysis, targeted actions, and vigilant monitoring, FP&A teams can not only elevate their function but also contribute more profoundly to their organization's strategic decision-making and future success.

Learning from Past Forecasting Inaccuracies in FP&A

In financial planning and analysis (FP&A), the ability to look back and learn from past forecasting inaccuracies is not just beneficial—it's imperative for the evolution and refinement of forecasting methodologies. Each misstep in a forecast, each variance from reality, holds invaluable lessons that, if properly analyzed, can lead to significant improvements in future forecasting accuracy and reliability.

Identifying Root Causes

The journey towards understanding past inaccuracies begins with a meticulous deconstruction of each forecasting error, identifying not just the 'what' but the 'why'. Was the inaccuracy a result of flawed data, optimistic assumptions, external market shocks, or perhaps a combination of these? For instance, a forecast might have failed to anticipate the impact of a sudden geopolitical event on market conditions, revealing a need for more agile, adaptive forecasting models that can incorporate real-time data and emerging trends.

Imagine a scenario where an FP&A team at a Vancouver-based tech firm failed to predict a sharp decline in hardware sales. On closer examination, it's discovered that the model didn't account for the rapid consumer shift towards cloud-based solutions, a trend that was gaining momentum worldwide. This oversight highlights the importance of incorporating broader market and technological trends into the forecasting process.

Transforming Insights into Action

Understanding the root causes of past inaccuracies is only half the battle; the next step is applying these insights to refine forecasting processes. This might involve:

1. Enhancing Data Quality: Ensuring that the data feeding into forecasts is accurate, up-to-date, and comprehensive. For instance, integrating more granular sales data or market intelligence into the forecasting model could improve its predictive accuracy.

2. Adapting Models to Incorporate External Factors: Adjusting models to better account for volatile external variables, such as economic indicators or industry trends, can make forecasts more resilient to unforeseen shifts.

3. Implementing Advanced Analytical Tools: Leveraging advanced forecasting techniques such as machine learning algorithms, which can analyze vast datasets and identify patterns that may not be apparent to human analysts.

4. Strengthening Scenario Planning: Developing a range of scenarios to understand the potential impact of various external shocks on financial outcomes. This approach allows FP&A teams to prepare more robust, flexible financial strategies.

Institutionalizing Learning

For organizations to effectively learn from past forecasting inaccuracies, they must cultivate an environment that encourages open dialogue, constructive feedback, and continuous learning. This involves:

- Creating a Culture of Transparency: Encouraging teams to share and discuss forecasting inaccuracies without fear of blame or retribution. This open environment fosters collaboration and collective problem-solving.

- Regular Review Cycles: Instituting regular, structured reviews of forecasts versus actuals, facilitating a routine examination of where and why divergences occurred.

- Knowledge Sharing: Organizing workshops or debrief sessions where teams can discuss past forecasts, share learnings, and brainstorm improvements. Leveraging insights from diverse departments can provide a more holistic view of the factors influencing forecasts.

- Continuous Professional Development: Investing in training for FP&A staff in the latest forecasting methodologies, analytical tools, and soft skills like critical thinking and communication. This ensures the team remains at the cutting edge of FP&A practice.

Learning from past forecasting inaccuracies is a critical component of a mature FP&A function. It's a process that demands rigor, openness, and a commitment to continuous improvement. By systematically analyzing where forecasts have gone awry, implementing targeted improvements, and fostering a culture of learning and adaptation, FP&A teams can enhance the accuracy of their future forecasts, thereby providing more reliable, actionable insights for decision-making. This adaptive approach not only mitigates future risks but also positions the organization to capitalize on opportunities in an ever-changing business landscape.

CHAPTER 8: MANAGING EXPECTATIONS AND NAVIGATING UNCERTAINTY

I n the meticulous world of Financial Planning & Analysis (FP&A), setting realistic expectations is paramount. This crucial step is less about taming ambition and more about finely balancing it with the practical realities of the market and the organization's capabilities. It's a dance between what is aspirational and what is achievable, informed by a deep understanding of past performance, current trends, and future potentials.

The foundation of setting realistic expectations lies in a comprehensive understanding of both the internal and external landscapes of the business. Internally, it requires an in-depth analysis of the company's historical performance data, identifying trends, and understanding the capabilities and limitations of its resources. Externally, it demands an acute awareness of the market dynamics, including competitor movements, regulatory changes, and economic indicators. For instance, a CFO in a Vancouver-based renewable energy firm must not only consider the firm's capacity for innovation and production but also the shifting global energy policies and the increasing competition in green technology.

Setting realistic forecasts is the leverage of data-driven insights. Utilizing advanced analytics and embracing technologies such as AI and machine learning can provide a more nuanced prediction model. These technologies have the power to sift through vast amounts of data to identify patterns and trends that may not be immediately apparent, offering a more substantiated basis for forecasts. By employing predictive analytics, FP&A professionals can generate forecasts that more accurately reflect the likely trajectory of the business, adjusting expectations to mirror these insights.

A key strategy in setting realistic expectations is the development and utilization of scenario planning. This involves creating a range of potential scenarios, from the most optimistic to the most pessimistic, each based on different sets of assumptions about future market conditions, competitive landscape, regulatory changes, and internal performance. By preparing for multiple outcomes, FP&A professionals can better understand the potential range of future states and set expectations that are realistic within that spectrum. For example, scenario planning can help a multinational corporation navigate uncertainties in trade policies by preparing for various scenarios of tariff changes and their impacts on supply chains and profitability.

In the dynamic realm of business, the ability to remain flexible and adapt expectations in real-time is invaluable. Setting realistic expectations is not a one-time task but a continuous process of adjustment and recalibration. This flexibility allows FP&A professionals to respond promptly to unforeseen changes, whether they are market downturns, disruptive technological innovations, or sudden shifts in consumer behavior. Incorporating rolling forecasts as part of the FP&A process can facilitate this flexibility, enabling more frequent adjustments to expectations based on the latest available data.

Cultivating a culture that values realism over unwarranted optimism is essential. It involves clear communication across all levels of the organization about the importance of setting achievable goals, grounded in empirical data and thorough analysis. Such a culture encourages transparency, where challenges and uncertainties are openly discussed, and forecasts are scrutinized constructively. It also involves training and development programs to equip the FP&A team with the skills required to analyze data critically, apply advanced forecasting techniques, and communicate findings effectively.

Setting realistic expectations in FP&A is a critical discipline that balances ambition with evidence-driven analysis. It involves a deep dive into both internal capabilities and external market conditions, the application of advanced analytics, and the strategic use of scenario planning to prepare for a range of future possibilities. By fostering a culture of realism and maintaining flexibility, organizations can navigate the complexities of the business environment with greater confidence and precision, turning forecasts into valuable strategic assets that drive informed decision-making.

The Dangers of Over-Optimism in Forecasts

Over-optimism in forecasting, while rooted in a natural

human inclination towards positive outcomes, can lead to perilous pitfalls for any organization. This tendency to view the future through rose-colored glasses often results from a combination of cognitive biases, pressure to meet stakeholder expectations, and sometimes, a genuine underestimation of the challenges ahead. The fine line between ambition and attainable goals becomes blurred, setting the stage for potential financial missteps and strategic errors.

One of the primary drivers of over-optimistic forecasts is cognitive bias. Confirmation bias, for instance, leads individuals to favor information that confirms their preconceptions or hypotheses, regardless of whether the information is true. In the context of FP&A, this might manifest in selectively focusing on data that supports aggressive growth predictions while ignoring signals that suggest a more conservative approach. Similarly, the planning fallacy, which causes planners to underestimate the time, costs, and risks of future actions, can severely distort forecasts. These biases not only jeopardize the accuracy of financial forecasts but also cloud judgment, leading to overconfident decision-making.

The consequences of over-optimistic forecasts can be far-reaching. At a strategic level, they can misguide the allocation of resources, leading to overinvestment in projects with overly ambitious returns that may never materialize. This misallocation further strains other potentially viable projects or areas of the business that are underfunded as a result.

Financially, over-optimism can lead to liquidity issues, as revenue projections fail to materialize, leaving the company struggling to cover operational costs or debt obligations. For publicly traded companies, failing to meet forecasted growth targets can also have a detrimental impact on stock prices and investor confidence.

Moreover, the cultural impact within an organization can be equally damaging. Persistent over-optimism can lead to a cycle of disappointment, where teams are repeatedly set up for failure, eroding morale and trust in leadership. This environment discourages realistic risk assessment and critical thinking, further embedding a culture of unrealistic forecasting.

Mitigating the Dangers through Rigorous Analysis and Diverse Perspectives

To combat the dangers of over-optimism, organizations must foster a culture of rigorous analytical thinking and encourage a diversity of perspectives. Implementing checks and balances through cross-departmental review processes can help mitigate individual biases. Encouraging a culture where questioning and critical assessment of forecasts are valued over conformity can further safeguard against over-optimism.

Scenario analysis emerges as a crucial tool in this context. By rigorously exploring a range of outcomes—from the most pessimistic to the most optimistic—organizations can better prepare for uncertainty. This approach also helps in tempering expectations by presenting a balanced view of potential futures, thus mitigating the risk of overly optimistic forecasts.

Case Study: The Tech Startup Pitfall

Consider the case of a tech startup, buoyed by initial success and venture capital interest, projecting exponential growth based on the optimistic assumptions of market capture and product adoption. Ignoring the historical data of similar ventures and market saturation levels led to an unrealistic forecast, compelling the company to scale operations prematurely. The result was an unsustainable burn rate, talent churn due to disillusionment, and eventual retrenchment—a cautionary tale highlighting the perils of over-optimism.

Over-optimism in financial forecasting is a treacherous path, leading to strategic misalignments, financial instability, and a disillusioned workforce. By promoting a culture of critical analysis, embracing diverse perspectives, and rigorously testing assumptions through scenario planning, organizations can navigate the fine line between ambition and realism. This balanced approach ensures that optimism, while a valuable trait, is always grounded in evidence and reality, safeguarding the organization's future and fostering sustainable growth.

Balancing Caution with Ambition

In financial planning and analysis (FP&A), striking a harmonious balance between caution and ambition is akin to walking a tightrope. This delicate equilibrium is pivotal in crafting forecasts that are not only aspirational but also grounded in the pragmatic realities of the market and organizational capabilities. The art of balancing these two facets involves a nuanced understanding of the organization's strategic objectives, risk tolerance, and the broader economic environment.

The Constituents of a Balanced Forecast

A balanced forecast recognizes the importance of ambition in driving growth and innovation, while caution serves as the anchor, ensuring that the organization remains resilient against unforeseen challenges. The synergy between these two elements fosters a forward-looking perspective that is both optimistic and realistic.

1. Ambition as the Growth Engine: Ambition propels the organization forward, setting high but attainable targets that challenge the status quo. It embodies the organization's aspirations for market expansion, product innovation, and revenue growth. Ambitious goals motivate teams, catalyze innovation, and attract investment by demonstrating the potential for significant returns.

2. Caution as the Stabilizer: Caution, on the other hand, introduces a layer of pragmatism into the forecasting process. It plays a critical role in risk management, ensuring that forecasts account for potential market fluctuations, competitive dynamics, and internal constraints. Caution is about preparing for the worst while striving for the best, thereby ensuring that the organization remains resilient and adaptable.

Integrating Scenario Planning for Balance

Scenario planning emerges as a crucial methodology in achieving this balance. By developing multiple scenarios that encompass a range of possible futures, organizations can explore the implications of various levels of ambition and caution. This process involves:

- Best-case scenarios that push the boundaries of ambition, illustrating what could be achieved in an optimal environment.

- Worst-case scenarios that apply a higher degree of caution, considering potential challenges and setbacks that could impact the organization.

- Realistic scenarios that find the middle ground, balancing ambition with a prudent level of caution.

Each scenario is accompanied by strategic plans and contingency measures, ensuring that the organization is well-prepared to pivot as circumstances change.

The Role of Data and Analytics

Advancements in data analytics and business intelligence tools have significantly enhanced the ability to balance caution with ambition. These technologies enable deeper insights into market trends, customer behaviors, and operational efficiencies. By leveraging predictive analytics, organizations can model the potential outcomes of various strategies, providing a data-driven foundation for balanced forecasting.

Cultivating a Culture of Balanced Optimism

Fostering a corporate culture that values balanced optimism is essential. This involves:

- Encouraging open dialogue about the assumptions and risks underpinning forecasts, promoting a culture where questioning and scrutiny are seen as constructive.

- Rewarding both innovation and risk management,

acknowledging that both elements are critical for sustainable growth.

- Investing in skills development, equipping teams with the analytical tools and strategic thinking capabilities needed to navigate the complexities of balanced forecasting.

Case Study: The Retail Giant's Strategic Pivot

Consider the case of a global retail giant facing the dual challenges of digital disruption and changing consumer behaviors. By adopting a balanced forecasting approach, the company set ambitious targets for online sales growth while also being cautious of the potential for market saturation and logistical challenges. Scenario planning enabled the organization to develop robust e-commerce strategies while also bolstering its brick-and-mortar operations against potential downturns. The result was a comprehensive growth strategy that capitalized on emerging opportunities while mitigating risks.

Balancing caution with ambition in financial forecasting is not about compromising one for the other but about finding the sweet spot where both can coexist. This balanced approach enables organizations to pursue growth aggressively while also building the resilience needed to navigate the inevitable ebbs and flows of the business landscape. Through rigorous analysis, scenario planning, and a culture of balanced optimism, organizations can forge a path toward sustainable success.

Communicating Uncertainties and Risks

Effective risk communication lies transparency. This is not

merely about presenting data and probabilities; it's about creating a narrative that elucidates the potential impacts of uncertainties on organizational objectives. Transparency involves:

1. Clear Articulation of Assumptions: Every financial forecast is underpinned by a set of assumptions. Clearly communicating these assumptions helps stakeholders understand the conditions under which the forecast might change.

2. Quantification of Risks: Where possible, risks should be quantified, providing stakeholders with a sense of magnitude. This could involve sensitivity analyses or scenario simulations that illustrate how changes in key variables affect the forecast.

3. Visual Depiction of Uncertainties: Utilizing charts, graphs, and heat maps to visualize the range of potential outcomes can be far more impactful than numbers alone. Visual tools help distill complex uncertainties into understandable insights.

Empowering Decision-Making with Scenario Analysis

Scenario analysis stands as a pivotal tool in the communication of uncertainties and risks. By presenting multiple potential futures – each with its own set of assumptions, risks, and outcomes – scenario analysis empowers stakeholders to make decisions with a comprehensive understanding of potential variability. This approach fosters a dynamic decision-making environment where strategies can be adapted in response to evolving circumstances.

Dialogue and Engagement: Beyond the Report

Communicating uncertainties and risks extends beyond the delivery of a report or presentation. It encompasses ongoing dialogue with stakeholders to explore the implications of these risks and uncertainties:

- Stakeholder Workshops: Interactive sessions with key stakeholders can facilitate a deeper understanding of the risks and uncertainties presented in the forecast. These workshops provide a forum for questions, clarifications, and collaborative exploration of mitigation strategies.

- Regular Updates: As the external environment changes, so too do the uncertainties and risks associated with a forecast. Regularly updating stakeholders on these changes ensures that decision-making is based on the most current understanding of the landscape.

Incorporating Feedback Loops

Effective communication is a two-way street. Incorporating feedback mechanisms into the risk communication process allows for the refinement of forecasts based on stakeholder insights and concerns. This iterative process not only enhances the accuracy and relevance of the forecasts but also builds trust and credibility.

Case Study: Navigating a High-Stakes Merger

Consider the scenario of a corporation contemplating a high-stakes merger in a volatile industry. The FP&A team developed a comprehensive forecast outlining the financial implications of the merger, including a detailed analysis of uncertainties and risks. By employing a transparent communication strategy, complete with scenario analyses and visual tools, the team facilitated a series of workshops with the board of directors. These discussions, rooted in a clear understanding of potential risks, ultimately guided a strategic decision that balanced ambition with a well-informed caution.

Communicating uncertainties and risks is an art that requires clarity, transparency, and ongoing engagement. By employing strategic methodologies such as scenario analysis and visual tools, FP&A professionals can equip stakeholders with the insights needed to navigate the complex terrain of financial decision-making. Through iterative dialogue and an emphasis on transparency, organizations can foster a culture of informed risk-taking that aligns with their strategic objectives.

Navigating Uncertain Environments

Central to navigating uncertain environments is the concept of adaptive forecasting. Unlike traditional forecasting methods, which often rely on static assumptions, adaptive forecasting embraces flexibility, allowing for real-time adjustments as new information becomes available. This approach involves:

1. Continuous Monitoring: Keeping a vigilant eye on market trends, regulatory developments, and internal performance metrics to identify signals of change early on.

2. Dynamic Scenarios: Developing a range of scenarios that reflect different possible futures, rather than a single, fixed outlook. This includes worst-case, best-case, and most-likely scenarios, enabling organizations to prepare for a variety of outcomes.

3. Feedback Loops: Implementing mechanisms to incorporate feedback from across the organization and its external environment. This ensures that forecasts remain relevant and responsive to new insights and emerging trends.

Leveraging Technology for Insight and Agility

Technological advancements play a crucial role in enabling FP&A teams to navigate uncertain environments. Tools such as predictive analytics, artificial intelligence (AI), and machine learning offer unparalleled insights into potential future trends and outcomes, while also enhancing the speed at which organizations can respond to change. Key technologies include:

- Predictive Analytics: Using historical data and statistical algorithms to forecast future events. This can help organizations anticipate market shifts or customer behavior changes.

- Artificial Intelligence and Machine Learning: AI and machine learning can analyze vast amounts of data to identify patterns and predict outcomes, offering a depth of insight beyond human analysis.

Building a Resilient Organization

Resilience is the capability to withstand and recover from disruptions. In FP&A, fostering organizational resilience requires a multi-faceted approach:

- Diversification: Spreading risk across different markets,

products, or investments to mitigate the impact of adverse events in any one area.

- Flexibility in Operations: Developing operational processes that can be quickly adapted or scaled in response to changing circumstances.

- Cultivating a Risk-aware Culture: Encouraging an organizational culture that understands and actively manages risk, promoting proactive rather than reactive responses.

Case Study: Pivoting in a Pandemic

The onset of the global pandemic serves as a poignant example of navigating uncertain environments. Faced with unprecedented disruptions, a multinational corporation utilized adaptive forecasting to revise its financial outlook, incorporating real-time data on lockdowns, supply chain disruptions, and consumer behavior changes. Leveraging AI-based predictive models, the FP&A team provided insights that guided the company's pivot to e-commerce, mitigating the impact of retail closures. This adaptive approach not only safeguarded the company's financial health but also positioned it for accelerated growth in the post-pandemic landscape.

Navigating uncertain environments demands a blend of strategic foresight, technological leverage, and organizational resilience. By adopting adaptive forecasting, embracing the insights offered by advanced technologies, and building a culture of flexibility and risk awareness, FP&A professionals can guide their organizations through the complexities of modern business landscapes. This strategic navigation empowers companies to not just survive but thrive amidst uncertainty, turning potential challenges into opportunities for growth and innovation.

Flexibility in Forecasting and Planning

Flexibility in forecasting and planning is not merely a strategy; it's a survival skill in today's fast-paced economic environment. This segment delves deep into the essence of flexibility within the FP&A domain, highlighting practical steps, methodologies, and tools that empower organizations to remain agile and responsive to the ever-changing business dynamics.

The Pillars of Flexible Forecasting

flexible forecasting lies the capacity to adapt plans based on evolving circumstances and new information. This dynamic approach is built on several key pillars:

1. Rolling Forecasts: Unlike traditional annual forecasts, rolling forecasts are updated regularly, often quarterly or monthly, to reflect the latest market conditions and performance data. This continual revision process ensures that forecasts are always current, providing a more accurate basis for decision-making.

2. Scenario Analysis: In addition to dynamic scenarios mentioned earlier, flexibility in forecasting necessitates a robust scenario analysis framework that can quickly adapt to changes. This involves regularly updating scenarios as new information becomes available and reassessing the probability of each scenario as conditions evolve.

3. Modular Planning: Designing business plans and budgets in a modular fashion allows for individual components to be adjusted, added, or removed without disrupting the overall plan. This modularity supports swift responses to unanticipated shifts in the business landscape.

Technological Enablers of Flexibility

Advancements in technology have significantly enhanced the ability of FP&A teams to forecast and plan with greater flexibility. Key enablers include:

- Cloud Computing: Cloud-based FP&A software facilitates real-time data sharing and collaboration across departments and locations, ensuring that decision-makers have access to the latest information.

- Data Visualization Tools: These tools enable complex data to be presented in an easily digestible format, allowing for quicker understanding and response to emerging trends.

- Simulation Software: Simulation and modeling tools offer the ability to test various scenarios and outcomes, helping organizations to assess the potential impacts of different strategies rapidly.

Cultural Shift Towards Flexibility

Cultivating a culture that embraces flexibility and change is crucial for the effective implementation of flexible forecasting and planning. This cultural shift involves:

- Encouraging openness to change among staff and management.

- Promoting ongoing learning and development to keep pace with new tools and methodologies.

- Fostering cross-departmental collaboration to ensure a holistic view of the organization in planning processes.

Real-world Application: Agile Response to Supply Chain Disruption

A compelling illustration of flexibility in action is seen in how a leading manufacturing firm adapted its forecasting and planning processes in response to a sudden supply chain disruption. By employing rolling forecasts and scenario analysis, the company quickly assessed the situation's impact on production schedules and demand forecasts. Modular planning allowed for rapid shifts in sourcing strategies, and advanced analytics provided insights into alternative suppliers. This flexible approach minimized the disruption's impact on operations and maintained service levels for customers.

Flexibility in forecasting and planning is the cornerstone of modern FP&A practice. It enables organizations to navigate the complexities of today's business environment with confidence, making informed decisions that drive strategic advantage. Through a combination of rolling forecasts, scenario analysis, modular planning, and leveraging the latest technological tools, companies can achieve a level of agility that supports sustained growth and resilience in the face of uncertainty.

The Role of the CFO in Crisis Management

At the core of effective crisis management is the CFO's ability to anticipate financial storms and prepare the organization to weather them. This involves:

1. Liquidity Management: Ensuring availability of cash reserves to meet short-term obligations without compromising long-term strategic goals. This requires astute management of working capital, strategic divestments, and securing credit lines well before the crisis hits.

2. Risk Assessment and Mitigation: Proactively identifying financial and operational risks through a comprehensive risk management framework. The CFO must evaluate the financial impact of potential crises and develop mitigation strategies to protect the organization's assets and reputation.

3. Strategic Cost Management: Balancing cost-cutting measures with investment in critical areas to ensure the organization emerges stronger post-crisis. The CFO needs to discern which costs are variable and can be temporarily reduced without affecting core operations.

Leadership and Communication

A crisis demands strong leadership from the CFO, characterized by:

- Decisive Action: The CFO must make rapid and informed decisions, often with incomplete information. This decisiveness, based on a clear understanding of the organization's financial health and market conditions, can steer the organization away from potential pitfalls.

- Transparent Communication: Keeping internal and external stakeholders informed is crucial during a crisis. The CFO should communicate the financial realities and the steps being taken to safeguard the organization's future, fostering trust and confidence among employees, investors, and customers.

- Cross-functional Collaboration: Working closely with other C-suite executives to ensure a cohesive response strategy. The CFO's insights can help align various departments' response efforts with the overall financial strategy.

Technological Leverage

In the digital age, a CFO's toolkit includes advanced technologies that support agile decision-making during a crisis:

- Financial Modeling Tools: Utilizing sophisticated financial models to simulate various crisis scenarios and their potential impacts on the organization's finances. This aids in developing contingency plans that are informed by data-driven insights.

- Real-time Reporting Systems: Implementing systems that provide real-time financial data, enabling the CFO to monitor the crisis's impact on cash flow, revenue, and expenses as it unfolds. This allows for timely adjustments to the financial strategy.

Case Study: Leading Through a Global Pandemic

The recent global health crisis serves as a prime example of the CFO's role in crisis management. A multinational corporation faced unprecedented supply chain disruptions and a sharp decline in consumer demand. The CFO led a cross-functional task force that quickly assessed the financial impact, secured additional liquidity through various financial instruments, and implemented a digital transformation initiative to adapt to the changing consumer behavior. Regular, transparent communication with all stakeholders kept the organization aligned and focused, enabling it to navigate through the crisis effectively.

The CFO's role in crisis management extends beyond financial oversight to strategic leadership, effective communication, and technological proficiency. By preparing for crises before they occur, responding decisively when they hit, and leading with transparency and foresight, CFOs can guide their organizations through challenging times, emerging more resilient and strategically positioned for the future.

Adjusting Forecasts in Real-Time: The CFO's Guide to Agile Financial Planning

The foundation of real-time forecast adjustment is an agile mindset. In contrast to traditional forecasting methods, which may rely on annual or quarterly projections, an agile approach emphasizes continuous review and adjustment. This paradigm shift enables CFOs to respond swiftly to market volatility, regulatory changes, and unexpected challenges.

1. Continuous Analysis: Implementing a practice of ongoing analysis rather than periodic review. This includes regular monitoring of key performance indicators (KPIs), market

trends, and internal performance metrics.

2. Flexibility in Planning: Developing financial plans that accommodate quick shifts in strategy. This flexibility involves setting aside resources for unforeseen events and maintaining a portfolio of initiatives that can be accelerated or decelerated based on real-time data.

Technological Tools for Real-Time Forecasting

Advancements in financial technology are pivotal in enabling CFOs to adjust forecasts in real-time. The integration of the following tools into the financial planning process is crucial:

- Cloud-based Financial Planning and Analysis (FP&A) Solutions: These platforms offer the advantage of scalability and accessibility, allowing finance teams to update forecasts anytime, anywhere, and providing a single source of truth for all stakeholders.

- Advanced Analytics and Predictive Modeling: Utilizing artificial intelligence (AI) and machine learning (ML) to analyze patterns in large datasets, predicting future trends, and identifying potential risks or opportunities for the business.

- Real-time Dashboards: Implementing dashboards that display real-time financial data, enabling the CFO and other decision-makers to have instant visibility into the organization's financial health.

Strategies for Implementing Real-Time Forecast Adjustments

Transitioning to a model that supports real-time forecast adjustments requires strategic planning and execution:

1. Cultivating Data-Driven Culture: Encouraging a culture where decisions are made based on data rather than intuition. This involves training and empowering finance teams to interpret data and understand its implications for the business.

2. Cross-Departmental Collaboration: Enhancing communication and collaboration between the finance department and other business units. This ensures that the finance team receives timely insights into operational changes that could impact financial forecasts.

3. Scenario Planning: Regularly engaging in scenario planning exercises to explore how different external and internal factors may impact the organization. This prepares the team to pivot strategies quickly when actual conditions change.

Case Example: Agile Forecasting in Action

Consider the case of a technology firm that experienced sudden shifts in demand due to global supply chain disruptions. The CFO utilized cloud-based FP&A software to gather real-time data from sales, operations, and external sources. By analyzing this data through AI-driven predictive models, the finance team was able to project various scenarios rapidly. This enabled the firm to adjust its forecasts and resource allocation on the fly, mitigating potential losses and capitalizing on emerging opportunities.

Adjusting forecasts in real-time is not merely about adopting new technologies; it's about transforming the financial planning process into a more agile, collaborative, and data-driven practice. By doing so, CFOs can ensure that their organizations are not just reacting to the world as it changes but proactively planning for a multitude of possible futures, staying ahead of the curve in a competitive and uncertain market landscape.

The Role of Leadership in Forecasting: Steering Through Uncertainty with Vision and Decisiveness

Forecasting, is about predicting the future—a task fraught with uncertainty and the potential for error. Visionary leadership stands out by not only acknowledging this uncertainty but embracing it as an opportunity for strategic advantage. A leader with a clear vision can set the direction for forecasting efforts, ensuring that the organization's financial strategy aligns with its long-term goals.

1. Strategic Alignment: Visionary leaders ensure that forecasting efforts are not siloed activities but integral parts of the organization's strategic framework. They align financial forecasts with the company's vision, mission, and strategic objectives, ensuring every financial decision propels the organization closer to its goals.

2. Innovation and Adaptation: Embracing innovative forecasting methods and technologies is crucial. Leaders must champion the adoption of AI, machine learning, and real-time analytics, pushing the boundaries of traditional forecasting to harness the power of these advancements.

Decisiveness in Uncertainty: The Role of the CFO

In FP&A, indecision can be as detrimental as an incorrect decision. The ability to make informed decisions swiftly, especially under conditions of uncertainty, defines effective leadership. The CFO, as the herald of financial strategy, must exhibit an unwavering commitment to decisiveness.

1. Risk Management: Effective leaders understand that forecasting is inherently tied to risk management. They use forecasts to identify potential risks and develop strategies to mitigate these risks, making decisions that balance risk and reward.

2. Agility: The financial landscape can change rapidly, requiring forecasts to be adjusted in real-time. Leaders must be agile, ready to make quick decisions based on the latest data and insights to steer the organization through volatility.

Navigating Through Uncertainty: Bridging Leadership and Data

The true test of leadership in forecasting lies in navigating through uncertainty. This involves a delicate balance between relying on data-driven insights and leveraging leadership intuition and experience.

1. Data-Driven Decision Making: Leaders foster a culture where decisions are grounded in data and analytics. They ensure that the organization's decision-making processes are structured around actionable insights derived from accurate, timely, and relevant data.

2. Leadership Intuition: While data is critical, effective leaders also know when to trust their intuition. They understand the

industry nuances and can read between the lines of what the data presents, using their experience to guide decisions when data may not give a clear direction.

Case Example: Leadership Driving Forecasting Success

Consider a multinational corporation facing economic turbulence in multiple markets. The CFO, leveraging a combination of real-time data analytics and seasoned judgment, quickly adjusted the company's financial forecasts. By reallocating resources towards more resilient markets and cutting costs in vulnerable areas, the CFO demonstrated decisive leadership. This swift action, grounded in both data and intuition, enabled the company to weather the storm and emerge in a stronger competitive position.

The role of leadership in forecasting transcends mere oversight. It embodies the vision to set the strategic direction, the decisiveness to act under uncertainty, and the wisdom to balance data with intuition. In the complex dance of FP&A, effective leadership is the compass that guides the organization through the ever-changing landscape of financial predictions, towards a future of prosperity and growth.

Leading Through Uncertain Times: A Blueprint for Navigating Financial Forecasts with Resilience

Resilient leadership is the cornerstone of effective forecasting during periods of uncertainty. It embodies the capacity to absorb stress, recover critical functionality, and thrive amidst changing circumstances. This resilience is not innate; it is cultivated through strategic foresight, emotional intelligence, and an unwavering commitment to the organization's vision.

1. Strategic Foresight: Leaders must cultivate an ability to look beyond the horizon, anticipating potential financial storms and preparing the organization accordingly. This foresight involves rigorous scenario planning, where multiple outcomes are considered and strategies are developed to address each potential future.

2. Emotional Intelligence: Navigating through uncertain times requires leaders to manage not only the financial aspects of the organization but also its human capital. Emotional intelligence—the ability to understand and manage one's own emotions and those of others—becomes a critical tool. It enables leaders to maintain team morale, foster a culture of trust and resilience, and communicate effectively even when the news is not favorable.

Implementing Adaptive Strategies

In the face of uncertainty, adaptive leadership strategies take precedence. These strategies are not static; they evolve as the external financial environment changes.

1. Flexibility in Forecasting: Traditional annual budgeting processes give way to more flexible, continuous forecasting methods. Rolling forecasts, for instance, allow leaders to adjust financial expectations in real-time, responding to emerging trends and unexpected challenges with agility.

2. Decentralized Decision-Making: Empowering teams by delegating decision-making authority can unleash innovative solutions that a centralized leadership model might overlook. This approach requires a balance, ensuring that decentralized decisions align with the organization's overall strategy and

financial goals.

Communication as a Leadership Tool

Amidst uncertainty, clear, transparent, and consistent communication becomes a powerful leadership tool. It bridges the gap between leadership's strategic vision and the operational realities of the team.

1. Transparent Reporting: Leaders should prioritize transparency in financial reporting, sharing not just the "what" but also the "why" behind financial forecasts and adjustments. This openness fosters a culture of trust and collective responsibility.

2. Continuous Dialogue: Regular, open channels of communication between leaders and their teams ensure that everyone is aligned with the current financial outlook and the rationale behind strategic decisions. This continuous dialogue facilitates swift collective action in response to changing forecasts.

Case Example: Adaptive Leadership in Action

Consider a tech start-up navigating the financial uncertainties triggered by a global economic downturn. The CFO, practicing resilient leadership, shifted the company's financial strategy from aggressive expansion to consolidation. Utilizing rolling forecasts, the leadership team was able to reallocate resources dynamically, focusing on core products that showed steady demand. Through transparent communication, the entire organization was aligned on these strategic shifts, enabling the company to weather the downturn and emerge in a position of strength.

Leading through uncertain times requires a multifaceted approach, blending strategic foresight, emotional intelligence, and adaptive strategies with effective communication. As the financial landscape continues to evolve, leaders who embody these principles will not only navigate through the storm but will also chart a course toward sustained organizational growth and resilience.

Building Trust in the Forecasting Process: Cultivating Confidence and Credibility

Trust in the forecasting process begins with the fundamental expectation of accuracy. Stakeholders, from executives to investors, need to feel confident that the forecasts they base their decisions on are not only carefully constructed but also reflect a realistic picture of the future.

1. Historical Accuracy Analysis: Regularly comparing forecasted outcomes with actual results serves as a critical trust-building exercise. It allows FP&A teams to refine their models based on historical data, enhancing the accuracy and reliability of future forecasts.

2. Methodological Transparency: Sharing the methodologies and assumptions underlying forecasts demystifies the process and invites constructive scrutiny. It demonstrates a commitment to intellectual honesty and opens the door to feedback, further refining the forecasting process.

Transparency: The Keystone of Trust

Transparency in the forecasting process involves more than just open communication; it's about creating an environment where information flows freely, and all contributions are valued.

1. Regular Updates and Revisions: Keeping stakeholders informed with regular updates and being upfront about revisions to forecasts fosters a culture of transparency. It reassures them that the forecasting process is dynamic and responsive to new information.

2. Explanation of Variances: When forecasts deviate from actual results, a thorough explanation of the variances can be a powerful trust-building tool. It shows a commitment to learning and improvement, key attributes of a trustworthy FP&A function.

Engaging Stakeholders: A Collaborative Approach

Building trust in the forecasting process extends beyond the confines of the FP&A team. Engaging a broad range of stakeholders throughout the forecasting cycle encourages a sense of ownership and accountability.

1. Inclusive Planning Sessions: Inviting input from various departments and stakeholders in the forecasting process ensures that multiple perspectives are considered. Such inclusivity can uncover insights that would otherwise be missed, leading to more accurate and comprehensive forecasts.

2. Clear Communication of Implications: Clearly communicating the strategic implications of forecasts helps stakeholders understand their significance. It bridges the gap between data-driven predictions and strategic actions, reinforcing the value of the forecasting process.

Case Example: A Tale of Restored Trust

Consider the case of a multinational corporation that faced skepticism over its forecasting accuracy after several quarters of missed targets. The FP&A team initiated a "Forecasting Transparency Initiative," where they openly shared methodologies, assumptions, and the rationale behind forecast adjustments. They also established a cross-departmental forecasting committee, including representatives from sales, operations, and marketing, to provide insights into the forecasting process. Over time, this approach not only improved the accuracy of forecasts but also restored trust among stakeholders, leading to more cohesive and strategic decision-making across the organization.

Trust in the forecasting process is not a given; it is earned through consistent accuracy, unwavering transparency, and inclusive stakeholder engagement. By embedding these principles into FP&A operations, organizations can ensure that their forecasting process is not just a procedural necessity but a strategic asset that commands confidence and drives informed decision-making.

Encouraging a Culture of Financial Foresight: Nurturing Anticipatory Finance Teams

Financial foresight goes beyond traditional forecasting; it involves a deep understanding of the potential future states of the market and how they might affect an organization's financial health. It's about creating a culture where every member of the finance team, from the CFO to junior analysts, is encouraged to think ahead, identify trends, and consider their implications.

1. Strategic Scenario Planning: Implementing regular strategic scenario planning sessions can empower finance teams to explore various future scenarios, including those that may seem unlikely. This practice not only prepares the team for a range of outcomes but also sharpens their ability to recognize early indicators of change.

2. Continuous Learning and Adaptation: Curating an environment that values continuous learning and adaptation is crucial for fostering financial foresight. Encouraging team members to stay informed about global economic trends, technological advancements, and regulatory changes can provide a broader perspective necessary for anticipatory thinking.

Leveraging Technology for Enhanced Foresight

The integration of advanced technologies plays a pivotal role in nurturing a culture of financial foresight. Tools such as predictive analytics and AI offer unprecedented capabilities in identifying patterns, trends, and potential future outcomes from vast datasets.

1. Predictive Analytics Workshops: Organizing workshops focused on predictive analytics can demystify these technologies for finance teams. By understanding how to use these tools, team members can more accurately project future financial trends and outcomes.

2. AI-Assisted Forecasting Models: Encouraging the use of AI-assisted forecasting models can enhance the accuracy of predictions and free up team members to focus on strategic analysis rather than data crunching. This shift can enable

teams to dedicate more time to interpreting data and developing forward-looking strategies.

Cultivating a Collaborative Forecasting Environment

Promoting a collaborative environment is key to fostering a culture of financial foresight. Collaboration encourages the exchange of diverse perspectives and ideas, which can lead to more innovative solutions and anticipatory strategies.

1. Cross-Departmental Engagement: Encouraging finance teams to work closely with other departments can provide valuable insights into potential future challenges and opportunities. For instance, collaboration with the R&D department might offer a glimpse into future product innovations that could impact the financial strategy.

2. Finance Foresight Forums: Establishing regular forums where finance teams can share insights, discuss potential future scenarios, and brainstorm strategic responses can reinforce a culture of foresight. These forums can also serve as a platform for recognizing and rewarding forward-thinking initiatives.

Case Example: Proactive Financial Strategy in Action

Consider the narrative of a tech company that successfully navigated a potential market downturn by fostering a culture of financial foresight. The CFO had implemented quarterly foresight forums, where the finance team, in collaboration with the marketing and product development teams, analyzed emerging market trends. This collaborative approach led them to anticipate a shift in consumer preferences early on, allowing them to adjust their financial strategy and product development plans accordingly. This proactive response not only mitigated the potential negative impact on their financial performance but also positioned them as market leaders in innovation.

Cultivating a culture of financial foresight enables organizations to not just react to market changes but to anticipate and strategically navigate them. By embracing strategic scenario planning, leveraging advanced technologies, and fostering collaboration, finance teams can become anticipatory rather than reactionary, positioning their organizations for long-term success and stability.

CHAPTER 9: LEGAL AND ETHICAL CONSIDERATIONS

Compliance lies the dual mandate of adhering to financial reporting standards while also ensuring that forecasts and projections reflect an ethical commitment to accuracy and transparency. This balance is critical, not just for the integrity of the financial system, but also for maintaining stakeholder trust—a currency as valuable as any financial asset.

The challenge of compliance is compounded by the international variations in financial regulations. What is permissible in one jurisdiction might be prohibited in another, and vice versa. For global enterprises, this necessitates a patchwork approach to financial forecasting, where strategies are tailored not just to the markets they operate in, but also to the regulatory environments of those markets.

For instance, the European Union's GDPR has profound implications for how data is handled, with significant repercussions for the data-driven aspects of forecasting. Similarly, the United States' Sarbanes-Oxley Act imposes rigorous requirements on financial reporting, impacting the forecasting process from data collection to final projection.

Adherence to financial reporting standards like IFRS (International Financial Reporting Standards) or GAAP (Generally Accepted Accounting Principles) is not merely a legal obligation; it's a cornerstone of credibility and reliability in financial forecasting. These standards ensure that forecasts are prepared using consistent, transparent methods, making them comprehensible and trustworthy to investors, regulators, and other stakeholders.

The integration of these standards into the forecasting process involves rigorous data validation, the application of consistent methodology, and a commitment to ethical financial practices. This integration is not static; as standards evolve, so too must the processes and systems used by FP&A teams.

The velocity of change in financial regulations and reporting standards is accelerating, driven by technological advancements, evolving market dynamics, and the increasing complexity of global finance. Staying abreast of these changes is a formidable challenge, requiring a proactive approach to compliance management.

One effective strategy is the establishment of a dedicated compliance function within the FP&A team, responsible for monitoring regulatory developments and ensuring that forecasting models and methodologies remain in compliance. This function can also serve as a focal point for compliance training and awareness, ensuring that the entire team understands the regulatory context of their work.

compliance and regulation is a dynamic and   component

of financial forecasting. Navigating it successfully requires a blend of vigilance, adaptability, and a deep commitment to ethical financial practices. By embedding these principles into the core of their operations, CFOs and their FP&A teams can not only avoid the pitfalls of non-compliance but also elevate the standard of their forecasting efforts, building a foundation of trust and integrity that benefits all stakeholders.

Adhering to Financial Reporting Standards

The cornerstone of any robust financial planning and analysis (FP&A) framework is its adherence to established financial reporting standards. These standards, such as the International Financial Reporting Standards (IFRS) and the Generally Accepted Accounting Principles (GAAP) in the United States, serve as the bedrock for ensuring consistency, transparency, and accountability in financial reporting across the globe. For CFOs and their FP&A teams, the commitment to these standards is not just about regulatory compliance; it's about reinforcing the integrity of the financial forecasting process.

IFRS and GAAP are more than just acronyms in the finance industry; they are comprehensive sets of accounting rules and standards that dictate how financial transactions and other accounting events should be reported in financial statements. The adoption of these standards ensures that an organization's financial statements are understandable and comparable across international boundaries.

The significance of adhering to these standards cannot be overstated. For multinational corporations, this adherence facilitates the comparison of financial statements with competitors, partners, and industry benchmarks, regardless of where these entities operate. It simplifies the process for investors and stakeholders to make informed decisions, as they can trust the consistency and reliability of the financial reports presented to them.

Integrating these reporting standards into the forecasting process involves several critical steps. First, it requires a deep understanding of the specific requirements of each standard, as well as how they apply to the unique circumstances of the organization. This understanding forms the basis for developing forecasting models that align with these standards.

Second, it necessitates robust data governance practices to ensure the accuracy, completeness, and integrity of the data used in forecasts. This is particularly challenging in today's digital age, where the volume and velocity of data can be overwhelming. FP&A teams must employ sophisticated data management tools and technologies to sift through this data, ensuring that only high-quality, relevant data informs their forecasts.

Third, the adoption of advanced technologies plays a pivotal role in adhering to financial reporting standards. Software solutions designed for FP&A, equipped with capabilities for real-time data analysis, scenario planning, and predictive analytics, can significantly enhance the accuracy and reliability of forecasts. These tools can automate the application of complex reporting standards, reducing the risk of human error and ensuring consistent compliance.

The landscape of financial reporting standards is not static. It evolves in response to changes in the global economic environment, advances in technology, and emerging challenges in the financial sector. As such, continuous education and training are vital for CFOs and their FP&A teams to stay abreast of these changes.

Regular training sessions, workshops, and seminars can equip finance professionals with the latest knowledge and skills required to navigate the complexities of financial reporting standards. Moreover, fostering a culture of continuous learning within the FP&A team can encourage proactive engagement with new standards and interpretations, ensuring that the organization remains at the forefront of best practices in financial forecasting.

The adherence to financial reporting standards is a multifaceted endeavor that extends beyond mere compliance. It is a commitment to excellence in financial forecasting, underpinned by a deep understanding of the standards, robust data governance, advanced technology, and a culture of continuous learning. For CFOs and FP&A teams, this commitment is instrumental in building trust with stakeholders, facilitating informed decision-making, and driving the strategic direction of the organization forward.

International Variations in Financial Regulations

Navigating the labyrinth of international financial regulations is a formidable challenge that CFOs and their FP&A teams face in today's globalized business environment. The variations in financial regulations across different jurisdictions can significantly impact the financial forecasting process, making it crucial for finance professionals to possess a nuanced understanding of these differences and their implications.

The international financial regulatory landscape is

characterized by a mosaic of rules and standards that govern financial reporting, auditing, taxation, and corporate governance. These regulations are not only country-specific but can also vary between regions within countries, adding layers of complexity to the compliance process. For instance, the European Union has its overarching regulatory framework, which coexists with the national regulations of its member states.

Key regulatory bodies such as the International Accounting Standards Board (IASB), the Financial Accounting Standards Board (FASB) in the United States, and the European Securities and Markets Authority (ESMA) play pivotal roles in setting and enforcing these standards. However, despite efforts to harmonize financial reporting standards through the adoption of IFRS, significant differences remain, particularly in areas such as revenue recognition, lease accounting, and financial instruments.

The variations in financial regulations have a direct impact on the financial forecasting process. For multinational corporations operating in multiple jurisdictions, this means that forecasts must be adaptable and sensitive to the regulatory requirements of each region. It necessitates a segmented approach to forecasting, where financial models are tailored to reflect the specific compliance obligations in each market.

This segmented approach, however, presents its own set of challenges. It requires FP&A teams to have a deep and up-to-date knowledge of the regulatory environments in which they operate. Moreover, it demands sophisticated forecasting tools that can accommodate different accounting standards, tax regimes, and compliance requirements without compromising the integrity and comparability of the financial data.

To effectively navigate the complexities of international financial regulations, CFOs and FP&A teams can adopt several strategies. Firstly, investing in continuous education and training is essential. Keeping abreast of regulatory changes and understanding their implications on financial forecasting is critical for maintaining compliance and ensuring the accuracy of financial forecasts.

Secondly, leveraging technology is key. Advanced FP&A software solutions equipped with features such as multi-GAAP reporting, tax planning modules, and regulatory compliance dashboards can streamline the forecasting process. These tools can automate the application of different regulatory standards, reducing the risk of non-compliance and freeing up valuable resources for strategic analysis.

Thirdly, cultivating a network of local experts and advisors in each jurisdiction can provide invaluable insights into the nuances of local regulations. These experts can offer guidance on best practices, alert teams to upcoming regulatory changes, and assist in interpreting complex regulations, thereby enhancing the quality and compliance of financial forecasts.

The variations in international financial regulations present a significant challenge to the financial forecasting process. However, by understanding the regulatory landscape, leveraging advanced technology, and drawing on the expertise of local advisors, CFOs and their FP&A teams can navigate these complexities effectively. This not only ensures compliance but also enhances the strategic value of financial forecasting as a tool for guiding multinational corporations through the global business environment.

Keeping Up with Changes in Compliance Requirements

In the ever-evolving world of finance, staying abreast of changes in compliance requirements is akin to navigating a river that changes its course daily. For CFOs and their FP&A teams, the task is not just about compliance for its own sake but about harnessing these changes as opportunities to enhance strategic planning and financial forecasting.

Compliance requirements in the financial world are not static. Driven by shifts in economic policies, geopolitical events, technological advancements, and societal demands, regulatory frameworks are continually updated to address emerging risks and opportunities. The introduction of regulations like GDPR in Europe and the CCPA in California, USA, exemplifies how digital privacy concerns have forced businesses worldwide to adjust their data handling and processing practices, directly impacting financial data gathering and forecasting processes.

The key to turning compliance from a challenge into an opportunity lies in its integration into the organization's strategic planning. This integration allows companies to not only foresee potential compliance issues but also adapt their financial forecasting and strategic planning processes to leverage these changes. For instance, the anticipation of tighter financial regulations can lead to the early adoption of more rigorous financial practices, setting a company apart from its competitors.

Advancements in technology offer powerful tools for managing compliance changes. Cloud-based financial planning and analysis (FP&A) platforms equipped with regulatory updates can help CFOs ensure that financial forecasts are always in alignment with the latest compliance requirements. Artificial Intelligence (AI) and Machine Learning (ML) can predict regulatory trends, allowing companies to prepare in advance for changes that may affect their financial operations.

Cultivating a culture that views compliance as an integral part of the business strategy is crucial. This involves training and developing a mindset among the FP&A team that is always alert to regulatory news and updates, understanding the implications of these changes, and being ready to adjust forecasts and strategies accordingly. Regular compliance audits, participation in financial regulation workshops, and engagement with regulatory bodies can also foster an atmosphere of proactive compliance.

A pertinent example of adapting to compliance changes is the financial industry's transition from the London Interbank Offered Rate (LIBOR) to alternative reference rates like SOFR (Secured Overnight Financing Rate). This transition demanded significant adjustments in financial forecasting models, contract renovations, and risk management strategies. Companies that proactively adjusted their FP&A processes to accommodate these new rates were able to mitigate risks more efficiently and seize the strategic advantages of early compliance.

Keeping up with changes in compliance requirements demands a dynamic approach to financial planning and analysis. By integrating compliance into strategic planning, leveraging modern technologies, and fostering a culture of proactive compliance, CFOs and their teams can transform regulatory challenges into strategic opportunities. This proactive stance not only ensures regulatory compliance but also positions the company for strategic advantage in the complex and competitive global business environment.

Ethical Considerations in Forecasting

The cornerstone of ethical forecasting is the commitment to accuracy. This doesn't merely imply avoiding errors but encompasses a deliberate effort to ensure that forecasts are as accurate as possible, without intentional over-optimism or undue pessimism. The temptation to present overly favorable forecasts to please stakeholders or to secure investments poses a significant ethical dilemma. Such practices not only mislead investors but can also destabilize markets and erode trust in the financial system. This principle was starkly highlighted in the aftermath of the 2008 financial crisis, where overly optimistic financial forecasts played a pivotal role in the market's collapse.

Transparency is another critical ethical pillar. It involves clear communication about the methodologies, assumptions, and uncertainties involved in the forecasting process. Too often, forecasts are presented as definitive predictions without adequate disclosure of the underlying variables and potential volatilities. This lack of transparency can lead stakeholders to make decisions based on incomplete or misleading information. A commitment to transparency ensures that all parties have a comprehensive understanding of the forecast's basis, fostering informed decision-making.

In an era where data is akin to currency, the ethical gathering, handling, and use of data in forecasting cannot be overstressed. With regulations like GDPR setting the precedent for data protection, FP&A teams must navigate the delicate balance between leveraging data for insights and respecting individual privacy rights. Moreover, accountability extends to how data-driven forecasts impact employees, customers, and the broader community. For instance, a forecast predicting significant downsizing can have profound implications on employee morale and community stability. Ethical forecasting demands a conscientious approach to such outcomes, ensuring that the human aspect of data-driven decisions is not overlooked.

A compelling illustration of ethical considerations in forecasting can be seen in the pharmaceutical industry. The pricing of new drugs involves complex forecasting models that predict R&D costs, market demand, and competitive pricing. However, ethical dilemmas arise when profit maximization forecasts lead to exorbitant pricing, placing life-saving drugs out of reach for many. Ethical forecasting in this context involves a balanced consideration of profitability and accessibility, ensuring that the pursuit of financial gains does not overshadow the societal obligation to provide equitable access to healthcare.

Ethical considerations in forecasting are the bedrock upon which trust and integrity in the financial planning process are built. It extends beyond mere compliance to embody a principled approach to accuracy, transparency, and accountability. As FP&A professionals navigate the challenges of financial forecasting, embracing these ethical principles ensures not only the reliability of forecasts but also upholds the broader ethical responsibilities towards stakeholders and society. In this dance of numbers and ethics, the path of integrity leads to sustainable success and trust in the financial landscape.

Avoiding Manipulation of Forecasts

Manipulated forecasts are not merely errors in judgment or miscalculations; they are calculated distortions designed to mislead. The motivation behind such manipulation can range from attempting to influence stock prices, securing loans under false pretenses, to meeting short-term financial targets to receive bonuses. The methods of manipulation are varied, including but not limited to, overstating sales forecasts, underestimating expenses, or employing overly optimistic economic assumptions.

The consequences of forecast manipulation are far-reaching. Initially, it may seem like a successful strategy for achieving financial or market advantages. However, the long-term repercussions can be devastating. Stakeholder trust, once eroded, is challenging to rebuild. Investors, lenders, and even internal team members become wary, impacting future fundraising efforts and internal morale. On a broader scale, manipulated forecasts can lead to market distortions, contributing to economic instability and eroding public trust in financial markets.

The defense against forecast manipulation is multi-faceted, requiring a combination of stringent governance, robust methodologies, and a strong ethical culture.

1. Governance and Oversight: Establishing strong governance structures is paramount. This includes oversight bodies such as audit committees equipped with the expertise to review and challenge forecasting processes and outcomes. External audits and reviews by independent parties also add a layer of scrutiny that can deter manipulation.

2. Methodological Rigor: Employing rigorous, transparent

methodologies for forecasting acts as a bulwark against manipulation. This involves clear documentation of assumptions, methodologies, and data sources. Adopting standardized forecasting models across the organization can reduce the room for individual manipulation.

3. Cultivating an Ethical Culture: Perhaps the most potent defense against manipulation is cultivating a culture of integrity and transparency. This involves setting clear ethical guidelines, providing training on ethical forecasting, and establishing channels for raising concerns about unethical practices without fear of reprisal.

4. Technological Safeguards: Leveraging technology can provide additional safeguards. Forecasting software that tracks changes, requires approval for adjustments, and maintains an audit trail can significantly deter attempts to manipulate forecasts. Advanced analytics and machine learning can also detect patterns indicative of manipulation.

At the helm of the endeavor to prevent forecast manipulation is senior management. Their commitment to transparency, integrity, and accountability sets the tone for the entire organization. Leading by example, they can instill a culture where ethical forecasting is valued and practiced universally. This commitment is communicated through clear policies, continuous education, and by rewarding transparency and honesty rather than just short-term financial achievements.

Avoiding the manipulation of forecasts is not merely about adherence to regulatory requirements; it is about ensuring the integrity of the financial planning and analysis process. It is about building and maintaining trust with stakeholders and contributing to the stability of financial markets.

By implementing robust defenses against manipulation, organizations can ensure that their forecasting processes remain transparent, accurate, and, most importantly, ethical. In the dynamic landscape of FP&A, integrity in forecasting is not just a regulatory obligation but a strategic asset that guides companies towards sustainable success.

Ethical Responsibilities of the CFO

The CFO's ethical responsibilities extend beyond mere compliance with laws and regulations. They embody the organization's ethical compass, guiding financial strategies, decisions, and practices with a steadfast commitment to integrity. This encompasses:

1. Transparency in Reporting: Ensuring that all financial reports accurately reflect the company's financial status without embellishment or omission. This includes providing clear explanations of accounting methodologies, disclosing potential conflicts of interest, and making all necessary information available to stakeholders.

2. Accountability: Taking responsibility for the financial health and reporting of the organization. This involves not only owning up to mistakes or oversights but also implementing corrective actions to prevent future occurrences.

3. Fair Financial Practices: Upholding fair financial practices that do not mislead stakeholders, manipulate stock prices, or unjustly enrich individuals at the company's or stakeholders' expense.

The CFO often faces complex ethical dilemmas where financial and ethical considerations might seem at odds. Navigating these challenges requires a nuanced approach:

1. Balancing Short-term Pressures with Long-term Ethics: The pressure to meet quarterly forecasts can be immense. CFOs must balance these short-term pressures with the long-term ethical considerations and health of the organization, avoiding practices that could compromise future integrity or stability.

2. Ethical Decision-Making in Ambiguous Situations: Not all decisions come with a clear ethical path. In such cases, the CFO must rely on a framework of ethical decision-making that considers the welfare of all stakeholders, the legal implications, and the alignment with the organization's values.

3. Whistleblower Protections: Encouraging a culture where employees feel safe to report unethical financial practices without fear of retaliation is crucial. The CFO plays a key role in establishing and enforcing policies that protect whistleblowers.

The CFO's influence extends beyond the confines of the finance department, shaping the ethical culture of the entire organization:

1. Setting the Tone at the Top: The CFO, alongside other senior leaders, must exemplify the ethical standards they expect to see throughout the organization. This "tone at the top" is critical in fostering an environment where ethical practices are the norm, not the exception.

2. Education and Training: Providing regular education and training on ethical financial practices, regulatory compliance,

and the importance of transparency helps embed an ethical mindset across the organization.

3. Open Lines of Communication: Maintaining open channels for discussion and questions about ethical concerns or financial practices encourages a proactive approach to ethical issues and reinforces the importance of integrity in financial operations.

The ethical responsibilities of the CFO are both broad and deeply consequential. In steering the financial direction of the company, the CFO must navigate the balance between financial performance and ethical integrity. By championing transparency, accountability, and ethical decision-making, the CFO not only safeguards the financial health of the organization but also upholds its moral compass, laying a foundation for long-term success and trust with all stakeholders. In the evolving landscape of global finance, the role of the CFO as an ethical leader has never been more critical.

Transparency and Accountability in Financial Reporting

Transparency in financial reporting is not merely about fulfilling regulatory obligations; it is about painting an accurate, unvarnished picture of the company's financial health and operations. Herein lies several key practices:

1. Comprehensive Disclosure: All financial statements should be complete, presenting both the favorable and unfavorable aspects of the company's financial position. This includes not only the mandatory financial disclosures but also voluntary information that could affect stakeholders' decisions.

2. Clarity and Understandability: Financial reports should be presented in a manner that is clear and understandable to all stakeholders, irrespective of their financial literacy. This might involve the use of plain language summaries alongside more complex financial analyses.

3. Timeliness: Reporting should be timely, providing stakeholders with relevant financial data when it is most needed for decision-making, rather than when it becomes less impactful or obsolete.

Accountability in financial reporting implies a willingness to be answerable for financial performance and decisions. This encompasses several critical elements:

1. Accuracy and Honesty: Ensuring that financial reports are accurate and honest, free from any form of manipulation to present a more favorable view than is warranted by reality.

2. Ethical Financial Practices: This involves adherence to ethical standards in financial reporting, including the avoidance of practices such as earnings management or "creative accounting" that could mislead or deceive stakeholders.

3. Responsiveness to Stakeholder Inquiries: A commitment to accountability means being responsive to stakeholders' questions and concerns regarding financial reports, providing clear and forthright explanations as needed.

The CFO plays a pivotal role in implementing best practices in financial reporting, which include:

1. Adopting High-Quality Financial Reporting Standards: Utilizing internationally recognized standards, like IFRS (International Financial Reporting Standards) or GAAP (Generally Accepted Accounting Principles), as the basis for financial reporting.

2. Continuous Improvement: Engaging in continuous improvement of financial reporting processes to enhance transparency and accountability. This could involve the adoption of new technologies, methodologies, or practices that improve the quality and efficiency of financial reporting.

3. Stakeholder Engagement: Regularly engaging with stakeholders to understand their needs and concerns regarding financial information, and adjusting reporting practices to better meet these needs.

4. Internal Controls and Audit: Establishing robust internal controls and facilitating regular internal and external audits to ensure the integrity and accuracy of financial reports.

The principles of transparency and accountability are not merely regulatory requirements; they are essential to building and maintaining trust with investors, regulators, employees, and the public. As the financial steward of the company, the CFO has a paramount responsibility to uphold these principles in all aspects of financial reporting. By doing so, they not only comply with legal obligations but also contribute to a culture of integrity and ethical behavior within the organization, ultimately enhancing its reputation and value in the eyes of all stakeholders.

Risk Management

Risk management, a cornerstone of astute financial planning and analysis (FP&A), stands as the fortress safeguarding an organization from the unpredictable waves that could potentially jeopardize its financial stability. This segment explores the dynamics of risk management within FP&A, emphasizing the structured methodologies and strategic approaches that Chief Financial Officers (CFOs) must employ to navigate the treacherous waters of financial uncertainty.

The first step in effective risk management is the identification and understanding of the myriad risks that an organization faces. These can be broadly categorized into market risks, credit risks, operational risks, and compliance risks. Each category requires a nuanced approach for identification, assessment, and mitigation. For instance:

1. Market Risks: These include risks from fluctuations in market prices, interest rates, and foreign exchange rates. Utilizing tools like Value at Risk (VaR) models can help in quantifying potential losses from market volatility.

2. Credit Risks: The risk of loss arising from a borrower's inability to repay a loan or meet contractual obligations. Credit risk assessment tools and credit rating systems are essential in evaluating and mitigating this risk.

3. Operational Risks: These involve risks from internal processes, people, and systems, or from external events. Implementation of robust internal controls and regular process audits are key in managing operational risks.

4. Compliance Risks: The risk of legal or regulatory sanctions, financial forfeiture, or material loss an organization faces

when it fails to comply with laws, regulations, codes of conduct, or standards of practice. Staying abreast of regulatory changes and fostering a culture of compliance are vital.

Once risks are identified and assessed, the next step is developing and implementing mitigation strategies. This involves:

1. Diversification: Spreading investments across various financial instruments, industries, and other categories to reduce exposure to any single asset or risk.

2. Hedging: Using financial instruments like futures, options, and swaps to offset potential losses in investments.

3. Insurance: Transferring risk to a third party by purchasing insurance policies for significant financial exposures.

4. Limit Setting: Establishing pre-defined limits for risk exposure to manage and control risk-taking activities.

In the digital age, leveraging technology is paramount in enhancing the efficiency and effectiveness of risk management processes. Financial technology (fintech) and regtech (regulatory technology) solutions can automate risk identification, enhance risk monitoring, and provide advanced analytics for better decision-making. For example:

1. Predictive Analytics: Using machine learning algorithms to predict potential future losses and identify risk trends based on historical data.

2. Blockchain: Enhancing transparency and reducing fraud

risks through decentralized ledger technology.

3. Regulatory Technology: Automated tools that help in monitoring compliance with ever-changing regulatory requirements.

Ultimately, the effectiveness of risk management is contingent upon the cultivation of a risk-aware culture within the organization. This involves:

1. Education and Training: Regularly educating employees about potential risks and training them on risk management practices.

2. Communication: Encouraging open communication about risks and fostering an environment where employees feel comfortable reporting potential issues.

3. Leadership: Demonstrating commitment from the top, with senior leaders championing risk management initiatives and setting the tone for a risk-aware culture.

Risk management in FP&A is not a static task but a dynamic process that requires continuous attention, adaptation, and improvement. By understanding the multifaceted nature of risks, employing strategic mitigation tactics, leveraging technological advancements, and fostering a culture that prioritizes risk awareness, CFOs can safeguard their organizations against financial perils. Through meticulous planning and vigilant oversight, risk management becomes not just a defensive strategy but a critical component of strategic decision-making, driving an organization towards its financial objectives with confidence and resilience.

Identifying and Mitigating Financial Risks

The initial phase in preempting financial calamities involves a meticulous process of risk identification. This process is multifaceted, employing both quantitative and qualitative analyses to uncover hidden risks and potential threats. Techniques include:

1. Financial Statement Analysis: A deep dive into financial statements can reveal insights into liquidity, solvency, and operational efficiency, highlighting potential vulnerabilities.

2. Industry and Market Analysis: Understanding broader market trends and industry-specific challenges can help in identifying external risks that might impact the organization.

3. Scenario Analysis: Constructing various financial scenarios, including worst-case, best-case, and most likely scenarios, to understand potential impacts on the organization's financial health.

4. Historical Trend Analysis: Analyzing historical data for patterns that might predict potential risks, leveraging statistical tools and models for predictive insights.

Identifying risks is only half the battle; the essence of risk management lies in the strategic implementation of mitigation techniques. These techniques are designed to either reduce the probability of a risk occurrence or lessen its impact on the organization. Key strategies include:

1. Establishing Risk Appetite and Tolerance Levels: Defining

clear boundaries for acceptable risk levels, ensuring that these are aligned with the organization's strategic objectives and capacity to bear risk.

2. Risk Transfer: Utilizing instruments like insurance or contracts to transfer the financial impact of certain risks to third parties.

3. Risk Avoidance: Making strategic decisions to avoid risk altogether, such as exiting from high-risk markets or discontinuing vulnerable product lines.

4. Risk Reduction: Implementing policies and procedures to reduce the likelihood or impact of risks. This could include diversifying investment portfolios, enhancing cybersecurity measures, or improving operational efficiencies.

Technology plays a pivotal role in modern risk management strategies. Innovative FinTech solutions offer advanced capabilities for real-time risk monitoring, predictive risk modeling, and streamlined compliance management. Noteworthy technologies include:

1. Artificial Intelligence and Machine Learning: AI and ML models can sift through massive datasets to identify risk patterns, forecast potential financial stress points, and recommend preemptive actions.

2. Big Data Analytics: Harnessing the power of big data for comprehensive risk assessment, providing a holistic view of risk exposure across all facets of the organization.

3. Robotic Process Automation (RPA): Automating routine risk

monitoring and compliance tasks, allowing risk management teams to focus on strategic risk mitigation efforts.

The linchpin of effective risk management is a proactive, risk-aware culture that permeates every level of the organization. Cultivating such a culture involves:

1. Leadership Commitment: Senior management must lead by example, demonstrating a steadfast commitment to risk management principles and practices.

2. Continuous Education and Awareness: Regular training sessions and workshops to keep all employees informed about potential risks and the importance of risk management.

3. Open Communication Channels: Creating an environment where employees feel empowered to report potential risks without fear of reprisal.

4. Rewarding Risk Management Excellence: Recognizing and rewarding individuals and teams who contribute significantly to risk identification and mitigation efforts.

Navigating the complexities of financial risk management requires a sophisticated blend of analytical prowess, strategic planning, and technological leverage. By meticulously identifying potential risks and deploying targeted mitigation strategies, organizations can not only shield themselves from financial adversities but also position themselves for sustainable growth and success in an unpredictable world. This proactive and comprehensive approach to financial risk management empowers CFOs and finance teams to steer their organizations with confidence, ensuring resilience and stability in the face of ever-evolving financial landscapes.

Legal Implications of Inaccurate Forecasting

In the dance of financial management, inaccurate forecasting can lead the unwary into a minefield of legal challenges, including:

1. Securities Fraud Allegations: Public companies that release financial forecasts that are knowingly false or misleading may face allegations of securities fraud under laws such as the Securities Exchange Act of 1934 in the United States. Similar regulations exist globally, where the intentional dissemination of inaccurate financial information to investors constitutes a legal violation.

2. Regulatory Sanctions: Regulatory bodies, including the Securities and Exchange Commission (SEC) in the U.S., have the authority to impose fines, sanctions, and other penalties on companies and their executives for the issuance of misleading financial forecasts. These sanctions can extend to barring executives from serving as officers or directors of public companies.

3. Shareholder Litigation: Shareholders may initiate class action lawsuits against a company and its executives if inaccurate forecasts lead to financial losses. These lawsuits can allege that the company failed to exercise due diligence in its forecasting process, thereby misleading investors.

4. Breach of Contract Claims: Inaccurate forecasts can also lead to breach of contract claims if financial projections are part of agreements with lenders, creditors, or other contractual partners. If these entities suffer losses due to reliance on erroneous forecasts, they may seek legal recourse.

To navigate the perilous legal implications of inaccurate forecasting, companies must fortify their defenses through:

1. Rigorous Forecasting Methodologies: Employing sophisticated, data-driven forecasting techniques that account for a wide range of variables and potential outcomes. This includes the use of advanced analytics, scenario planning, and sensitivity analysis.

2. Transparency and Disclosure: Clear, transparent communication about the assumptions underlying financial forecasts, the methodologies employed, and the potential risks and uncertainties. This transparency is crucial in demonstrating due diligence and mitigating allegations of misleading investors.

3. Regular Updates and Revisions: Frequent review and adjustment of financial forecasts in light of new financial data, market trends, and emerging risks. Timely updates can help in managing stakeholders' expectations and reducing the risk of legal challenges.

4. Legal and Compliance Oversight: Engaging legal and compliance teams in the forecasting process to ensure that all regulatory requirements are met and that forecasts are presented in a manner that is consistent with legal obligations.

mitigating the legal implications of inaccurate forecasting lies the commitment to ethical financial practices. This commitment involves:

1. Cultivating a Culture of Integrity: Fostering an organizational culture where honesty, transparency, and

273

ethical conduct are paramount, especially in the realms of financial reporting and forecasting.

2. Stakeholder Education: Educating stakeholders, including investors and employees, about the inherent uncertainties in financial forecasting and the potential for revisions as new information emerges.

3. Proactive Risk Disclosure: Diligently identifying and disclosing potential risks that could impact financial outcomes, thereby providing stakeholders with a comprehensive understanding of the forecasting landscape.

The legal implications of inaccurate financial forecasting underscore the critical importance of precision, transparency, and ethical conduct in FP&A. By navigating the legal landscape with diligence and foresight, organizations can mitigate the risks associated with financial projections, safeguarding their legal standing and fostering trust among investors, regulatory bodies, and other stakeholders. As the financial markets continue to evolve, the imperative for accurate, compliant, and ethically grounded financial forecasting becomes ever more pronounced, serving as a cornerstone of corporate governance and strategic financial management.

Ensuring Ethical Use of Predictive Technologies

The ethical deployment of predictive technologies in FP&A requires a robust framework that encompasses:

1. Transparency: Clearly communicate the use, scope, and limitations of predictive technologies to all stakeholders. Transparency is pivotal in ensuring that stakeholders understand how predictions are generated, the data sources

utilised, and the potential biases inherent in the technology.

2. Accountability: Establish clear lines of accountability for decisions made based on predictive technology forecasts. While these technologies can significantly enhance decision-making processes, it is crucial that human oversight remains a core component, ensuring accountability for the outcomes of these decisions.

3. Data Privacy and Security: Rigorous standards for data privacy and security are essential in the ethical use of predictive technologies. This involves not only protecting the data from unauthorised access but also ensuring that the data collection and processing practices respect individual privacy rights and comply with applicable regulations.

To operationalise these ethical frameworks, organisations must undertake the following practices:

1. Bias Mitigation: Actively work to identify and mitigate biases in predictive models. This involves diversifying data sets and employing techniques such as fairness-aware algorithms to ensure that forecasts do not perpetuate or amplify existing inequalities.

2. Stakeholder Engagement: Engage with a wide range of stakeholders, including ethicists, technologists, and the end-users of financial forecasts, to gather diverse perspectives on the ethical use of predictive technologies. This engagement helps in identifying ethical dilemmas and exploring solutions collaboratively.

3. Continuous Monitoring and Evaluation: Establish mechanisms for the ongoing monitoring and evaluation

of predictive models to ensure they operate within the established ethical frameworks. This includes regular audits of both the models and their outcomes, as well as the adaptation of models in response to changing ethical standards and societal norms.

At the core of ensuring the ethical use of predictive technologies lies the commitment to principled decision-making. This commitment involves:

1. Scenario Analysis: Conducting scenario analysis to understand the potential impacts of predictive technology forecasts on different stakeholder groups. This aids in anticipating ethical challenges and strategising on how to address them.

2. Ethical Training: Providing training for teams involved in FP&A on ethical considerations specific to predictive technologies. This training should cover not only the theoretical aspects of ethics but also practical decision-making frameworks.

3. Ethical Audits: Implementing periodic ethical audits of predictive technologies and their applications. These audits, conducted by internal or external ethics experts, can provide an objective assessment of the ethical considerations at play and recommend improvements.

Ensuring the ethical use of predictive technologies in FP&A is not merely a regulatory requirement but a strategic imperative that can enhance trust, credibility, and transparency in financial forecasting. By embedding ethical considerations into predictive technology deployment, organisations can navigate the complex interplay between innovation and ethics, thereby forging a path towards responsible and sustainable financial planning and analysis practices. This ethical foundation not only reinforces the integrity of the FP&A function but also aligns it with broader organisational values and societal expectations.

CHAPTER 10:
SUCCESS STORIES

A t the center of transformative forecasting initiatives is the integration of advanced technologies such as artificial intelligence (AI), machine learning (ML), and big data analytics. These technologies facilitate the analysis of vast datasets, enabling the identification of patterns and trends that were previously undetectable. For instance, AI and ML algorithms can predict market movements with a higher degree of accuracy by analyzing historical data, current trends, and even sentiments expressed in news articles and social media.

1. Tech Giant's Leap: A notable example is a leading tech company that revamped its entire forecasting process by incorporating AI-driven algorithms. This initiative not only improved the precision of its financial forecasts but also reduced the time required for the forecasting process by half, thereby significantly enhancing operational efficiency.

2. Retail Revolution: Another example is a global retail chain that implemented a machine learning model to forecast demand for over 10,000 products across different regions. This initiative allowed for more accurate stock management,

reduced waste, and optimized supply chain operations, leading to substantial cost savings and increased customer satisfaction.

3. Data Integration and Quality: Successful forecasting initiatives begin with the integration of high-quality, diverse data sources. This includes internal financial data, industry trends, macroeconomic indicators, and even non-traditional data such as weather patterns and geopolitical events.

4. Cross-functional Collaboration: Effective forecasting requires input from various departments within an organization, including finance, operations, sales, and marketing. Cross-functional collaboration ensures that forecasts are comprehensive and reflect the multifaceted nature of business operations.

5. Scalability and Flexibility: Transformative forecasting initiatives are designed with scalability in mind, capable of adapting to the organization's growth and evolving market conditions. Flexibility in adjusting forecasting models and assumptions is crucial to staying relevant and accurate.

While transformative forecasting initiatives offer immense benefits, they also present challenges such as the need for substantial initial investment, the complexity of integrating new technologies with existing systems, and the requirement for specialized skills to develop and manage advanced forecasting models. Overcoming these challenges necessitates a strategic approach, including phased implementation, ongoing training and development for staff, and possibly partnerships with technology providers.

Transformative forecasting initiatives have a profound

impact on organizations, driving more informed strategic decisions, optimizing resource allocation, and enhancing competitive advantage. As technology continues to evolve, the future of forecasting looks even more promising, with potential advancements such as real-time forecasting and the integration of quantum computing offering the possibility of even greater accuracy and insights.

The advent of transformative forecasting initiatives marks a significant evolution in the field of FP&A. By harnessing the power of advanced technologies and embracing innovative methodologies, organizations can achieve a level of forecasting accuracy and efficiency that was once beyond reach. These initiatives not only underscore the strategic value of accurate forecasting but also exemplify how embracing change can lead to remarkable improvements in decision-making, operational efficiency, and overall organizational success.

Companies that Reinvented Their Forecasting Processes

The journey to reinvent forecasting processes often starts with a bold vision for the future—one that acknowledges the limitations of traditional forecasting methods and the potential of new technologies to surmount these challenges. Companies leading the charge in this transformation recognize the value of predictive analytics, artificial intelligence, and machine learning as tools not just for enhancing forecasting accuracy but also for aligning financial planning with strategic objectives.

1. Global E-commerce Titan: A pioneering instance is an e-commerce behemoth that redefined its forecasting model by deploying sophisticated machine learning algorithms. The

company developed a system capable of analyzing consumer behavior, seasonal trends, and market dynamics in real-time, leading to a dramatic improvement in inventory management and demand forecasting. This initiative significantly minimized overstock and stockouts, ensuring optimal inventory levels and enhancing customer satisfaction.

2. Innovative Automotive Manufacturer: Another example involves an automotive leader that integrated predictive analytics into its sales forecasting process. By leveraging data on past sales, economic indicators, and consumer trends, the company was able to forecast demand for various models with unprecedented accuracy. This allowed for more precise production planning, reducing both surplus inventory and shortages, and thus optimizing manufacturing efficiency.

3. Pharmaceutical Pioneer: In the pharmaceutical industry, where forecasting accuracy is critical to managing complex supply chains and ensuring drug availability, one company stands out. It implemented an AI-driven forecasting system that considers factors such as drug trial outcomes, regulatory approvals, and market competition. This approach not only improved forecast accuracy but also enabled the company to better navigate the highly regulated pharmaceutical landscape.

- Data Democratization: These companies made a strategic move to democratize data access across their organizations. By breaking down silos and ensuring that relevant data is accessible to all stakeholders involved in the forecasting process, they fostered a more collaborative and informed approach to forecasting.

- Adaptive Learning Models: The use of adaptive learning

models that continuously refine forecasts based on new data and outcomes was a game-changer. This dynamic approach allows models to become more accurate over time, adapting to changing market conditions and internal variables.

- Scenario Planning: Incorporating scenario planning into the forecasting process enabled these companies to anticipate and prepare for a range of potential futures. By evaluating different scenarios and their financial implications, they could make more robust strategic decisions.

The overhaul of forecasting processes by these companies led to significant benefits, including enhanced decision-making capabilities, improved financial performance, and a stronger competitive position. Furthermore, by aligning their forecasting processes more closely with strategic goals, they could pivot more swiftly in response to market changes, seizing opportunities and mitigating risks more effectively.

The experiences of these companies underscore the transformative potential of reimagining forecasting processes. As we look to the future, it is clear that the journey of forecasting innovation is far from complete. Emerging technologies and methodologies promise to further refine and enhance the art and science of forecasting, offering new avenues for companies willing to invest in their future.

the companies that have boldly reinvented their forecasting processes serve not only as beacons of success in the present landscape but also as harbingers of the evolving future of financial planning and analysis. Their journeys highlight the importance of embracing change, investing in technology, and fostering a culture of innovation to remain competitive and resilient in a constantly shifting business environment.

THE CFO GUIDE TO FORECASTING IN FP&A

Implementing AI and Machine Learning in Forecasting

The integration of AI and ML into forecasting signifies a paradigm shift from traditional, often manual, forecasting methods to more dynamic, data-driven approaches. The journey begins with the recognition of the potential these technologies hold for deciphering complex patterns in vast datasets, enabling predictive insights that were previously unattainable.

1. Data Infrastructure Overhaul: A foundational step for many companies has been the modernization of their data infrastructure. This involves the aggregation and cleaning of data from disparate sources to create a unified, accessible data repository. Such a repository is crucial for training ML models and for ensuring the consistency and reliability of AI-driven forecasts.

2. Model Development and Training: Developing bespoke AI and ML models tailored to specific forecasting needs is a complex, iterative process. It involves selecting the appropriate algorithms, training the models with historical data, and continuously refining them based on their performance and accuracy in predicting future outcomes.

3. Integration with Existing Systems: Seamlessly integrating AI and ML models into existing FP&A systems poses both technical and operational challenges. Companies have navigated these by developing interfaces and protocols that allow for the smooth exchange of data between AI/ML models and traditional financial planning tools.

The path to successfully implementing AI and ML in

forecasting is fraught with challenges, from technical hurdles to organizational resistance.

- Skillset and Knowledge Gap: One of the primary challenges has been the skillset and knowledge gap within existing teams. Overcoming this has required significant investment in training and sometimes bringing in external expertise to bridge the gap.

- Data Quality and Availability: Ensuring the quality and availability of data for training AI and ML models has been another significant challenge. Companies have addressed this by implementing rigorous data governance frameworks and investing in data cleaning and preparation technologies.

- Change Management: Perhaps the most underestimated challenge has been managing the change within organizations. Transitioning to AI-driven forecasting requires shifts in workflows, responsibilities, and decision-making processes. Successful companies have navigated this through transparent communication, stakeholder engagement, and phased implementation strategies.

The implementation of AI and ML in forecasting has had a transformative impact on companies, yielding benefits that extend beyond improved forecast accuracy.

- Strategic Decision Making: Enhanced forecasting capabilities have empowered companies to make more informed strategic decisions, with a deeper understanding of potential future scenarios and their implications.

- Operational Efficiency: Automation of routine forecasting tasks has freed up valuable resources, allowing finance teams to focus on analysis and strategic activities rather than data compilation and basic number crunching.

- Resilience and Agility: With the ability to rapidly update forecasts in response to new data, companies have become more resilient and agile, better equipped to navigate the uncertainties of today's business environment.

As companies continue to navigate the implementation of AI and ML in their forecasting processes, the journey is characterized by continuous learning and adaptation. The future promises even greater integration of advanced analytics, with potential developments in areas such as neural networks and deep learning offering the prospect of even more accurate and nuanced forecasts.

The adoption of AI and ML in forecasting is not just about technological change; it's about reimagining the future of business planning and decision-making. For companies willing to embrace these changes, the rewards are substantial, positioning them at the leading edge of innovation and strategic foresight in their respective industries.

Overcoming Challenges Through Innovative Strategies

Data lies AI and ML applications, yet its management presents a significant challenge due to issues of quality, integration, and accessibility. Innovative companies have tackled this by adopting advanced data management technologies such as data lakes and cloud-based platforms, enabling the centralization and efficient processing of vast amounts of data. Furthermore, the use of data virtualization techniques has allowed for real-time access to data across various systems without the need for physical data movement, significantly enhancing the speed and flexibility of data analysis for forecasting purposes.

The successful implementation of AI and ML in forecasting requires a deep understanding of both financial principles and advanced analytics. To bridge the gap between these domains, pioneering firms have established cross-functional teams comprising members from finance, IT, and data science backgrounds. These teams employ agile methodologies, fostering an environment of rapid experimentation and iteration. By doing so, they facilitate the seamless integration of financial acumen and technical expertise, driving the development of more accurate and robust forecasting models.

The field of AI and ML is characterized by rapid advancements, with new algorithms and techniques constantly emerging. Recognizing this, forward-thinking companies have invested in sandbox environments where data scientists can safely experiment with cutting-edge algorithms. Such experimentation has not only allowed firms to improve the accuracy of their forecasts but also to discover novel applications of these technologies, such as anomaly detection and predictive maintenance, which further enhance operational efficiency and strategic decision-making.

One of the critical challenges in adopting AI and ML models is the "black box" nature of these technologies, which can hinder their acceptance among stakeholders. To address this, companies have focused on developing models that prioritize explainability and transparency. Techniques such as feature importance analysis and model-agnostic explanation tools have been employed to demystify the forecasting process. This approach has facilitated greater trust and confidence in AI-driven forecasts, enabling more widespread adoption across the organization.

The dynamic nature of AI and ML technologies necessitates a commitment to continuous learning and adaptation. Companies leading the way in forecasting innovation have established dedicated centers of excellence (CoEs) focused on AI and ML. These CoEs serve as hubs for knowledge sharing, training, and research, ensuring that the organization remains at the cutting edge of technological advancements. Moreover, they play a crucial role in fostering a culture of innovation, encouraging employees to explore new applications of AI and ML and continuously refine their forecasting methodologies.

Overcoming the challenges associated with implementing AI and ML in forecasting has required companies to think creatively and act decisively. Through innovative data management solutions, cross-functional collaboration, advanced algorithm experimentation, a focus on explainability, and a commitment to continuous learning, these organizations have not only navigated these hurdles but have also set new standards for excellence in FP&A. As we look to the future, these innovative strategies will undoubtedly continue to evolve, driving the next wave of advancements in financial forecasting.

Strategic Wins Through Effective Forecasting

Imagine a world where a company can foresee market shifts before they occur, where financial downturns are not threats but opportunities for growth. This is not the domain of fantasy but the practical reality for firms that have harnessed the power of effective forecasting. A pivotal case that exemplifies this is the story of a tech giant that stood at the brink of bankruptcy in the early 2000s. Through the implementation of a revolutionary forecasting model that leveraged both quantitative and qualitative data, the company not only averted financial disaster but also positioned itself as a market leader. By predicting consumer trends and aligning their product development pipeline accordingly, they achieved a strategic win that has become a legend in the annals of corporate history.

The foundation of any successful forecasting endeavor is built upon three crucial pillars: the integration of comprehensive data analysis, the adoption of advanced forecasting tools, and the establishment of a culture that embraces flexibility and innovation.

1. Comprehensive Data Analysis: The first pillar involves the aggregation and analysis of both internal and external data sources. This includes not only financial metrics but also non-financial indicators such as social media sentiment, geopolitical events, and competitor movements. For instance, a Vancouver-based renewable energy company utilized local economic data and global energy consumption trends to predict a surge in demand for green technology, positioning themselves strategically to capitalize on this uptick.

2. Advanced Forecasting Tools: The second pillar focuses on the technological aspect, where AI and machine learning models come into play. These tools can unearth patterns invisible to the human eye, offering predictions with astonishing accuracy. A healthcare firm, by integrating AI into its forecasting models, was able to predict patient admission rates and optimize staffing levels accordingly, leading to operational efficiency and increased patient satisfaction.

3. Culture of Flexibility and Innovation: The third pillar is perhaps the most critical yet the most challenging to cultivate. A culture that encourages experimentation and learning from

failures is essential for forecasting success. This involves a shift in mindset from viewing forecasting as a mere financial exercise to appreciating it as a strategic tool.

The real-world implications of effective forecasting are vast and varied. In mergers and acquisitions, accurate forecasts can identify potential targets before they come onto the market radar, allowing companies to make strategic moves. In product development, forecasting can predict shifts in consumer preferences, enabling firms to innovate ahead of the curve. Moreover, in risk management, forecasting plays a defensive role by identifying potential threats and allowing firms to mitigate them before they materialize.

A profound example of strategic wins through forecasting was demonstrated during the global financial crisis of 2008. A multinational corporation, through its advanced forecasting models, predicted the downturn earlier than its competitors. This foresight allowed it to adjust its investment strategies, hedge against the worst impacts of the crisis, and even find growth opportunities amidst the economic turmoil.

The journey towards strategic wins through effective forecasting is complex and fraught with challenges. However, the rewards justify the endeavor. It enables organizations not just to survive but to thrive and lead in an ever-changing global landscape. As we continue to advance in our capabilities and understanding, the potential for forecasting to drive strategic wins is boundless, limited only by our willingness to embrace change and look beyond the horizon.

Navigating Financial Crises

The history of financial markets is punctuated with crises,

each unique in its genesis but common in its capacity for disruption. From the dot-com bubble burst at the turn of the millennium to the global financial meltdown of 2008, each crisis has imparted valuable lessons. One of the most critical insights is the importance of maintaining a healthy liquidity reserve. Companies that navigated these crises successfully had often prioritized liquidity management as a core component of their financial planning, allowing them to weather periods of credit crunch and market volatility.

Another lesson is the significance of diversification—not just in terms of investment portfolios but also concerning revenue streams and supply chains. The global financial crisis underscored how interconnected and vulnerable the global economy could be. Organizations that had diversified their operations and supply chains across various geographies and sectors were better equipped to manage the disruptions.

In today's digital age, data analytics and forecasting tools have become indispensable in the arsenal against financial crises. Real-time data analysis allows organizations to monitor their financial health continuously and spot early warning signs of trouble. Predictive analytics can forecast potential market downturns, enabling companies to adjust their investment strategies and operational expenditures proactively.

A contemporary approach to crisis management also emphasizes the importance of stakeholder communication. Transparent, timely, and honest communication with investors, employees, and customers can help maintain trust and confidence during uncertain times. For instance, during the COVID-19 pandemic, companies that communicated effectively with their stakeholders, providing regular updates and clear information on their response strategies, were often seen in a more favorable light.

Scenario planning emerges as a powerful tool in the context of financial crises. By preparing for multiple potential futures, organizations can develop flexible strategies that can be quickly deployed as circumstances evolve. This involves not just forecasting different scenarios but also stress-testing financial models against various crisis conditions to understand potential impacts on liquidity, cash flow, and profitability.

Incorporating scenario planning into the financial forecasting process requires a shift in mindset—from a linear approach to financial planning to a more dynamic, iterative process. It also necessitates a culture that values agility and encourages continuous learning from both successes and failures.

The unprecedented nature of the COVID-19 pandemic presented a litmus test for companies worldwide. One notable success story is that of a global e-commerce giant that utilized its advanced forecasting models to predict shifts in consumer behavior. Anticipating an increase in online shopping, the company swiftly adjusted its logistics and supply chain operations to meet the surging demand. Moreover, by stress-testing its financial models against various pandemic scenarios, the company could maintain a solid liquidity position, ensuring its ability to invest in strategic opportunities even amidst the crisis.

Navigating financial crises requires a multifaceted approach that combines historical insights, contemporary strategies, and forward-thinking methodologies. The ability to anticipate potential crises, prepare for various outcomes through scenario planning, and maintain flexibility in strategic decisions is integral to steering an organization through the storm. As financial landscapes continue to evolve, so too must the strategies of CFOs and financial professionals, always with an eye towards resilience, adaptability, and strategic foresight.

Successful Mergers and Acquisitions Guided by Forecasting

The inception of any successful M&A venture lies in the meticulous analysis and forecasting of potential outcomes. It's a rigorous process that involves evaluating the financial health, market position, and growth prospects of the target company. However, the forecasting for M&A extends beyond these fundamentals. It encompasses a comprehensive analysis of how the integration will synergize with the acquiring company's existing operations, culture, and long-term strategic goals.

A vital tool in this process is the discounted cash flow (DCF) model, which helps in determining the present value of the target company based on projected future cash flows. Adjustments are made for potential synergies, risks, and the strategic fit between the companies. This quantitative forecasting is complemented by qualitative insights into the market dynamics, competitor strategies, and regulatory landscapes to ensure a multidimensional evaluation.

One illustrative example is the acquisition of WhatsApp by Facebook in 2014. Facebook's strategic forecasting identified the exponential growth trajectory of mobile messaging apps and the potential for significant synergies between WhatsApp and Facebook's broader ecosystem. The forecasting models projected not only the financial benefits but also the strategic advantage of owning a dominant player in mobile communication, which was critical in justifying the $19 billion price tag. This acquisition has since become a textbook case of successful M&A, driven by visionary forecasting and strategic alignment.

Another noteworthy example is the merger between Exxon and Mobil in 1999, one of the largest mergers in history. The strategic forecasting leading up to the merger intricately analyzed the potential for operational synergies, cost savings, and the combined entity's enhanced capacity to navigate the volatile oil market. The merger's success, resulting in ExxonMobil becoming one of the world's leading energy companies, underscores the importance of thorough forecasting in identifying and capitalizing on strategic M&A opportunities.

The synergy between forecasting and due diligence cannot be overstated in the context of M&A. While forecasting provides a vision of the potential future, due diligence grounds that vision in reality, assessing the tangible and intangible assets of the target company. It's a symbiotic process where forecasting informs the areas of focus for due diligence, and the findings from due diligence refine the assumptions underpinning the forecasts.

For instance, in the due diligence phase of the acquisition of LinkedIn by Microsoft in 2016, Microsoft conducted an exhaustive analysis of LinkedIn's data assets, user engagement metrics, and integration potential with Microsoft's suite of productivity tools. This due diligence, informed by strategic forecasting, validated the acquisition's premise, leading to a highly successful integration that significantly enhanced Microsoft's product ecosystem.

Forecasting in the domain of M&A is a multifaceted discipline that blends financial acumen with strategic vision. Successful mergers and acquisitions, guided by robust forecasting, stand as testaments to the power of informed, forward-looking decision-making. As the business landscape evolves, the role of forecasting in M&A will only grow in importance, enabling companies to identify, execute, and integrate strategic opportunities with unparalleled precision and insight.

Achieving Sustainability Goals through ESG-Focused Forecasting

ESG-focused forecasting is the recognition that sustainable practices are not only ethically imperative but also fundamentally linked to long-term financial success. This forecasting approach incorporates ESG metrics alongside traditional financial indicators to provide a more holistic view of a company's potential for sustainable growth. It shifts the narrative from viewing sustainability as a cost to recognizing it as an investment in future viability.

For instance, a company may use ESG-focused forecasting to evaluate the financial implications of reducing carbon emissions, considering factors such as potential savings from energy efficiency improvements, the cost of transitioning to renewable energy sources, and the impact on brand reputation and market positioning. This comprehensive analysis allows for informed decision-making that balances short-term financial considerations with long-term sustainability goals.

One of the critical methodologies in ESG-focused forecasting is scenario analysis, which involves creating multiple forward-looking scenarios based on varying levels of ESG integration. This technique allows companies to explore the potential financial outcomes of different sustainability strategies, assessing risks and opportunities under various global economic and environmental conditions.

Another vital tool is materiality assessment, which helps companies identify the ESG factors most relevant to their business and industry. By prioritizing these factors in their forecasting models, companies can focus their resources on the sustainability initiatives that will have the most significant impact on financial performance and stakeholder value.

A landmark example of successful ESG-focused forecasting is the case of Unilever. By embedding sustainability into its core business strategy and forecasting, Unilever has achieved substantial cost savings, reduced environmental impact, and enhanced its brand image, resulting in a strong market position and resilient financial performance.

Similarly, Ørsted, a leading energy company, transformed its business model from fossil fuels to renewable energy, guided by ESG-focused forecasting. The forecasting provided insights into the long-term viability and profitability of renewable energy, driving strategic decisions that have positioned Ørsted as a global leader in clean energy.

While the benefits of ESG-focused forecasting are clear, companies face challenges in implementation, including data availability and quality, integrating ESG metrics with financial planning, and aligning with evolving regulatory standards. Addressing these challenges requires a commitment to transparency, continuous improvement, and stakeholder engagement.

ESG-focused forecasting represents a paradigm shift in how companies plan for the future, merging financial performance with sustainability objectives. By incorporating ESG metrics into their forecasting models, companies can navigate the complexities of the modern business landscape, achieving sustainable growth that benefits shareholders, stakeholders, and the planet alike. As more companies embrace this approach, ESG-focused forecasting will undoubtedly play a crucial role in shaping the global economy's trajectory towards sustainability.

Lessons Learned

The quintessential lesson is the imperative to adopt a holistic approach to ESG-focused forecasting. Companies that have successfully integrated ESG considerations into their forecasting mechanisms understand that sustainability is not a siloed entity but a pervasive element influencing all aspects of business operations. For instance, Patagonia's commitment to environmental sustainability has permeated its supply chain operations, product design, and customer engagement strategies, demonstrating the power of a holistic approach in driving financial and sustainability outcomes.

A recurring theme in ESG-focused forecasting is the challenge of data – its acquisition, integrity, and interpretation. The lesson here is twofold: firstly, the need for rigorous data management practices to ensure the reliability and accuracy of ESG data; and secondly, the importance of developing sophisticated analytical capabilities to translate data into actionable insights. Companies like Salesforce have leveraged cloud-based platforms to enhance their data management and analytics capabilities, exemplifying how technological innovation can address the data challenge.

Another critical lesson is the invaluable role of stakeholder engagement. Companies that have thrived in integrating

ESG into their financial forecasting attribute a significant part of their success to actively involving stakeholders – investors, customers, employees, and communities – in their sustainability journey. This engagement has not only enriched the forecasting process with diverse perspectives but also bolstered stakeholder trust and commitment. The journey of Unilever underlines the impact of stakeholder engagement, with its sustainable living brands growing 69% faster than the rest of the business.

The evolving regulatory landscape around sustainability and financial reporting has emerged as both a challenge and a guiding compass. Navigating this landscape requires a proactive and agile approach, adapting forecasting models to meet regulatory requirements while seizing opportunities for strategic advantage. Lessons from companies like Ørsted illustrate the strategic foresight in anticipating regulatory shifts, positioning them as leaders in renewable energy and benefiting from early compliance.

Perhaps the most poignant lesson is the imperative of flexibility in ESG-focused forecasting. The dynamic nature of sustainability issues – from climate change impacts to social justice movements – demands that companies remain adaptable, ready to adjust their forecasts and strategies in response to emerging trends and challenges. This lesson is vividly exemplified by the automotive industry's pivot towards electric vehicles, with companies like Tesla leading the charge by integrating sustainability trends into their strategic forecasting.

The journey of ESG-focused forecasting is fraught with challenges, yet it is also marked by significant achievements and profound learning. The lessons distilled from this journey underscore the importance of a holistic approach, rigorous data management, stakeholder engagement, regulatory agility, and strategic flexibility. As companies venture further into sustainability, these lessons serve as guideposts, illuminating the path towards a future where financial forecasting and sustainability objectives are inextricably linked, driving towards a more sustainable and financially robust world.

Common Pitfalls and How to Avoid Them

One of the most prevalent pitfalls is the overreliance on historical data. In the rapidly evolving landscape of ESG, yesterday's data can often be a misleading guide for tomorrow's strategy. Avoid this trap by incorporating real-time data streams and predictive analytics into your forecasting models. For example, companies like Google have employed real-time environmental data to adjust their operational strategies, significantly reducing their carbon footprint.

ESG data is inherently complex and multifaceted, encompassing a wide range of social, environmental, and governance factors. A common mistake is treating this data with oversimplification. To avoid this, invest in advanced analytical tools and expertise to decode the nuances of ESG data. This includes leveraging AI and machine learning techniques to identify patterns and insights that can inform more nuanced and effective forecasting.

While quantitative data is vital, qualitative ESG factors such as brand reputation, employee satisfaction, and community impact also play a critical role in forecasting. A pitfall here is overlooking these qualitative aspects. Counteract this by incorporating stakeholder interviews, surveys, and social media analysis into your ESG assessment, ensuring a more comprehensive forecast. Patagonia's approach of integrating customer feedback on sustainability practices into their product development and marketing strategies illustrates the value of qualitative insights.

Another pitfall is the misalignment of ESG goals with overarching business objectives, leading to disjointed strategies and missed opportunities. Avoid this by ensuring that ESG forecasting is integrated into the broader strategic planning process. This alignment ensures that sustainability initiatives drive not just compliance but also competitive advantage. IKEA's strategy of designing products to be sustainable and affordable is a testament to the power of alignment between ESG goals and business objectives.

The regulatory environment for ESG is in constant flux, and a failure to stay ahead of these changes can lead to compliance risks and missed opportunities. Avoid this pitfall by establishing a dedicated team to monitor and analyze regulatory trends, ensuring your forecasting models are both compliant and strategically positioned to leverage new opportunities. Ørsted's proactive adjustment to its forecasting in anticipation of regulatory changes in the renewable energy sector is a prime example of turning potential pitfalls into strategic advantages.

Navigating the complexities of ESG-focused forecasting is fraught with potential pitfalls, but awareness and strategic action can turn these challenges into opportunities for growth and innovation. By recognizing and addressing the common missteps outlined above, companies can enhance the accuracy and strategic value of their ESG forecasting, positioning themselves as leaders in the nexus of sustainability and financial performance. This journey is not without its hurdles, but with the right approach, the path forward leads to a future where ESG integration is not just a mandate but a strategic differentiator.

The Impact of Strong Leadership and Clear Communication

At the helm of ESG integration, leadership is not merely a position but a voyage into uncharted waters, requiring a captain who can see beyond the horizon. A visionary leader understands that ESG forecasting is not a mere tactical adjustment but a strategic reorientation towards sustainability. They champion ESG initiatives, embedding them into the corporate DNA and making sustainability a shared vision rather than a siloed responsibility.

For instance, consider the transformative journey of Unilever under the leadership of Paul Polman. Polman's visionary approach pivoted Unilever towards sustainability, making it the cornerstone of their business strategy. Under his guidance, Unilever launched the Sustainable Living Plan, ambitiously committing to decouple environmental impact from growth and increase social impact. This visionary leadership catalyzed a cultural shift within Unilever, propelling it towards sustainable profitability.

Clear communication is the backbone that supports the body of ESG forecasting. It involves articulating the importance of ESG metrics, not just as a compliance or reporting requirement, but as integral to the strategic fabric of the organization. Effective communication demystifies ESG for stakeholders at all levels, from the boardroom to the break room, ensuring that everyone understands their role in achieving the ESG objectives.

The power of clear communication is exemplified in the case of Salesforce, a company that has placed a high emphasis on transparent and effective communication regarding its sustainability goals. Salesforce regularly publishes comprehensive reports detailing their ESG strategies, progress, and future plans. This open communication fosters a culture of accountability and engagement, encouraging every employee to contribute towards the common goal of sustainability.

The relationship between strong leadership and clear communication in ESG-focused forecasting is symbiotic. Visionary leaders use effective communication as a tool to inspire, engage, and mobilize their organization towards ESG goals. Conversely, clear and transparent communication reinforces leadership's commitment to ESG, enhancing trust and credibility among stakeholders.

This symbiosis is crucial in navigating the uncertainties and complexities inherent in ESG forecasting. For example, when an organization faces a dilemma between short-term financial gains and long-term sustainability goals, strong leadership, backed by clear communication, can guide the organization towards decisions that align with its ESG vision. This ensures that ESG forecasting transcends being a mere exercise in compliance to become a strategic lever for sustainable growth.

The journey towards ESG-focused forecasting is punctuated with challenges that test the mettle of organizations. However, under the aegis of strong leadership and bolstered by the clarity of purposeful communication, these challenges can be transformed into opportunities. The impact of strong leadership and clear communication in ESG forecasting is profound, driving not just compliance and reporting, but shaping a sustainable future. As organizations navigate the complexities of integrating ESG into their forecasting models, the beacon of visionary leadership combined with the compass of clear communication will be indispensable in charting a course towards lasting success.

Adapting to a Rapidly Changing Business Environment

The relentless pace of technological innovation is reshaping industries, making it imperative for organizations to stay abreast of emerging technologies and integrate them into their operational and strategic frameworks. The adoption of AI and machine learning in financial forecasting provides a case in point. These technologies enable real-time data analysis, enhance predictive accuracy, and offer insightful scenario planning capabilities, thus empowering decision-makers to anticipate changes and make informed strategic decisions.

For example, the financial sector has witnessed a profound transformation with the advent of fintech innovations. Companies like Stripe and Square have revolutionized payment processing and financial services, compelling traditional banks to rethink their operational models and embrace digital transformation. This shift underscores the importance of technological agility in maintaining competitive advantage and fostering innovation.

Adapting to a rapidly changing business environment requires strategic flexibility – the ability to pivot and realign strategies in response to evolving external conditions. Integrating scenario planning into the strategic planning process is crucial in this context. Scenario planning involves developing detailed, plausible models of possible futures, allowing organizations to explore and prepare for various contingencies.

Take, for instance, the global response to the COVID-19 pandemic. Organizations that had embraced scenario planning were better positioned to navigate the uncertainties of the pandemic. They were able to quickly adapt their operations, whether through shifting to remote work, reconfiguring supply chains, or pivoting to new business models, thereby minimizing disruptions and capturing new opportunities.

In a rapidly changing business environment, organizational resilience becomes paramount. This resilience is underpinned by a culture of continuous learning and innovation. Encouraging a mindset of curiosity and openness to new ideas among employees fosters an environment where adaptive strategies can be quickly developed and deployed.

Google's approach to innovation exemplifies this principle. By allocating resources to "moonshot" projects and fostering an internal culture that values risk-taking and experimentation, Google continues to expand the boundaries of its core business and explore new markets, thereby ensuring its adaptability and resilience.

Ultimately, the ability of an organization to adapt to a rapidly changing environment hinges on the quality of its leadership. Leaders must embody adaptability, demonstrating a willingness to challenge the status quo, embrace new ideas, and lead by example in the face of change. They must also possess the foresight to anticipate shifts in the business landscape and the decisiveness to act swiftly and strategically.

Consider the leadership of Satya Nadella at Microsoft. By

shifting the company's focus towards cloud computing and embracing a "growth mindset" culture, Nadella revitalized Microsoft, steering it through a period of significant industry change and positioning it for future success.

Adapting to a rapidly changing business environment is an imperative for organizational survival and success. It necessitates a proactive approach to technological innovation, strategic flexibility, a culture of continuous learning, and visionary leadership. By embedding these principles into their strategic planning and operational practices, organizations can navigate the complexities of change, turning potential threats into opportunities for growth and innovation.

CHAPTER 11:
FAILURES AND
LESSONS

O ne prevalent misstep in financial forecasting is an overreliance on historical data. While past performance can provide valuable insights, it is not always a reliable predictor of future outcomes, especially in an era characterized by rapid technological change and market volatility. Kodak's downfall is a poignant example. Once a titan in the photography industry, Kodak failed to anticipate the digital revolution, relying too heavily on its historical dominance in film photography. This oversight in forecasting led to the company's eventual bankruptcy in 2012, a stark reminder of the limitations of historical data as a sole forecasting tool.

Another critical misstep is the failure to account for external factors that could impact financial projections. Nokia's experience serves as a cautionary tale. Before the advent of smartphones, Nokia was the leading mobile phone manufacturer. However, the company did not fully appreciate the potential impact of smartphones on the market and was overtaken by competitors like Apple and Samsung. Nokia's oversight in recognizing and adapting to these external changes underscored the importance of incorporating a broad range of external factors into financial forecasts.

Forecasters often fall prey to confirmation bias, the tendency to favor information that confirms pre-existing beliefs or hypotheses. This bias can lead to skewed forecasts that do not accurately reflect reality. A notable example of confirmation bias impacting financial forecasts occurred with the dot-com bubble of the late 1990s. Many investors and analysts continued to project astronomical growth for internet companies, ignoring warning signs of overvaluation. The eventual bursting of the dot-com bubble resulted in significant financial losses, highlighting the dangers of confirmation bias in financial forecasting.

A rigid adherence to initial forecasts without considering new information is another common pitfall. Blockbuster's inability to adapt its business model and forecasting in the face of Netflix's rise is a case in point. Blockbuster's leadership dismissed the threat posed by Netflix's subscription-based, mail-order rental service and later, its streaming platform. This lack of adaptability in forecasting and strategy ultimately led to Blockbuster's decline.

The key to avoiding these forecasting missteps lies in adopting a flexible, forward-looking approach that considers a wide range of variables, including technological advancements, market trends, and emerging competitor strategies. Employing a mix of quantitative and qualitative forecasting methods can provide a more nuanced view of potential futures. Additionally, fostering a culture that encourages questioning assumptions and biases will enhance the accuracy and reliability of financial forecasts.

while financial forecasting is fraught with challenges, understanding and learning from past missteps can significantly improve the accuracy and relevance of future forecasts. By recognizing the limitations of reliance on historical data, incorporating a broad analysis of external factors, mitigating confirmation bias, and maintaining adaptability in their forecasting models, organizations can navigate the uncertainties of the financial landscape with greater confidence and strategic insight.

Analyzing Failures in Financial Forecasting

The first step in analyzing failures in financial forecasting is to establish a robust framework. This framework should encompass both quantitative and qualitative dimensions. Quantitively, it examines the statistical methods used, the accuracy of data inputs, and the mathematical models applied. Qualitatively, it delves into the decision-making processes, the assumptions made, and the adaptability of the forecasting model to changing circumstances. For instance, a comprehensive analysis of the 2008 financial crisis reveals both a reliance on flawed risk assessment models and a systemic underestimation of the interconnectedness of global financial markets.

The 2008 financial crisis provides a fertile ground for analysis, illustrating how a combination of complex financial instruments, lack of regulation, and flawed forecasting models can lead to catastrophic outcomes. Financial institutions and regulators failed to forecast the risk posed by mortgage-backed securities and the potential for a domino effect within the global financial system. This failure was partly due to overreliance on historical housing price data and risk models that did not adequately account for extreme, yet plausible, market conditions.

A critical aspect of analyzing failures in financial forecasting is the identification of methodological shortcomings. Time series models, for example, are often criticized for their heavy reliance on past data, potentially obscuring forward-looking insights. The introduction of machine learning and AI in forecasting has mitigated this to an extent, yet these technologies bring their own challenges, such as overfitting and a lack of transparency in decision-making processes. A balanced critique of Enron's collapse highlights both the misuse of financial instruments for speculative forecasting and the failure to incorporate ethical considerations into forecasting methodologies.

Beyond methodologies and models, the human element plays a pivotal role in forecasting failures. Cognitive biases, such as overconfidence and herd mentality, can skew forecasts away from rational expectations. The downfall of Bear Stearns and Lehman Brothers showcases how leadership's dismissal of warning signs and overconfidence in market resilience contributed to their collapse. Analyzing these failures requires a critical examination of organizational culture, leadership decision-making, and the psychological biases at play.

The goal of analyzing failures in financial forecasting is not to assign blame but to learn and adapt. This involves developing a culture that encourages transparency, questioning assumptions, and continuous learning. Incorporating scenario analysis, stress testing, and a range of forecasting models can build resilience into financial forecasting efforts. Furthermore, fostering interdisciplinary collaboration can bring diverse perspectives into the forecasting process, challenging conventional wisdom and uncovering blind spots.

The analysis of failures in financial forecasting is a multi-faceted endeavor that requires a comprehensive approach, combining quantitative analysis, qualitative insights, and a deep understanding of human behavior. By dissecting these failures with a keen eye and a commitment to learning, organizations can enhance their forecasting capabilities, making them more adaptable to the complexities of the modern financial landscape.

The Consequences of Ignoring Market Indicators

Market indicators are not just numbers on a chart; they are the pulse of economic and financial health. From interest rates, inflation figures, to stock market trends, these indicators provide a dashboard for navigating the financial future. They signal shifts in economic conditions, offering predictive insights that are crucial for making informed decisions. Ignoring these signals can be likened to sailing blindfolded; the chances of hitting an iceberg increase exponentially.

The dot-com bubble of the late '90s and early 2000s serves as a stark reminder of the consequences of ignoring market indicators. The exuberant investment in internet-based companies, fueled by unrealistic expectations of growth, ignored fundamental indicators such as earnings and price-to-earnings ratios. When the bubble burst, it wiped out trillions of dollars in market value, leading to the collapse of many firms and severe financial turmoil for investors.

Similarly, the subprime mortgage crisis of 2007-2008 underscored the catastrophic results of overlooking market warnings. Here, the disregard for increasing default rates and the unsustainable rise in property prices set the stage for a global financial crisis. The fallout was devastating, with a cascade of bank failures, significant job losses, and economies around the world plunging into recession.

Understanding and respecting market indicators necessitate a nuanced approach. It's not merely about reacting to every fluctuation but discerning which trends signal a genuine need for strategic adjustment. For instance, short-term volatility in stock markets may not necessarily indicate a looming crisis, but a consistent downward trend coupled with deteriorating economic fundamentals should not be ignored.

The case of Kodak's decline illustrates the peril of ignoring the subtler indicators of technological change and market shifts towards digital photography. Despite early innovations in digital cameras, Kodak clung to its film-based business model too long, ultimately leading to its downfall. This example highlights that market indicators extend beyond numbers; they encompass broader technological, social, and economic trends.

The key to leveraging market indicators lies in building responsive forecasting models that can adapt to changing signals. This involves integrating a wide spectrum of indicators, applying analytical rigor to distinguish noise from genuine trends, and incorporating flexibility into forecasting methodologies. Scenario planning and stress testing, based on varying market conditions, can prepare organizations for different futures, reducing the risk of being caught off-guard.

Moreover, fostering a culture that values data-driven decision-making and encourages vigilance in monitoring market indicators is essential. This culture must be supported by continuous learning and an openness to adjust forecasts as new information becomes available.

Ignoring market indicators is a perilous path that has led many organizations astray. The consequences, as history has shown, can range from missed opportunities to complete financial ruin. The wisdom gleaned from past oversights underscores the necessity of heeding these signals, integrating them into forecasting models, and maintaining an adaptive approach to financial planning. In doing so, organizations can navigate the uncertain waters of the future with greater confidence and resilience, ensuring that they not only survive but thrive in the ever-changing financial landscape.

Misunderstanding Technological Impacts

The advent of technologies such as Artificial Intelligence (AI), machine learning, blockchain, and big data analytics has not merely added tools to the arsenal but fundamentally altered the battleground. These technologies offer unprecedented capabilities in predictive analytics, real-time data processing, and scenario planning, promising a horizon brimming with insights and foresight. Yet, the failure to grasp the extent and nature of these technological impacts can lead to strategic missteps and operational obsolescence.

Consider the tale of a once-thriving financial firm, whose leadership viewed AI and machine learning as mere buzzwords rather than the harbingers of change they were. This firm continued to rely on static, quarterly forecasts, ignoring the dynamic, real-time predictive models that competitors were adopting. As the market's volatility increased, their outdated methods led to inaccurate forecasts, missed opportunities, and eventually, a loss of client trust and market share.

On another front, the misunderstanding of blockchain technology's potential in enhancing transparency and security in transactions led some institutions to dismiss it as applicable only to cryptocurrencies. This oversight precluded them from pioneering decentralized finance solutions that could have significantly reduced fraud and transaction costs, providing a competitive edge in an increasingly digital world.

A common underpinning of these pitfalls is not merely the misinterpretation of technology's current state but a gross underestimation of its growth trajectory. The exponential pace at which technology evolves means that today's cutting-edge tool can become tomorrow's industry standard. Companies that failed to anticipate the rapid adoption of cloud computing found themselves burdened by costly on-premise infrastructure, unable to scale or adapt swiftly to market changes.

Echoing the earlier discussion of Kodak's oversight of digital photography's rise, this moment serves as a poignant reminder that the failure to understand technological impacts can extend beyond financial forecasts. It can spell the existential crisis for businesses. Kodak's leadership did not fully comprehend the disruptive potential of digital technology, mistaking it for a supplemental rather than a substitutive innovation. This miscalculation led to a historic downfall from market leadership to obsolescence.

To avoid such pitfalls, organizations must cultivate a culture of technological fluency, where understanding and adapting to technological trends are integral to strategic planning. This entails ongoing education and engagement with emerging technologies, fostering partnerships with tech companies, and investing in R&D to explore new applications within the

THE CFO GUIDE TO FORECASTING IN FP&A

financial domain.

Moreover, adopting a mindset of adaptability, where business models and strategies are regularly evaluated against the backdrop of technological evolution, is crucial. This adaptability should be embedded in the FP&A processes, ensuring that forecasts and plans remain relevant, resilient, and responsive to the rapid technological shifts.

Misunderstanding the impacts of technology in financial forecasting and planning carries dire consequences. It is a misstep that can lead organizations into strategic cul-de-sacs, operational inefficiencies, and competitive disadvantage. By embracing technological fluency and adaptability, companies can navigate modern financial landscapes, leveraging technology not just as a tool, but as a compass guiding them towards innovation, insight, and informed decision-making in the ever-evolving dance of finance and technology.

Recovery and Adaptation

Recovery from a forecasting failure is a multistage process that begins with an unvarnished analysis of what went wrong. This involves dissecting the forecasting models, the assumptions that underpinned them, and how the technological landscape was misinterpreted. For instance, a financial institution that underestimated the impact of fintech innovations on consumer behavior might analyze the gaps in their market analysis and forecasting methodologies.

The next step is the recalibration of forecasting models. This recalibration isn't merely about adjusting numbers but involves a fundamental reassessment of the technological drivers of market trends. It might include incorporating real-time data analytics, adopting more agile forecasting methodologies, or integrating AI for better predictive insights.

Once recovery mechanisms are set in motion, the focus shifts to adaptation. This phase is characterized by the strategic integration of technology into forecasting models and operational processes. A pivotal strategy here is the adoption of an iterative, agile approach to forecasting. Unlike traditional models, agile forecasting allows for rapid adjustments based on real-time market feedback and technological trends, thereby enhancing resilience and responsiveness.

Another adaptive strategy is fostering cross-functional collaboration. Integrating insights from technology teams, market analysts, and financial planners can create a more holistic understanding of technological impacts on financial forecasts. For example, collaboration with IT departments can provide early insights into emerging technologies, while dialogue with market analysts can offer a deeper understanding of competitive dynamics.

The crux of adaptation lies in leveraging technology not as an adjunct but as a core component of the forecasting process. This includes harnessing AI and machine learning for dynamic scenario planning, deploying blockchain for secure and transparent record-keeping, or utilizing big data analytics for comprehensive market insights. The key is to ensure that technology adoption is aligned with strategic goals and enhances forecasting accuracy and efficiency.

A practical illustration of recovery and adaptation can be seen in a company that initially resisted cloud computing, only to face scalability issues and increased costs. Post-failure, the company not only shifted its infrastructure to the cloud but also adopted cloud-based analytics for flexible, scalable, and cost-effective forecasting. This move not only addressed the immediate challenges but also positioned the company to rapidly adapt to future technological advancements.

Recovery and adaptation is a culture that values continuous learning and innovation. Encouraging teams to stay abreast of technological trends, invest in professional development, and learn from industry best practices can transform forecasting failures into opportunities for growth. This culture fosters resilience, ensuring that organizations not only bounce back from setbacks but also emerge stronger, more agile, and better equipped to navigate the future.

Recovery and adaptation in the face of forecasting failures demand a strategic, integrated approach to technology. By analyzing failures without bias, recalibrating forecasting models, and embracing technological integration, companies can turn missteps into stepping stones towards forecasting excellence. In the ever-evolving landscape of finance and technology, adaptability is not just an asset; it is a necessity for survival and success.

Strategies for Rebounding After a Forecasting Failure

The journey to rebound begins with a thorough root cause analysis. This is not about assigning blame but understanding the specific factors that led to the forecasting failure. Did the failure stem from an overreliance on historical data without accounting for new market variables? Was there a technological oversight, such as failing to incorporate the latest data analytics tools or AI capabilities? Identifying these root causes is paramount to preventing recurrence.

With the root causes identified, the next step involves refining forecasting models. This refinement process might include integrating more sophisticated data analytics tools or revisiting the model's assumptions to align with current and predicted market realities. For example, incorporating machine learning algorithms can significantly enhance the accuracy of predictive models by learning from past forecasting errors.

A common pitfall in forecasting is relying on incomplete or siloed data. Post-failure, it's imperative to enhance both the quality and integration of data. This might involve establishing more robust data governance protocols or investing in technology platforms that enable seamless data integration across departments. High-quality, integrated data is the backbone of accurate forecasting.

Moving beyond a single-point forecast to a scenario-based planning approach can significantly improve resilience. This involves creating multiple forecasts based on different assumptions and scenarios, ranging from the most likely to the most pessimistic. This not only prepares the organization for a variety of outcomes but also provides a clearer picture of potential risks and opportunities.

Agility is key in the volatile world of FP&A. Cultivating an agile forecasting culture means moving away from annual forecasting cycles to more frequent, perhaps quarterly or even monthly, cycles. It also means being open to revisiting and adjusting forecasts as new information becomes available, rather than sticking rigidly to a set forecast.

Often, forecasting failures can be traced back

to communication breakdowns. Strengthening internal communication channels ensures that all relevant stakeholders are on the same page regarding assumptions, data sources, and the rationale behind forecasts. Equally important is external communication, especially with investors and stakeholders, to manage expectations and maintain trust in the event of a forecasting failure.

Lastly, leveraging the failure as a learning opportunity is crucial. Organizing workshops or training sessions to dissect what went wrong and what could be done differently in the future turns a negative experience into a powerful tool for organizational growth. Encouraging a culture that views failure as a stepping stone rather than a setback fosters innovation and continuous improvement.

Rebounding from a forecasting failure is not an overnight process. It requires a systematic approach, starting from understanding the failure's root causes to implementing strategic adjustments and fostering a culture of agility and continuous learning. By adopting these strategies, finance teams can not only recover from setbacks but also enhance their forecasting capabilities, making them more resilient and adaptive to future challenges.

Adjusting Processes and Assumptions Post-Failure

In the wake of a forecasting failure, the recalibration of processes and assumptions is not merely a corrective action but a strategic imperative. This segment explores the nuanced approach required to reassess and modify the underpinnings of financial forecasting methods. It's through this meticulous process that organizations can transform their forecasting framework into one that is not only more reliable but also resilient to the unpredictabilities of the financial landscape.

The foundation of any forecasting model is built on assumptions - about market conditions, customer behavior, economic factors, and more. A critical step post-failure is to rigorously re-evaluate these assumptions. Are they still relevant in the current market context? For instance, if previous forecasts assumed steady market growth but overlooked potential economic downturns, it's time to consider more conservative, varied economic scenarios.

This re-evaluation also extends to the assumptions about the data sources being used. It's crucial to scrutinize the relevance, timeliness, and accuracy of the data upon which forecasts are built. This may involve diversifying data sources or placing greater emphasis on real-time data analytics.

Adjusting the forecasting process involves scrutinizing each step of the workflow for inefficiencies or outdated practices. It's about asking hard questions: Are there bottlenecks that delay the forecasting process? Is the organization using the most up-to-date technology for data analysis and forecast generation?

One practical step might involve adopting more agile forecasting methodologies, such as moving from static annual forecasts to dynamic, rolling forecasts that can be updated more frequently based on current data. This not only allows for more accurate predictions but also provides the flexibility to quickly adjust to unforeseen changes.

Forecasting cannot operate in isolation. A post-failure adjustment should include strengthening cross-functional collaboration within the organization. This means ensuring that departments such as sales, marketing, and operations are not only contributors but also active participants in the forecasting process. Their insights and frontline data can provide valuable context that enhances the accuracy of financial forecasts.

The complexity of today's financial environment often surpasses the capabilities of traditional forecasting tools. In adjusting post-failure processes, there's a clear opportunity to incorporate advanced analytical tools, such as predictive analytics, AI, and machine learning. These technologies can handle vast amounts of data and identify patterns that might not be apparent to human analysts, providing a more nuanced and accurate forecasting capability.

Adjustment post-failure is not a one-time task but an ongoing process of learning and development. Cultivating a culture that encourages experimentation, accepts failure as a learning opportunity, and is committed to continuous improvement is pivotal. This involves setting up mechanisms for regular review and feedback on forecasting performance, encouraging team members to stay updated with the latest in financial forecasting methodologies and technologies, and promoting an environment where innovative ideas are welcomed and tested.

Adjusting processes and assumptions post-forecasting failure is a critical step towards not just recovery, but future-proofing an organization's financial forecasting capabilities. By re-evaluating assumptions, optimizing processes, enhancing collaboration, embracing advanced technologies, and fostering a culture of continuous learning, organizations can turn past failures into powerful catalysts for transformation. This approach not only mitigates the risk of future forecasting errors but also positions organizations to navigate the uncertainties of the financial landscape with greater agility and confidence.

Learning to Predict and Respond to Disruptors

Strategic foresight involves looking beyond the immediate horizon and envisioning future scenarios that could disrupt the financial ecosystem. This requires a blend of qualitative and quantitative analysis, encompassing everything from geopolitical shifts and regulatory changes to technological advancements and societal trends.

A practical approach to this is the development of an 'early warning system' within the organization. This system hinges on the continuous monitoring of key indicators that signal potential disruptors. For example, a sudden change in consumer behavior, a new regulatory framework in a significant market, or the emergence of a groundbreaking technology could all serve as early warnings.

The advent of big data and advanced analytics has transformed the landscape of financial forecasting. Organizations can now harness these technologies to sift through vast amounts of data, identify patterns, and predict potential disruptors before they fully manifest. Techniques such as predictive analytics, scenario modeling, and sentiment analysis play a crucial role in this process.

For instance, sentiment analysis of social media and news sources can provide early indications of changing consumer sentiments or emerging political and economic issues. Similarly, scenario modeling can help in simulating the potential impact of various disruptors, enabling organizations to prepare multiple response strategies.

The traditional annual budgeting and forecasting process is often too rigid to accommodate the rapid changes brought about by disruptors. Hence, there is a growing shift towards more agile forecasting models such as rolling forecasts, which are updated on a continuous basis to reflect the latest data and insights.

This agility allows organizations to adjust their strategies in real-time, ensuring they are always aligned with the current business environment. It also facilitates a more dynamic allocation of resources, enabling companies to rapidly respond to opportunities and threats as they arise.

Predicting and responding to disruptors is not solely the responsibility of the finance team but requires a collaborative effort across the entire organization. Cultivating a culture of innovation and openness is critical in this regard. Employees at all levels should be encouraged to share their insights and observations about potential disruptors.

Moreover, organizations should foster an environment where experimentation is valued, and failure is seen as a learning opportunity. This involves setting up cross-functional teams to explore new ideas and technologies and investing in continuous learning and development programs.

An effective tool for learning to predict and respond to disruptors is scenario planning. This involves developing detailed scenarios based on various potential disruptors and their likely impact on the organization. These scenarios can then be used to conduct stress tests on the organization's financial models, assessing their resilience under different conditions.

This process not only highlights vulnerabilities but also identifies potential opportunities for growth, enabling organizations to develop more robust strategies that can withstand the test of time.

Learning to predict and respond to disruptors is a complex but essential process for modern finance organizations. It requires a multifaceted approach that combines strategic foresight, advanced data analytics, agile forecasting models, a culture of innovation, and rigorous scenario planning. By mastering these elements, organizations can position themselves to not just survive but thrive in an ever-evolving financial landscape, turning potential threats into opportunities for growth and innovation.

Preventative Measures

In the dance of financial forecasting, where precision meets the unpredictable nature of markets, preventative measures stand as the guardians of accuracy and reliability. They are not merely strategies, but a set of meticulously crafted approaches designed to anticipate and mitigate the myriad risks that can distort the forecasting process. Here, we delve deep into the fabric of these measures, exploring their significance, implementation, and impact on financial planning and analysis (FP&A).

Preventative strategies lies the critical process of risk identification and assessment. It's a proactive step that demands a keen understanding of both internal and external environments. One illustrative example can be drawn from the unpredictable weather in Vancouver, where sudden shifts can mirror the volatile nature of financial markets. Just as the city's residents prepare for rain or shine, companies must scan their horizons for potential threats, ranging from market fluctuations to regulatory changes, and assess their potential impact on financial outcomes.

Scenario analysis emerges as a robust tool in this preventive arsenal. It involves constructing various plausible future states, not to predict, but to prepare. Each scenario, be it a best-case, worst-case, or something in between, is equipped with specific strategies to navigate potential financial landscapes. For instance, a company might develop a scenario where a new regulation could significantly increase operational costs. By preparing for this possibility, the company can devise contingency plans, such as cost-cutting measures or alternative revenue streams, ensuring resilience no matter which direction the regulatory winds blow.

Stress Testing: The Art of Resilience

Closely related to scenario analysis, stress testing evaluates a company's financial robustness under extreme conditions. It's akin to testing the structural integrity of bridges in Vancouver against the most severe earthquakes. By pushing financial models to their limits, companies can identify potential breakpoints and reinforce their strategies accordingly. This process not only reveals vulnerabilities but also strengthens the company's financial health, making it more adaptable to sudden economic tremors.

Continuous Monitoring and Feedback Loops

Preventative measures thrive on the principle of continuous improvement. The financial landscape is ever-evolving, and as such, forecasting models must be dynamic, adapting to new information as it becomes available. This requires a system of continuous monitoring, where real-time data feeds into forecasting models, allowing for adjustments on the fly. Moreover, establishing feedback loops, where outcomes are regularly compared against forecasts, can unveil patterns of discrepancies, providing valuable insights for refining future forecasts.

Educating and Aligning Stakeholders

A critical, often overlooked aspect of preventative measures is the alignment and education of stakeholders. Forecasting is not a solitary endeavor but a collective responsibility. From the C-suite to the finance team, all stakeholders must understand the importance of accuracy in forecasting and the role of preventative measures in achieving it. Regular training sessions, workshops, and transparent communication channels can foster a culture of vigilance and proactive risk management.

Technological Leverage

In the digital age, technology plays a pivotal role in implementing preventative measures. Advanced analytics, artificial intelligence, and machine learning offer unprecedented capabilities in identifying patterns, predicting risks, and automating parts of the forecasting process. For example, AI algorithms can continuously analyze market trends, competitor actions, and economic indicators, providing early warnings of potential disruptions. By integrating these technologies, FP&A teams can significantly enhance the accuracy and reliability of their forecasts.

Preventative measures in financial forecasting are not just

strategies; they are an ethos that encapsulates the proactive, vigilant, and adaptive mindset required in modern FP&A. By identifying risks early, preparing for multiple scenarios, stress-testing for resilience, continuously monitoring, aligning stakeholders, and leveraging technology, companies can shield their forecasts from the caprices of uncertainty. In doing so, they not only safeguard their financial health but also position themselves to navigate the future with confidence and agility.

Building Resilience into Forecasting Models

In the quest to fortify forecasting models against the tumult of financial markets, building resilience stands paramount. This endeavor is akin to constructing a lighthouse, steadfast amidst the stormy seas, guiding the financial planning and analysis (FP&A) vessel safely to harbor. The process of embedding resilience into forecasting models demands a meticulous and holistic approach, one that encompasses not only the financial aspects but also the operational and strategic facets of an organization. Herein, we explore the strategies and methodologies pivotal in crafting forecasting models that can withstand the vagaries of economic climates.

Central to resilient forecasting models is the diversification of data sources. Just as a financier in Vancouver might analyze both the local and global economic indicators to gauge market health, FP&A professionals must incorporate a broad spectrum of data. This includes not just historical financial data but also leading indicators, competitor benchmarks, and macroeconomic trends. By widening the data aperture, models gain the ability to capture early signals of change, thus enhancing their predictive power and adaptability.

Beyond static scenarios, resilient forecasting models employ dynamic scenario planning. This technique allows models to adjust in real-time to changing conditions, recalibrating forecasts based on new data inputs. Imagine a scenario where sudden geopolitical tensions disrupt supply chains. A dynamic model would immediately assess the implications on costs, revenue, and margins, adjusting forecasts accordingly. This agility turns forecasting models into living systems, continuously evolving with the business landscape.

Monte Carlo simulations offer a powerful means to embed flexibility into forecasting models. By running thousands of simulations, each based on a different set of random variables, these models provide a probability distribution of outcomes. This method offers a nuanced view of the future, highlighting not just a single forecast but a range of possible outcomes. For instance, when assessing the impact of a new product launch, Monte Carlo simulations can reveal the spectrum of potential revenue outcomes, from the most pessimistic to the most optimistic scenarios, thus preparing FP&A teams for various market receptions.

Sensitivity analysis plays a critical role in identifying vulnerabilities within forecasting models. By systematically altering one variable at a time while keeping others constant, FP&A teams can discern which inputs have the most significant impact on the forecast. This analysis can illuminate potential risk areas, such as undue reliance on a single revenue stream or exposure to currency fluctuation risks. With this knowledge, companies can strategize on risk mitigation, such as diversifying income sources or hedging financial risks.

The integration of artificial intelligence (AI) and machine learning (ML) propels forecasting models into a new echelon of resilience. These technologies enable models to learn from patterns, predict future trends with greater accuracy, and automate the adjustment of forecasts based on emerging data. For example, AI-driven models could predict customer demand shifts due to changing preferences or economic downturns, allowing FP&A teams to proactively adjust inventory levels, pricing strategies, and marketing efforts.

Lastly, the resilience of forecasting models is profoundly influenced by the culture within which they operate. A forward-looking culture, characterized by continuous learning, open communication, and cross-departmental collaboration, ensures that insights generated by resilient models are effectively translated into strategic decisions. Engaging diverse teams in the forecasting process, from sales to operations, enriches the model with varied perspectives, making it more robust and aligned with the ground realities of the business.

Building resilience into forecasting models is a complex, multifaceted endeavor that transcends mere mathematical adjustments. It requires an orchestration of diversified data, dynamic planning, advanced simulations, sensitivity analysis, cutting-edge technology, and, crucially, a culture attuned to forward-thinking. Such models stand as lighthouses in the turbulent seas of the financial world, guiding businesses toward sustainable growth and strategic agility. In crafting these resilient forecasts, FP&A professionals do not just predict the future; they prepare their organizations to thrive in it, regardless of the storms that may come.

Enhancing Risk Management Practices

Enhanced risk management is the strategic integration of

predictive analytics. Leveraging historical data, statistical algorithms, and machine learning techniques, predictive analytics can foresee potential risk factors before they crystalize into tangible threats. For example, by analyzing patterns of market behavior, FP&A teams can predict currency fluctuations and adjust their financial strategies accordingly. Predictive analytics transforms risk management from a reactive measure into a forward-looking tool, enabling organizations to navigate through the financial ebbs and flows with informed confidence.

Breaking the silos between departments to adopt a holistic view of risk is crucial. Traditional risk management often operates in compartmentalized domains, such as financial, operational, or strategic risks. However, enhancing risk management necessitates a panoramic view that encompasses all facets of an organization. By fostering inter-departmental collaborations, FP&A teams can gather a multi-dimensional understanding of risks. This approach not only identifies potential threats across the spectrum but also uncovers synergistic opportunities for mitigating risks. For instance, what may appear as an operational risk in supply chain logistics could have significant financial implications, underscoring the need for a unified risk assessment strategy.

Scenario analysis emerges as a pivotal tool in the arsenal of enhanced risk management. By constructing detailed scenarios of various plausible futures, organizations can prepare for a range of outcomes. This methodology extends beyond static 'best' and 'worst-case' scenarios to include dynamic, evolving narratives that adapt to new information and trends. Scenario analysis aids in stress-testing strategies against different risk scenarios, ensuring that contingency plans are both robust and flexible. For instance, scenario analysis might reveal vulnerabilities in a company's reliance on a single supplier, prompting diversification to mitigate supply chain risk.

Enhancing risk management practices is intrinsically tied to cultivating a culture of risk awareness throughout the organization. This entails embedding risk considerations into the decision-making process at all levels, from the C-suite to front-line employees. By empowering employees with the knowledge and tools to identify and communicate risks, FP&A teams can tap into a wealth of insights and foster a proactive stance towards risk management. Workshops, training sessions, and regular communication channels dedicated to risk awareness can facilitate this cultural shift, transforming risk management into a collective endeavor rather than a centralized function.

In an era where regulatory landscapes are ever-evolving, ensuring compliance and adherence to ethical standards is paramount in risk management. Enhanced practices involve not only keeping abreast of regulatory changes but also integrating these considerations into financial forecasting and planning. This proactive compliance strategy mitigates the risk of legal repercussions and reputational damage, safeguarding the organization's financial health and integrity. Moreover, adhering to ethical standards enhances trust among stakeholders, a critical asset in navigating the complexities of the financial domain.

Enhancing risk management practices within FP&A requires a multifaceted approach that blends predictive analytics, holistic risk assessment, scenario analysis, cultural transformation, and ethical governance. By adopting these practices, organizations equip themselves with the foresight, flexibility, and resilience needed to turn risks into opportunities. The ultimate goal is not merely to defend against potential threats but to forge a strategic advantage that propels the organization forward in its financial journey, regardless of the uncertainties that lie ahead.

CHAPTER 12:
ADAPTING TO
GLOBAL CHANGES

G eopolitical events, ranging from trade wars to political upheavals, can unsettle markets and disrupt global supply chains, presenting both challenges and opportunities for FP&A professionals. The key to adapting in this volatile landscape lies in dynamic scenario planning. By constructing a range of scenarios that account for possible geopolitical developments, organizations can prepare flexible strategies that allow for rapid adjustments. For instance, an FP&A team might develop scenarios based on potential outcomes of trade negotiations, enabling the company to swiftly recalibrate its supply chain strategy in response to new tariffs.

Economic cycles and shocks, whether they are localized recessions or global financial crises, demand a robust financial forecasting framework that incorporates leading indicators and macroeconomic trends. Advanced analytics and AI-driven tools play a pivotal role in deciphering these complex, interwoven economic signals. By leveraging real-time data and predictive modeling, FP&A teams can anticipate economic downturns or upswings and adjust their financial strategies accordingly. This might involve revising investment plans, optimizing cash flow management, or exploring new markets to hedge against regional economic instabilities.

With climate change ushering in a new era of environmental challenges, adopting sustainable practices has become essential for long-term financial planning. FP&A professionals are at the forefront of integrating environmental considerations into financial forecasts, assessing risks and opportunities associated with climate change. This includes evaluating the financial impact of transitioning to renewable energy sources, pricing carbon risk into investment decisions, and exploring opportunities in emerging green markets. Moreover, scenario analysis focused on environmental trends helps organizations prepare for regulatory changes and shifts in consumer preferences towards sustainability.

The digital revolution continues to redefine the landscape of FP&A through the advent of new technologies. Blockchain, for instance, offers unprecedented transparency and efficiency in financial transactions, while AI and machine learning enhance predictive capabilities in forecasting. Adapting to these technological changes requires not only an investment in new tools and systems but also a commitment to upskilling finance teams. Cultivating a culture of continuous learning and innovation ensures that organizations can harness these technologies to improve their forecasting accuracy, streamline operations, and drive strategic growth.

Adapting to global changes demands a proactive, strategic approach to FP&A that embraces scenario planning, leverages technological innovations, and fosters a culture of agility. By anticipating and preparing for the myriad challenges and opportunities presented by geopolitical, economic, and environmental shifts, organizations can not only weather the storms of change but also emerge stronger, more resilient, and poised for growth in the dynamic global landscape.

Anticipating and Planning for Global Economic Shifts

Anticipating economic shifts is the development of a 'global economic radar' system, a comprehensive framework that continuously monitors and analyses a spectrum of economic indicators and trends. This system integrates data from diverse sources, including international economic reports, market trends, currency fluctuations, and geopolitical events, to provide a holistic view of the global economic landscape. For instance, an FP&A team might use advanced data analytics to track leading indicators of economic health across key markets, such as consumer confidence indexes or manufacturing activity, enabling the organization to anticipate downturns or opportunities for expansion.

Armed with insights from the global economic radar, FP&A teams can engage in scenario planning, developing detailed financial models that account for a range of potential global economic conditions. This approach allows organizations to test their financial resilience under various scenarios, from mild recessions to severe financial crises, and to plan for contingencies. Stress testing, a critical component of scenario planning, involves simulating extreme economic conditions to assess the robustness of the organization's financial strategies, ensuring that it can withstand sudden economic shocks.

One of the fundamental strategies for mitigating the risks associated with global economic shifts is diversification. This extends beyond investment portfolios to encompass diversification of markets, revenue streams, and supply chains. By spreading operations and investments across different geographic regions and sectors, organizations can reduce their vulnerability to economic downturns in any single market or industry. For example, an FP&A team may advise expanding into emerging markets with high growth potential or diversifying product lines to cater to a broader range of consumer needs, thereby stabilizing revenue in the face of economic fluctuations.

The advent of AI and machine learning has significantly enhanced the predictive capabilities of financial forecasting. FP&A professionals are increasingly relying on these technologies to sift through vast amounts of economic data, identifying patterns and insights that can forecast future economic shifts. Machine learning models, for instance, can predict currency movements or stock market trends based on historical data, enabling more accurate financial planning and strategic investment decisions.

The cornerstone of successfully navigating global economic shifts lies in building a finance function that is both flexible and adaptive. This entails creating streamlined processes and systems that can be quickly adjusted as economic conditions change. It also involves cultivating a mindset of agility within the FP&A team, encouraging innovative thinking and rapid decision-making. By fostering a culture that values adaptability, organizations can respond to global economic shifts with strategic agility, adjusting their financial and operational strategies to seize opportunities and mitigate risks.

Anticipating and planning for global economic shifts is a complex, yet indispensable component of strategic financial planning. It requires a multifaceted approach that combines the development of a global economic radar, scenario planning, strategic diversification, leveraging predictive technologies, and fostering a culture of flexibility and adaptability. By embedding these strategies into their FP&A practices, organizations can not only safeguard against the uncertainties of the global economic landscape but also position themselves to thrive amidst its inevitable fluctuations.

The Impact of Geopolitical Tensions on Financial Planning

Geopolitical tensions encompass a broad range of events, from military conflicts and political unrest to economic sanctions and trade wars. Each of these events can have a significant impact on financial markets, affecting currency values, commodity prices, and investment flows. For instance, a sudden imposition of trade sanctions on a country can lead to immediate volatility in commodity markets, affecting global supply chains and causing a ripple effect across numerous industries. FP&A professionals must, therefore, cultivate a deep understanding of the geopolitical landscape and its potential impacts on financial markets and organizational operations.

The first step in mitigating the impact of geopolitical tensions is to assess their potential effects on global markets. This involves analyzing past events to identify patterns and outcomes, and employing sophisticated financial models to predict future market reactions. For example, by examining the impact of previous trade embargoes, FP&A teams can forecast the possible outcomes of new sanctions and develop strategies to hedge against these risks. This analysis must be comprehensive, considering the direct impacts on trade and supply chains, as well as the indirect effects on investor confidence and market sentiment.

Diversification as a Risk Mitigation Strategy

One of the most effective strategies for mitigating the risk of geopolitical tensions is diversification. This can be achieved through diversifying investments across different asset classes, geographic regions, and industries. By spreading exposure, organizations can reduce the impact of any single geopolitical event on their overall financial performance. For example, an organization with significant operations in a region experiencing political unrest may mitigate risk by expanding its operations into more stable regions, thereby ensuring continuity of operations and revenue streams.

Leveraging Technology for Real-Time Monitoring and Analysis

In the fast-paced world of global finance, the ability to monitor geopolitical developments in real-time and analyze their potential impacts is invaluable. Advanced technologies, including AI and machine learning, enable FP&A teams to track geopolitical events as they unfold, assessing their likely impacts on financial markets and the organization. Real-time monitoring allows for rapid response, adjusting financial plans and operational strategies to mitigate risks as they emerge.

Fostering a Culture of Agility and Resilience

Ultimately, the ability to navigate the complexities of geopolitical tensions hinges on an organization's culture. Cultivating a culture of agility and resilience empowers FP&A teams and the wider organization to adapt quickly to unforeseen geopolitical events, making strategic adjustments to safeguard financial and operational stability. This includes fostering open communication, encouraging innovative problem-solving, and developing flexible financial models that can be quickly recalibrated in response to changing global dynamics.

Geopolitical tensions present significant challenges to financial planning, requiring a nuanced understanding of global affairs and a proactive approach to risk management. Through comprehensive analysis, scenario planning, diversification, and the leveraging of advanced technologies, FP&A professionals can navigate the uncertainties of geopolitical risks, ensuring organizational resilience and strategic adaptability in an ever-changing global landscape.

Preparing for Environmental and Regulatory Changes

The first step in preparing for environmental and regulatory changes is developing a comprehensive understanding of the regulatory environment. This includes staying informed about current regulations, monitoring proposed changes, and assessing their potential impacts on the organization. For FP&A teams, this means establishing a proactive monitoring system, often leveraging technology to track regulatory developments in real-time. Such systems enable organizations to anticipate changes rather than react to them, providing a strategic advantage in financial planning.

Integrating Environmental Considerations

Environmental sustainability has become a central concern for businesses worldwide, driven by both regulatory requirements and consumer demand. FP&A professionals play a pivotal role in integrating environmental considerations into financial planning processes. This involves evaluating the financial impacts of environmental risks and opportunities, such as the potential costs of compliance with new environmental regulations or the benefits of investing in sustainable technologies. By incorporating environmental considerations into financial models, FP&A teams can help guide strategic decisions that align with sustainability goals and regulatory requirements.

Scenario Planning for Regulatory Changes

To effectively prepare for environmental and regulatory changes, FP&A professionals must employ robust scenario planning techniques. This involves creating detailed financial models that simulate various regulatory scenarios, including stringent environmental regulations, carbon pricing mechanisms, and subsidies for sustainable practices. These models help organizations assess the potential financial impacts of different scenarios and develop contingency plans. Scenario planning enables FP&A teams to identify strategic investments and operational adjustments that can mitigate risks and capitalize on opportunities arising from regulatory changes.

Leveraging Regulatory Changes for Competitive Advantage

Adapting to environmental and regulatory changes is not only about compliance and risk management; it also presents opportunities for competitive advantage. FP&A professionals can identify opportunities for innovation and differentiation by closely analyzing regulatory trends. For example, early adoption of cleaner technologies or sustainable practices can enhance brand reputation, open new markets, and attract environmentally conscious consumers and investors. Furthermore, proactive compliance can lead to cost savings through efficiency improvements and avoidance of penalties, contributing to improved financial performance.

Collaboration and Stakeholder Engagement

Effective preparation for environmental and regulatory changes requires collaboration across departments and engagement with external stakeholders. FP&A teams should work closely with legal, operations, and sustainability departments to understand the implications of regulatory changes and integrate environmental considerations into financial planning. Engaging with regulators, industry groups, and sustainability experts can provide valuable insights into regulatory trends and best practices. Additionally, transparent communication with investors and customers about the organization's environmental initiatives and regulatory compliance can enhance trust and support.

Preparing for environmental and regulatory changes is a complex but essential aspect of modern FP&A practice. By developing a deep understanding of the regulatory landscape, integrating environmental considerations into financial planning, employing scenario planning, leveraging regulatory changes for competitive advantage, and fostering collaboration and stakeholder engagement, FP&A professionals can ensure that their organizations are not only compliant but also positioned for sustainable success in a rapidly evolving environmental and regulatory context.

Embracing Innovation

Cultivating an Innovative Mindset in FP&A

Innovation begins with a mindset — a willingness to

challenge the status quo, explore uncharted territories, and embrace the risks associated with change. FP&A professionals, traditionally seen as guardians of financial stability, must now also champion innovative practices that drive strategic decision-making and operational efficiency. This involves nurturing a culture of curiosity, where questioning existing processes and seeking out improvements are encouraged and rewarded. By embracing a mindset that views change as an opportunity rather than a threat, FP&A teams can become pivotal in steering their organizations towards new horizons of financial performance and strategic agility.

Technological Advancements as Catalysts for Innovation

The accelerating pace of technological advancement offers unprecedented opportunities for FP&A to refine its practices and deliver deeper insights. Artificial intelligence (AI), machine learning (ML), blockchain, and predictive analytics are among the technologies reshaping the FP&A landscape. These tools not only enhance the accuracy of financial forecasts but also provide the agility to respond to market dynamics in real-time. For instance, AI and ML can automate routine data analysis tasks, freeing up FP&A professionals to focus on strategic analysis and decision support. Blockchain technology, on the other hand, offers a secure and transparent way to manage contracts and transactions, reducing the risk of financial discrepancies.

Implementing a Framework for Continuous Innovation

To harness the benefits of innovation, FP&A teams must establish a structured framework that supports the continuous exploration and integration of new ideas and technologies. This includes setting aside resources for innovation projects, establishing cross-functional innovation teams, and creating a process for evaluating and prioritizing innovative initiatives. Regular training and upskilling programs are essential to ensure that FP&A professionals remain adept at using new technologies and methodologies. Moreover, fostering partnerships with fintech startups and academic institutions can provide access to fresh perspectives and cutting-edge research.

Overcoming Barriers to Innovation

While the pursuit of innovation is critical, it is not without its challenges. Organizational resistance to change, budget constraints, and the complexity of integrating new technologies into existing systems can impede innovation efforts. To overcome these barriers, FP&A leaders must articulate a clear vision of how innovation can drive value for the organization, backed by tangible success stories and ROI analyses. Gaining executive buy-in and ensuring alignment with the organization's strategic objectives are crucial steps in securing the necessary resources and support for innovation initiatives.

Measuring the Impact of Innovation

Evaluating the impact of innovation on FP&A and the broader organization involves more than just financial metrics. While cost savings and revenue growth are important indicators, the benefits of innovation also manifest in improved decision-making speed, enhanced forecast accuracy, and increased organizational agility. Establishing key performance indicators (KPIs) specific to innovation outcomes can help quantify these benefits, providing a compelling case for continued investment in innovative practices.

Embracing innovation within FP&A is a strategic imperative that requires a deliberate approach, encompassing a culture shift, investment in new technologies, and a framework for continuous improvement. By fostering an innovative mindset, leveraging technological advancements, and overcoming barriers to change, FP&A teams can significantly contribute to their organizations' strategic objectives and resilience in the face of disruption. The future of FP&A lies in its ability to innovate — to reimagine its role and capabilities in a way that propels organizations towards sustainable growth and competitive advantage in the digital age.

Staying Ahead of Technological Advancements

The first step in staying ahead is to develop a keen sense of anticipation for technological trends that could impact FP&A and the broader financial sector. This requires a continuous scanning of the technological horizon, including academic research, patents, fintech startups, and industry thought leaders' insights. Engaging with tech forums, attending fintech conferences, and participating in industry consortiums can provide early warnings of disruptive technologies. Moreover, FP&A teams should cultivate a network of technology scouts and partners, including technology providers and innovation labs, to gain insights into potential applications and implications of new technologies.

Not every technological innovation will be relevant or beneficial for every organization. Thus, FP&A must evaluate technologies not just for their novelty or technical capabilities, but for their strategic fit and potential to address specific business challenges. This involves assessing technologies against criteria such as scalability, security, compliance, and integration with existing systems. A structured evaluation process, involving pilot projects and feasibility studies, can help determine the potential ROI and impact on processes, decision-making, and competitive positioning.

Once a technology is deemed beneficial, the focus shifts to integration. Seamless integration of new technologies into FP&A workflows requires careful planning, change management, and often, re-engineering of processes. This phase should begin with a clear roadmap that outlines the steps from pilot testing to full-scale deployment, including milestones for measuring progress. Training and upskilling of FP&A staff are paramount, as is the alignment of IT infrastructure and data governance policies to support the new tools. Moreover, a phased implementation approach can help manage risks and allow for adjustments based on feedback and initial outcomes.

Staying ahead of technological advancements is a dynamic and ongoing process that requires vigilance, strategic thinking, and adaptability. By anticipating technological shifts, evaluating their strategic implications, integrating them seamlessly, and fostering a culture of agility, FP&A can lead the way in harnessing technology to drive organizational success. The journey of technological advancement is perpetual, and FP&A's role is to navigate this journey with foresight, ensuring the organization not only keeps pace but sets the pace in a digitally driven world.

Encouraging Innovation Within the Finance Team

The foundation of fostering innovation lies in creating a safe environment where team members feel comfortable sharing their ideas without fear of criticism or failure. This involves recognizing and celebrating creative efforts, even when they do not result in immediate success. Establishing regular "innovation meetings" where team members can pitch new ideas, no matter how unconventional, can stimulate creative thinking and collaborative problem-solving.

Innovation thrives on diversity of thought. Forming a cross-functional task force that includes members from different departments within the organization can bring fresh perspectives to the finance team. This task force can focus on identifying challenges within the finance function and exploring technological or procedural innovations to address them. By involving members from various backgrounds, the task force can tap into a wider range of experiences and insights, driving more effective and holistic solutions.

A team that continuously learns is more likely to innovate. Investing in professional development opportunities, such as workshops, courses, and seminars focusing on the latest financial technologies and methodologies, can keep the finance team at the cutting edge. Encouraging certifications in areas such as data analytics, machine learning, and blockchain can also enhance the team's skill set, enabling them to explore new ways of solving problems and adding value.

Technology itself can be a powerful tool in encouraging innovation. Implementing collaborative platforms where ideas can be shared and developed in a communal space facilitates ongoing dialogue and idea maturation. Tools that enable simulation and modeling can help finance team members experiment with different scenarios and outcomes, encouraging a hands-on approach to innovation.

Recognition plays a crucial role in motivating team members to think outside the box. Developing a system to reward innovative ideas and implementations can further encourage creativity within the team. Rewards can vary from financial incentives to public acknowledgment in team meetings or company-wide communications. Highlighting successful innovations in internal case studies or newsletters can also provide team members with the recognition they deserve and inspire others to contribute their ideas.

To truly embed innovation within the finance team, it should be incorporated into performance reviews and goal setting. Setting specific innovation-related objectives, such as the number of new ideas proposed, the implementation of new processes, or the successful adoption of new technologies, can help align individual contributions with the broader goal of fostering innovation.

Encouraging innovation within the finance team is a multifaceted endeavor that requires creating a supportive environment, promoting cross-functional collaboration, investing in continuous learning, leveraging technology, and recognizing innovative efforts. By adopting these strategies, finance leaders can cultivate a team that not only adapts to the evolving financial landscape but actively shapes it, driving the organization towards future success with ingenuity and foresight.

Leveraging Data Analytics for Enhanced Decision-Making

At the core of leveraging data analytics is the comprehension of its key components: descriptive, diagnostic, predictive, and prescriptive analytics. Each layer builds upon the last to offer deeper insights into financial data, enabling CFOs and finance teams to navigate through past performance, understand current dynamics, forecast future trends, and recommend actions to achieve strategic goals. Grasping these fundamentals allows teams to identify which analytical approaches best align with their decision-making needs.

The selection of analytical tools is critical in the journey towards data-driven decision-making. Today's market offers a plethora of advanced software solutions equipped with AI and machine learning capabilities, designed to process large datasets with precision and speed. Tools such as SAP Analytics Cloud, IBM Cognos Analytics, and Tableau enable finance teams to perform complex analyses, including cash flow forecasting, risk assessment, and trend analysis. Choosing the right tool requires a balance between functionality, scalability, and user-friendliness, ensuring the team can harness its full potential.

Shifting towards a data-driven decision-making framework necessitates a cultural transformation within the finance team and the broader organization. This involves fostering a mindset that values data as a critical asset for strategic planning and operational efficiency. It requires regular training and development programs to enhance the team's data literacy, ensuring members are proficient in interpreting data analytics and translating them into strategic actions.

Data analytics must be intricately woven into the fabric of the finance function's strategic planning activities. By establishing clear protocols for data collection, analysis, and interpretation, finance teams can ensure that every financial plan and forecast is underpinned by solid data insights. This integration empowers CFOs to present substantiated strategies to stakeholders, illustrating scenarios, risks, and opportunities with clarity and confidence.

Enhanced decision-making is not confined to the finance team alone; it extends across the entire organization. Data analytics offers a common language for cross-departmental collaboration, enabling teams to align their strategies and objectives. Through shared dashboards and reports, finance can communicate financial insights and projections that influence marketing, operations, HR, and other functions, fostering a unified approach to achieving the organization's goals.

As data analytics becomes integral to decision-making, its ethical implications must not be overlooked. Ensuring data privacy, security, and compliance with regulatory standards is paramount. The finance team must establish rigorous data governance frameworks to manage data ethically, safeguarding against misuse and ensuring transparency in how data insights are derived and applied.

Leveraging data analytics for enhanced decision-making is a transformative journey for the finance function. It requires a profound understanding of analytical methodologies, the adoption of advanced tools, a cultural shift towards data-centricity, and the ethical management of data. By embracing data analytics, finance leaders can ensure their teams are equipped to navigate the complexities of the modern business landscape, making informed decisions that drive strategic success and sustainable growth.

Building a Sustainable Forecasting Culture

The first step in building a sustainable forecasting culture is to evolve beyond traditional mindsets that view forecasting as a purely numerical or administrative task. In the modern financial landscape, forecasting is a strategic function that combines quantitative analysis with qualitative insights. It requires a shift towards understanding forecasting as a dynamic and integral part of strategic management, essential for navigating through market volatilities and capitalizing on emerging opportunities.

A robust forecasting culture thrives on collaboration. It necessitates breaking down silos between the finance team and other departments, ensuring that forecasting becomes a cross-functional effort. By involving diverse perspectives from operations, sales, marketing, and HR, forecasts can encompass a broader view of the organization's ecosystem, enhancing their accuracy and relevance. Creating interdisciplinary teams focused on forecasting can facilitate this integration, promoting a shared responsibility towards achieving organizational objectives.

The landscape of financial forecasting is perpetually evolving, with new technologies, methodologies, and regulatory environments emerging. A sustainable forecasting culture is one that prioritizes continuous learning and development. This involves regular training sessions, workshops, and exposure to industry best practices, ensuring that the finance team and stakeholders across the organization stay abreast of advancements in forecasting techniques and tools. Encouraging certifications and professional development in areas such as data analytics, AI, and machine learning can further empower individuals, fostering a culture of expertise and innovation.

Technology plays a pivotal role in building a sustainable forecasting culture by democratizing data access and analysis. Implementing cloud-based forecasting tools and platforms can enable real-time data sharing and collaboration across departments. By making data accessible and understandable, technology can empower decision-makers at all levels, ensuring that forecasting influences day-to-day decisions as well as long-term strategic planning. Selecting scalable and user-friendly tools is crucial to ensure broad adoption and effective utilization.

A key characteristic of a sustainable forecasting culture is the establishment of feedback loops and continuous improvement mechanisms. This involves regularly reviewing forecasting processes, outcomes, and their impact on decision-making and business performance. Encouraging open dialogue about forecasting accuracy, variances, and lessons learned can foster an environment of transparency and continuous enhancement. Incorporating feedback from a wide range of stakeholders, including those outside the finance function, can provide diverse insights that drive iterative improvements.

Lastly, building a sustainable forecasting culture means fostering resilience and adaptability among team members and across the organization. This cultural aspect emphasizes the ability to respond to and recover from forecasting inaccuracies, market changes, and unforeseen challenges. Celebrating successes, learning from misses, and remaining agile in the face of uncertainty can galvanize a team's commitment to a forward-looking, adaptive approach to forecasting.

Establishing a sustainable forecasting culture is a multifaceted endeavor that extends beyond technical proficiency to encompass organization-wide engagement, continuous learning, technological empowerment, and an adaptive mindset. By embedding these principles into the fabric of the organization, leaders can ensure that forecasting becomes a vital pillar supporting strategic decision-making, resilience, and long-term success. In doing so, they not only enhance their organization's forecasting capabilities but also contribute to a more dynamic, informed, and forward-thinking business environment.

Enshrining adaptability and flexibility in corporate culture

An adaptable and flexible corporate culture lies a forward-looking mindset that anticipates change. Cultivating this mindset requires leaders to champion a vision that transcends the present, focusing on future possibilities and emerging trends. It involves encouraging curiosity, open-mindedness, and proactive thinking among team members, enabling them to envisage potential scenarios and prepare for various outcomes.

Central to enhancing adaptability and flexibility is the decentralization of decision-making. By empowering employees at all levels to make decisions, organizations can become more responsive and agile. This empowerment fosters a sense of ownership and accountability, driving individuals to act decisively and innovatively. Training and trust-building are pivotal in ensuring that employees are equipped and confident to make sound decisions aligned with strategic objectives.

A culture that prizes adaptability and flexibility also recognizes the value of experimentation and learning from failure. Establishing a safe space where taking calculated risks is encouraged, and failures are viewed as learning opportunities, can significantly contribute to an adaptive culture. This approach not only accelerates innovation but also demystifies failure, cultivating a resilient workforce that is not deterred by setbacks.

Effective communication channels and the free flow of information are indispensable for adaptability and flexibility. Transparent communication ensures that all members of the organization are aligned with its goals and aware of changes in the external environment. Utilizing digital tools and platforms can facilitate seamless information sharing, fostering a well-informed and cohesive team that can swiftly adjust to changing circumstances.

The velocity of technological advancements and changing industry dynamics necessitate continuous learning and skills development. Investing in training programs that enhance digital literacy, strategic thinking, and change management can equip employees with the necessary tools to adapt and thrive. Moreover, promoting cross-functional learning and job rotations can provide employees with a broader perspective, enhancing their ability to contribute innovatively across different facets of the organization.

Adaptability extends to organizational structures and work arrangements. Embracing flexible work models such as remote work, flexible hours, and project-based assignments can make the organization more resilient to external shocks. This flexibility supports a work-life balance, attracts diverse talent, and fosters a high-performance culture where productivity is measured by outcomes rather than hours spent in the office.

Ingraining adaptability and flexibility in corporate culture is a strategic necessity in today's fast-paced and uncertain business environment. By developing a forward-looking mindset, empowering decision-making, creating a safe space for experimentation, enhancing communication, investing in continuous learning, and incorporating flexible work arrangements, organizations can cultivate a dynamic and resilient culture. This cultural foundation not only enables businesses to withstand disruptions but also to emerge stronger, more innovative, and better positioned for future growth.

Investing in Training and Development

The inception of any impactful training and development program commences with its alignment to the overarching strategic goals of the organization. This alignment ensures that the learning objectives are not orthogonal to the direction in which the business aspires to move but are, in fact, propelling it forward. By closely integrating training programs with strategic objectives, organizations can create a symbiotic ecosystem where growth in individual competencies directly contributes to the realization of business goals.

Understanding that one size does not fit all is paramount in the design of training initiatives. The development of customized learning pathways that cater to the diverse needs, roles, and career aspirations within the finance team fosters a more engaged and motivated workforce. These pathways could range from mastering cutting-edge financial modeling techniques to leadership development programs for aspiring finance leaders. The customization of these pathways encourages a more personal investment in learning, leading to higher retention rates and a more profound impact on performance.

The advent of digital learning platforms has revolutionized the accessibility and scalability of training programs. Organizations can leverage these platforms to deliver a blend of synchronous and asynchronous learning experiences that cater to various learning styles and schedules. Through the use of AI-driven personalized learning recommendations, gamification, and social learning networks, these platforms can significantly enhance the learning experience, making it more interactive, engaging, and effective.

Cultivating a culture that prizes continuous learning demands more than just providing access to training resources. It requires the creation of an environment where curiosity is encouraged, where time is allocated for learning, and where knowledge sharing is celebrated. Leadership plays a critical role in modeling these behaviors, demonstrating a commitment to their own development, and recognizing and rewarding learning achievements within their teams.

To justify ongoing investment in training and development, it is crucial to measure its impact on both individual and organizational performance. This can be achieved through a variety of metrics, including but not limited to, improvements in productivity, the achievement of learning objectives, employee retention rates, and the overall financial performance of the organization. Regularly reviewing these metrics provides valuable insights into the effectiveness of training programs and identifies areas for further enhancement.

Investing in training and development is not merely an expenditure but a strategic investment in the future of the organization. By aligning training initiatives with strategic goals, customizing learning pathways, harnessing digital platforms, fostering a culture of continuous learning, and measuring the impact, organizations can ensure their finance teams are not only prepared for the challenges of today but are also equipped to lead in the dynamic landscape of tomorrow's financial world. This proactive approach to training and development is indispensable for organizations aiming to maintain a competitive edge in the fast-paced world of finance, technology, and global business operations.

The Evolving Role of the CFO in Shaping Future Leaders

The journey towards leadership often begins under the tutelage of a seasoned mentor. CFOs, with their expansive understanding of the financial and strategic underpinnings of a business, are uniquely positioned to guide aspiring leaders. Mentorship, in this context, extends beyond mere skill transfer; it is about instilling a strategic mindset, a knack for problem-solving, and the ability to foresee and navigate the future challenges of the business landscape. CFOs can initiate mentorship programs, offering direct engagement through project collaborations, shadowing opportunities, and regular one-on-one coaching sessions.

The creation of structured leadership development frameworks is vital in systematically identifying and nurturing high-potential individuals within the finance team and beyond. These frameworks often encapsulate a blend of formal training, experiential learning, and personal development plans tailored to the individual's aspirations and the organization's needs. CFOs play a crucial role in designing these frameworks, ensuring they are aligned with the company's strategic vision and incorporate finance's pivotal role in decision-making processes.

A forward-thinking CFO envisages a robust pipeline of finance leaders who can sustain and propel the organization's growth. This involves recognizing talent early, providing them with challenges that stretch their capabilities, and exposing them to cross-functional projects that broaden their perspective.

Importantly, it also means facilitating a culture where failure is seen as a stepping stone to learning, thereby encouraging innovation and risk-taking.

As the finance function increasingly embraces technology and data analytics, the CFO's role in leader development includes ensuring future leaders are proficient in these areas. This involves not just training in the use of new tools but fostering a mindset that leverages data-driven insights for strategic decision-making. CFOs can champion initiatives like hackathons and innovation labs that encourage experimentation and hands-on learning in these rapidly evolving domains.

The most potent tool a CFO has in shaping future leaders is their own example. Demonstrating ethical leadership, a commitment to continuous learning, and a strategic vision in their actions inspires those around them to emulate these qualities. CFOs who are transparent about their decision-making processes, who actively seek feedback, and who demonstrate resilience in the face of setbacks provide powerful lessons in leadership.

The role of the CFO is undergoing a significant evolution, expanding to encompass the critical function of developing future leaders. By actively engaging in mentorship, establishing leadership development frameworks, fostering a leadership pipeline, emphasizing the importance of technology and analytics, and leading by example, CFOs can ensure that the next generation of leaders is well-equipped to navigate the complexities of a rapidly changing business environment. This proactive approach not only secures the organization's future but also cements the CFO's legacy as a builder of leaders.

ADDITIONAL RESOURCES

Books

1. "Financial Forecasting, Analysis, and Modelling: A Framework for Long-Term Forecasting" by Michael Samonas.

   - Provides a thorough approach to financial forecast modeling and analysis, essential for high-level forecasting work.

2. "FP&A - Certified Corporate FP&A Professional" by Association for Financial Professionals.

   - A guide for those seeking certification, covering everything from basic concepts to advanced forecasting techniques.

3. "The Data-Driven CFO: Financial Leadership in the Age of Big Data" by Anders Liu-Lindberg and Michael J. Huthwaite.

   - Focuses on how CFOs can use big data analytics in financial forecasting and decision making.

Articles

1. "Beyond Budgeting: The Way Forward for Forecasting?" in the Financial Management (CIMA) magazine.

   - Discusses alternative forecasting methodologies aligning with modern business agility needs.

2. "Enhancing Financial Planning and Analysis with Machine Learning" in the Harvard Business Review.

   - Explores advanced techniques like machine learning in FP&A forecasting and its potential.

Websites

1. AF4S (Association for Financial Professionals) - Forecasting & Planning Section

   - URL: https://www.afponline.org/trends-topics/topics/forecasting-planning

   - Offers articles, guides, and training materials specifically aimed at forecasting and planning within finance.

2. Corporate Finance Institute (CFI)

   - URL: https://corporatefinanceinstitute.com/resources/knowledge/planning-forecasting/

   - Provides resources, free courses, and articles on financial forecasting and model building.

Organizations

1. Association for Financial Professionals (AFP)

   - Serves professionals in finance, including FP&A, offering certification, training, and networking opportunities.

2. Institute of Management Accountants (IMA)

   - Offers the CMA (Certified Management Accountant) credential which includes components relevant to forecasting and strategic financial management.

Tools

1. Adaptive Insights

   - A cloud-based software for business planning, including FP&A forecasting. Provides real-time analytics and scenario modeling.

2. Anaplan

   - Offers a platform for business planning across finance, sales, supply chain, and HR, with robust capabilities in forecasting and scenario analysis.

3. Prophix

   - A solution focusing on automating financial processes including budgeting, planning, forecasting, and reporting.

Online Courses and Certifications

1. FP&A Certification by the Association for Financial Professionals

  - An in-depth certification program focusing specifically on the skills required for advanced financial planning and analysis.

2. Advanced Financial Modeling & Valuation Course - Corporate Finance Institute

  - Teaches complex financial modeling skills, vital for accurate and effective forecasting.

FORECASTING
GUIDES

HISTORICAL TREND ANALYSIS

Step 1: Data Collection

- **Gather Historical Data**: Collect past data on the metric you wish to forecast, such as sales or revenue. The data should cover a sufficiently long period to identify patterns and trends accurately. Typically, 3-5 years of monthly data is a good starting point.

- **Ensure Data Quality**: Verify that the data is accurate, complete, and consistent. Cleanse any anomalies or outliers that do not reflect normal business operations.

Step 2: Data Preparation

- **Format Data**: Organize your data in a chronological order. Use a spreadsheet or statistical software for easy manipulation and analysis.

- **Adjust for Seasonality**: Identify any seasonal patterns in your data and adjust for them. This may involve calculating seasonal indices or using statistical methods to deseasonalize the data.

Step 3: Trend Analysis

- **Plot the Data**: Create a time series plot of your data to visually inspect trends, seasonal patterns, and cyclical fluctuations.

- **Calculate Trend Components**: Use statistical

methods to quantify the trend. This could involve fitting a linear regression model to the data or using moving averages to smooth out short-term fluctuations and highlight the underlying trend.

Step 4: Forecasting

- **Extrapolate the Trend**: Based on the identified trend, project future values. If you used a linear regression model, you could extend the trend line into the future. For moving averages, you might project the trend based on the slope of the recent period.

- **Adjust for Seasonality**: If you previously deseasonalized your data, now adjust your forecasted values to account for seasonal effects.

Step 5: Validation and Refinement

- **Back-Testing**: Validate your forecast by comparing it against a subset of historical data that was not used in the trend analysis. This will help you evaluate the accuracy of your forecasting model.

- **Refine the Model**: Based on the back-testing results, refine your model as necessary. This might involve adjusting for outliers, reconsidering the period used for moving averages, or incorporating additional variables that could impact the forecast.

Step 6: Documentation and Presentation

- **Document Your Process**: Keep detailed records of the data sources, assumptions, methods, and adjustments used in your analysis.

- **Prepare Your Forecast Presentation**: Create a clear and concise presentation of your forecast, including visualizations of the trend analysis, the rationale behind your model, and any assumptions or limitations.

Step 7: Monitoring and Updating

- **Monitor Performance**: Regularly compare actual outcomes against your forecasted values to monitor the performance of your model.

- **Update the Forecast**: As new data becomes available, update your forecast to reflect the most current information. This may involve repeating the analysis periodically to adjust for any changes in trends or business conditions.

Historical Trend Analysis is both an art and a science, requiring both quantitative analysis and qualitative judgment. By following these steps, you can leverage past data to make informed predictions about future trends, providing valuable insights for strategic planning and decision-making in FP&A.

REGRESSION ANALYSIS

Regression analysis is a statistical method used for forecasting when you want to understand the relationship between a dependent variable (what you want to forecast) and one or more independent variables (factors that might influence that forecast). It's particularly useful when you want to forecast a variable based on the linear relationship with other variables.

Step 1: Define the Variables

- **Dependent Variable (DV)**: Identify the metric you want to forecast, such as sales revenue.

- **Independent Variables (IVs)**: Identify factors that could influence your DV, such as advertising spend, market trends, economic indicators, etc.

Step 2: Data Collection

- **Gather Data**: Collect historical data for both your DV and IVs. The quality and granularity of your data can significantly impact the accuracy of your regression model.

- **Data Cleaning**: Ensure the data is clean, removing any outliers or errors that could distort the analysis.

Step 3: Choose the Type of Regression

- **Simple Linear Regression**: Use if you have one IV. It explores the linear relationship between the DV and the IV.

- **Multiple Linear Regression**: Use if you have two or more IVs. It examines how multiple factors collectively impact the DV.

Step 4: Develop the Regression Model

- **Statistical Software**: Use statistical software (e.g., Excel, R, SPSS) to input your data and run the regression analysis.

- **Interpret Coefficients**: The output will include coefficients for each IV, indicating how much the DV is expected to change with a one-unit change in the IV, holding all other variables constant.

Step 5: Model Validation

- **R-Squared**: Check the R-squared value to assess how well your model explains the variation in the DV. A higher R-squared value indicates a better fit.

- **P-Values**: Review the p-values of the coefficients to determine the statistical significance of each IV. A lower p-value (typically <0.05) indicates a significant impact on the DV.

Step 6: Forecasting

- **Predictive Forecasting**: Use the regression equation (model) to forecast the DV based on future values or expected changes in the IVs.

- **Sensitivity Analysis**: Conduct sensitivity analyses to understand how changes in the IVs impact the DV, which can help in scenario planning.

Step 7: Documentation and Presentation

- **Documentation**: Document your methodology, including the selection of IVs, data sources, and any assumptions made in the model.

- **Presentation**: Present the model, its findings, and the forecast in a clear and understandable manner, including visualizations like scatter plots showing the relationship between the DV and IVs.

Step 8: Monitoring and Updating

- **Monitor and Compare**: Regularly compare actual outcomes against forecasted values to assess the model's performance.

- **Update the Model**: Update your model as new data becomes available or as changes occur in the variables or their relationships. Continuous refinement is crucial for maintaining accuracy.

DELPHI METHOD

The Delphi Method is a forecasting process framework based on the results of multiple rounds of questionnaires sent to a panel of experts. Several characteristics define the Delphi method:

1. **Anonymity of the Respondents**: Experts answer questionnaires in multiple rounds. After each round, a facilitator provides an anonymous summary of the experts' forecasts and reasons. Participants are encouraged to revise their earlier answers in light of the replies of other members of their panel.

2. **Iteration and Controlled Feedback**: The process is iterative, with each round refining the forecasts based on the panel's collective information. The feedback is controlled and systematically processed.

3. **Statistical Aggregation of Group Response**: The final forecast is created by aggregating the responses statistically. This approach is used to achieve a consensus forecast.

Steps to Implement the Delphi Method:

1. **Choose a Panel of Experts**: Select experts based on their knowledge, experience, and expertise relevant to the forecast. The panel should be diverse to cover different perspectives.

2. **First Round of Questionnaires**: The initial questionnaire is broad, aiming to gather as much information as possible without influencing the experts with preconceived notions.

3. **Analysis and Feedback**: Analyze the responses, summarize them, and feed the summary back to the panelists. Highlight areas of agreement and disagreement.

4. **Subsequent Rounds**: Refine the questionnaires based on the feedback, focusing on areas of disagreement to narrow down the differences. Continue this process until a consensus is reached or diminishing returns are observed.

5. **Final Forecast**: Once the rounds are complete, aggregate the data to form a forecast. This may involve using median scores, mean values, or other statistical measures to summarize the panel's final opinions.

6. **Document and Present the Findings**: Prepare a detailed report on the forecast, including the methodology, the consensus reached, and any significant divergences among the panelists. Present this to the decision-makers.

Applications and Limitations:

- **Applications**: The Delphi Method is particularly useful for long-term forecasting and in situations where there is little historical data to inform predictions. It's often used for technological forecasting, demand forecasting in new markets, and assessing the impact of future trends.

- **Limitations**: The quality of the forecast depends heavily on the experts' selection. The process can be time-consuming and may suffer from biases if the panel is not properly managed.

The Delphi Method is a powerful qualitative forecasting technique that leverages expert opinions to make informed predictions about the future. It's particularly useful in scenarios where quantitative data is sparse or non-existent, allowing organizations to make strategic decisions based on expert insight.

MOVING AVERAGE

The Moving Average technique is a simple yet powerful forecasting method used to smooth out short-term fluctuations and highlight longer-term trends in data. It's particularly useful in inventory management, sales forecasting, and any situation where you want to understand the underlying direction in which data is moving, free from the "noise" of short-term variations. Here's a step-by-step guide to implementing the Moving Average technique:

Step 1: Choose Your Data

- **Select Your Time Series Data**: This could be monthly sales, daily inventory levels, or any other metric you're interested in forecasting.

Step 2: Determine the Moving Average Period

- **Select the Period Length**: The period (or window) length is how many consecutive data points you will use to calculate each moving average value. Common periods include 3-month, 6-month, and 12-month averages. The choice depends on the cycle of your data and how smooth you want the moving average to be. A longer period will smooth out the data more, but it can also lag more behind sudden changes.

Step 3: Calculate the Moving Averages

- **Simple Moving Average (SMA)**: For each point in time, calculate the average of the data points within the selected period. For example, a 3-month SMA at the end of March would be the average of January, February, and March data points.

The formula for a simple moving average is:

$$SMA = P1 + P2 + \cdots + Pn n SMA = n P1 + P2 + \cdots + Pn$$

where P1,P2,...,PnP1,P2,...,Pn are the data points in the period, and nn is the number of periods.

- **Calculate for Each Point**: Slide the window across your data set, calculating a new average each time you move one period forward in time.

Step 4: Plot Your Moving Averages

- **Visualize the Trend**: Plot the moving average values on a graph alongside the original data points. This will help you see the smoothed trend and compare it to the actual data fluctuations.

Step 5: Analyze and Forecast

- **Identify Trends**: Use the moving average line to identify trends in your data. An upward trend in the moving average might indicate increasing sales or inventory needs, while a downward trend could signal a decrease.

- **Forecasting**: While moving averages can help you understand past trends, they can also be used as a basis for forecasting. One simple approach is to project the moving average trend forward. However, be cautious, as this method assumes that past trends will continue unchanged.

Step 6: Adjust and Refine

- **Adjust the Period**: If the moving average is too smooth or too volatile, adjust the period length and recalculate. Finding the right balance may require some experimentation.

- **Consider Weighted Moving Averages**: For more refined analysis, consider using weighted moving averages (WMA) or exponential moving averages

(EMA), which give more weight to recent data points, potentially providing a more responsive trend line.

Step 7: Continuous Monitoring and Updating

- **Update Your Averages Regularly**: As new data comes in, update your moving averages to keep your forecasts current.

- **Monitor Changes in Trend**: Pay attention to shifts in the moving average trend, as these can indicate changes in the underlying data that might require action or adjustment in your planning.

The Moving Average technique is a versatile tool in the FP&A toolkit, offering a straightforward way to smooth data and identify trends. By carefully selecting the averaging period and regularly updating your analysis, you can gain valuable insights into your data's underlying movements, aiding in more accurate and timely decision-making.

EXPONENTIAL SMOOTHING

Exponential Smoothing is a forecasting technique that, like Moving Averages, aims to smooth time series data. However, it introduces a key improvement by giving more weight to recent observations, making it more responsive to changes in the data trend. This method is particularly useful for sales, inventory levels, and other financial data forecasting where recent changes are more indicative of future trends. Here's a guide to implementing Exponential Smoothing:

Step 1: Understand the Concept

- **Weighting**: Unlike simple moving averages that treat all data points equally, Exponential Smoothing assigns exponentially decreasing weights as you go back in time. The most recent data points have the highest weight, and the weight decreases exponentially for older data points.

Step 2: Choose the Smoothing Constant

- **Alpha (α)**: The first step in applying Exponential Smoothing is to choose the smoothing constant α, which ranges between 0 and 1. A higher α gives more weight to recent data, making the forecast more responsive to changes. The choice of α can be based on historical data performance, with some trial and error to find the optimal value.

Step 3: Calculate the Exponential Smoothed Series

- **Initial Setup**: You need an initial value to start the calculation. This could be the actual value of the first data point in your series, or it can be computed as an average of the initial period.

- **Formula**: The formula for Exponential Smoothing is given by:

$$S_t = \alpha \cdot Y_t + (1-\alpha) \cdot S_{t-1}$$

where S_t is the smoothed value at time t, Y_t is the actual value at time t, and S_{t-1} is the previous smoothed value.

Step 4: Forecasting

- **One-Step-Ahead Forecast**: In its simplest form, the forecast for the next period (F_{t+1}) is equal to the most recent smoothed value (S_t). This makes the method particularly suited for short-term forecasting.

- **Forecast Formula**: The forecast for any future period is given by:

$$F_{t+m} = S_t$$

for a simple exponential smoothing model, where m is the number of periods into the future you wish to forecast.

Step 5: Model Refinement

- **Adjust α**: If the forecasts are not as responsive as desired or are too reactive to random fluctuations, adjust the smoothing constant α and reevaluate.

- **Advanced Models**: For data with trends or seasonal patterns, consider using advanced exponential smoothing models like Double Exponential Smoothing (for trends) or Holt-Winters Exponential Smoothing (for trends and seasonality).

Step 6: Evaluation and Use

- **Accuracy Assessment**: Evaluate the accuracy of your

forecasts using measures such as Mean Absolute Error (MAE), Mean Squared Error (MSE), or Mean Absolute Percentage Error (MAPE).

- **Continuous Updating**: As new actual data becomes available, update the smoothed values and forecasts to maintain the accuracy and relevance of your predictions.

Step 7: Application

- **Decision Making**: Use the forecasts from Exponential Smoothing to inform decision-making processes in inventory management, budgeting, sales planning, and other areas requiring accurate future estimates.

Implementation Note:

Implementing Exponential Smoothing can be straightforward with spreadsheet software that supports it (like Excel) or programming languages with statistical libraries (like Python's Pandas and StatsModels). Careful selection of the smoothing constant ($\alpha\alpha$) and continuous refinement based on the performance of the model are key to effective forecasting.

Exponential Smoothing offers a robust and flexible approach to time series forecasting, especially when dealing with data that exhibits random variability or when you need a method that can quickly adapt to recent changes.

SEASONAL ADJUSTMENT

Seasonal Adjustment is a statistical technique used to remove the seasonal component of a time series to better understand underlying trends and cyclic effects. It's particularly valuable in industries with clear seasonal patterns, such as retail, tourism, and agriculture, enabling more accurate predictions for future periods by accounting for expected seasonal fluctuations. Here's a guide to implementing Seasonal Adjustment:

Step 1: Identify Seasonal Patterns

- **Analyze the Data**: Begin by examining your data for seasonal patterns. This could involve plotting the data over time to visually identify periods of regular increases or decreases that correspond to specific seasons or times of the year.

Step 2: Decomposition of Time Series

- **Decompose Your Time Series**: Time series decomposition involves breaking down the observed time series into three components: trend, seasonal, and random (irregular) components. This can be done using statistical software or programming languages like Python or R, which offer built-in functions for time series decomposition.

Step 3: Seasonal Component Estimation

- **Calculate Seasonal Indices**: Once the time series is

decomposed, calculate the seasonal component for each period. This involves averaging the seasonal effects over all cycles to get a single seasonal index for each period within the cycle (e.g., months in a year, days in a week).

Step 4: Seasonal Adjustment

- **Remove the Seasonal Component**: Adjust the original time series by removing the seasonal component, leaving the trend and random components. This is often done by dividing the original series by the seasonal index if the model is multiplicative, or subtracting if the model is additive.
  - **Additive Model**: $Y_t = T_t + S_t + E_t$, where the seasonal component is subtracted from the original data.
  - **Multiplicative Model**: $Y_t = T_t \times S_t \times E_t$, where the original data is divided by the seasonal component.

Step 5: Analyze and Forecast

- **Use the Adjusted Data for Forecasting**: With the seasonal effects removed, you can now apply other forecasting techniques to the seasonally adjusted data to predict future trends more accurately.

- **Reintroduce Seasonality for Future Periods**: For actual forecasting, after applying your chosen forecasting technique to the seasonally adjusted data, reintroduce the seasonal component based on historical seasonal patterns to make the forecast applicable to future periods.

Step 6: Continuous Monitoring and Model Updating

- **Review and Update Regularly**: Seasonal patterns can evolve over time. Regularly review and, if necessary, recalibrate your seasonal adjustment factors to ensure they remain accurate and reflective of current patterns.

Step 7: Documentation and Reporting

- **Document Your Process**: Keep detailed records of the methodologies, calculations, and adjustments made during the seasonal adjustment process. This documentation is crucial for transparency, repeatability, and future audits.

Implementation Tools and Software

- **Statistical Software**: Many statistical software packages and programming languages (like R, Python's Statsmodels, and SAS) offer built-in functionalities for seasonal decomposition and adjustment.

- **Excel**: For simpler analyses, Excel can perform basic seasonal adjustment calculations, especially when used in conjunction with Excel's Analysis ToolPak.

Seasonal Adjustment is a critical step in preparing time series data for accurate forecasting, particularly when dealing with seasonal businesses. By identifying and removing the seasonal component, analysts and planners can focus on the underlying trends and random fluctuations in the data, leading to more informed decision-making and strategic planning.

SCENARIO PLANNING

Scenario Planning is a strategic planning method that organizations use to envision and prepare for multiple future scenarios. It helps in understanding how different trends, uncertainties, and strategic choices could impact the future. By creating detailed hypothetical scenarios, organizations can develop flexible strategies that are robust across various possible futures. Here's how to implement Scenario Planning:

Step 1: Identify Objectives and Scope

- **Clarify Objectives**: Define what you want to achieve with scenario planning. Are you exploring future growth opportunities, assessing risks, or preparing for potential disruptions?

- **Determine the Scope**: Specify the time frame and the aspects of the business or environment you're focusing on (e.g., market trends, technological advancements, regulatory changes).

Step 2: Gather and Analyze Information

- **Research**: Collect data and insights on key forces, trends, and uncertainties that could impact your organization. This can include economic, political, technological, and social factors.

- **Stakeholder Input**: Engage stakeholders from different parts of the organization to provide diverse perspectives on potential future changes and impacts.

Step 3: Identify Key Drivers and Uncertainties

- **Drivers of Change**: From your research, identify the key factors that could drive change in your industry or organization. These are variables that have the potential to significantly impact your objectives.

- **Uncertainties**: Highlight the major uncertainties that could affect the future. These are factors with unpredictable outcomes but significant potential impacts.

Step 4: Develop Scenarios

- **Create Scenario Framework**: Using the key drivers and uncertainties, construct a framework for generating distinct scenarios. This often involves focusing on two or three critical uncertainties and creating a matrix to explore different combinations of these uncertainties.

- **Develop Detailed Scenarios**: For each scenario, build a detailed narrative that describes a plausible future state. Include how key drivers and uncertainties might evolve, and the potential impacts on your organization or industry. Typically, organizations develop three to five scenarios to capture a wide range of possibilities.

Step 5: Analyze Scenarios and Implications

- **Impact Analysis**: For each scenario, assess the implications for your organization. Consider how each scenario could affect your strategic objectives, operations, and competitive position.

- **Identify Indicators**: Determine which indicators could signal that a particular scenario is becoming more likely. This will help you monitor changes in the environment and adjust your strategies accordingly.

Step 6: Develop Strategies and Plans

- **Formulate Strategies**: Develop strategic options that could be effective across multiple scenarios. Focus on flexible, adaptive strategies that can be tweaked as the future unfolds.

- **Action Planning**: For each scenario, outline specific actions, initiatives, or investments that could position your organization to capitalize on opportunities or mitigate risks.

Step 7: Implement and Monitor

- **Implementation**: Integrate scenario planning into your strategic planning process. Ensure that your organization's strategic plans are robust against the various scenarios.

- **Continuous Monitoring**: Regularly monitor the indicators identified during the analysis phase to track which, if any, of the scenarios are becoming more likely. Be prepared to adjust your strategies in response to emerging trends or signals.

Step 8: Review and Update

- **Periodic Review**: Scenario Planning is not a one-time exercise. Periodically revisit your scenarios and the assumptions behind them, updating them as needed based on new information or changes in the environment.

Scenario Planning is a powerful tool for navigating uncertainty and fostering strategic agility. By preparing for a range of possible futures, organizations can better withstand shocks, seize opportunities, and steer towards desired outcomes, regardless of what the future holds.

MONTE CARLO SIMULATION

Monte Carlo Simulation is a quantitative technique that uses random sampling and statistical modeling to estimate the behavior of complex systems and evaluate the impact of uncertainty on models. It's widely used across various fields such as finance, engineering, project management, and risk analysis, enabling decision-makers to understand the likelihood of different outcomes in the face of uncertainty. Here's a guide to implementing Monte Carlo Simulation:

Step 1: Define the Problem

- **Objective**: Clearly define the objective of the simulation. What are you trying to measure or predict? This could be project completion times, investment returns, risk exposure, etc.

- **Variables**: Identify the key variables that influence the outcome of your model. Determine which variables are uncertain and will be varied in the simulation.

Step 2: Model the System

- **Develop a Mathematical Model**: Create a mathematical model that represents the system or process you're analyzing. This model should include the relationships between your input variables and the outcome.

- **Identify Distributions**: For each uncertain variable,

choose a probability distribution that best represents its uncertainty. Common distributions include normal, log-normal, uniform, and triangular.

Step 3: Simulate Random Inputs

- **Generate Random Samples**: Using the selected distributions, generate random inputs for each uncertain variable. This is where the Monte Carlo aspect comes into play, as you're using random sampling to explore a wide range of possible scenarios.

- **Software Tools**: Utilize software tools like Excel, R, Python, or specialized simulation software to perform the sampling and computations. These tools can efficiently generate random samples and automate the simulation process.

Step 4: Run the Simulation

- **Compute Outcomes**: For each set of random inputs generated, calculate the outcome using your mathematical model. This step is repeated many times (thousands or even millions) to explore a wide range of possible outcomes.

- **Record Results**: Keep track of the results from each simulation run. This data will be used to analyze the probability of different outcomes.

Step 5: Analyze the Results

- **Statistical Analysis**: Once the simulation runs are complete, analyze the results statistically. This can involve calculating the mean, median, variance, and other statistical measures of the outcomes.

- **Probability Distributions**: Plot the outcomes to visualize the probability distribution of the results. This will help you understand the range of possible outcomes and their likelihoods.

- **Risk Analysis**: Identify the risk levels associated with different outcomes. For example, you might calculate the probability of a project exceeding a certain cost or a portfolio falling below a target return.

Step 6: Interpret and Apply the Findings

- **Decision Making**: Use the insights gained from the simulation to inform decision-making. The results can help identify areas of high risk, guide risk management strategies, and support strategic planning.
- **Sensitivity Analysis**: Consider performing sensitivity analysis to understand how changes in input variables impact the outcomes. This can help identify which variables have the most significant effect on the model's results.

Step 7: Review and Refine

- **Validate the Model**: Where possible, validate the model by comparing its predictions against real-world outcomes or other models.
- **Iterative Process**: Monte Carlo Simulation is often an iterative process. Based on the results and any new information, you may need to refine your model and run additional simulations.

Monte Carlo Simulation is a powerful tool for understanding the impact of uncertainty and variability in complex systems. By providing a probabilistic range of outcomes rather than a single deterministic forecast, it offers a more nuanced view of risk and uncertainty, enabling more informed decision-making.

DRIVER-BASED FORECASTING

Driver-Based Forecasting is a strategic approach to financial forecasting that concentrates on understanding and modeling the primary factors or "drivers" that significantly impact business performance. This method enables organizations to focus their forecasting efforts on the variables that truly matter, making the forecasting process more efficient and the outcomes more actionable. Here's how to implement Driver-Based Forecasting:

Step 1: Identify Key Business Drivers

- **Understand Your Business Model**: Begin with a thorough analysis of your business model to identify which variables most directly influence your financial outcomes. These could be sales volume, price points, cost of goods sold (COGS), labor costs, or any other factors critical to your business's performance.

- **Engage Stakeholders**: Collaborate with stakeholders across the business to ensure a comprehensive understanding of the factors that drive performance. This can include sales, marketing, operations, finance, and any other relevant departments.

Step 2: Quantify Relationships Between Drivers and Financial Outcomes

- **Model the Relationships**: Once key drivers are

identified, quantify how changes in these drivers impact financial outcomes. This often involves statistical analysis or regression models to understand the sensitivity of financial results to changes in each driver.

- **Develop Assumptions**: For each key driver, develop assumptions about future performance. These assumptions can be based on historical data, industry benchmarks, and future expectations.

Step 3: Build the Forecasting Model

- **Create a Driver-Based Model**: Integrate the relationships and assumptions into a cohesive financial model. This model should allow for the input of various scenarios for each driver to see how they would impact financial forecasts.

- **Software Tools**: Leverage financial modeling software or spreadsheet tools like Excel to build your model. Ensure the model is flexible enough to update assumptions or add drivers as needed.

Step 4: Scenario Analysis

- **Run Scenarios**: Use the model to run different scenarios by varying the assumptions for your key drivers. This can help understand the range of possible outcomes and the sensitivity of your financial forecasts to changes in each driver.

- **Identify Leverage Points**: Pay particular attention to drivers that have a significant impact on financial outcomes. These are areas where strategic initiatives or operational improvements can have the most substantial effect on performance.

Step 5: Continuous Monitoring and Updating

- **Monitor Key Drivers**: Establish a process for regularly monitoring the performance of your key drivers. This involves setting up KPIs (Key Performance Indicators) that can give you real-time insights into how these drivers are performing.

- **Update Forecasts Regularly**: As actual data comes in or as the business environment changes, update your forecasts to reflect new information. This will help keep your forecasts accurate and relevant.

Step 6: Integrate into Decision Making

- **Use Forecasts for Strategic Planning**: Leverage your driver-based forecasts in strategic planning and decision-making. The insights gained from understanding the impact of key drivers can inform business strategy, investment decisions, and operational adjustments.

- **Communicate with Stakeholders**: Share insights from your driver-based forecasting with stakeholders across the organization. A clear understanding of how key drivers impact financial outcomes can align efforts and focus on areas that will drive performance.

Step 7: Review and Refine

- **Iterative Process**: Driver-based forecasting is an iterative process. Regularly review and refine your model and assumptions based on new data, changing market conditions, and improved understanding of your business drivers.

Driver-Based Forecasting provides a focused and flexible approach to financial forecasting, allowing organizations to concentrate on what's most important to their success. By understanding and modeling the impact of key business drivers, companies can make more informed strategic decisions, respond more quickly to changes in the business environment, and drive improved financial performance.

ROLLING FORECASTS

Rolling Forecasts represent a dynamic approach to financial forecasting, designed to offer a more flexible and adaptive view of the future by updating forecasts at regular intervals. Unlike traditional static forecasts that are anchored to a fiscal year, rolling forecasts extend continuously over a set period (e.g., 12 months, 18 months) into the future, adjusting as new data becomes available. This method ensures that the forecasts always reflect the most current information and can be a powerful tool for agile decision-making. Here's how to implement Rolling Forecasts:

Step 1: Define the Forecast Horizon

- **Select a Time Horizon**: Decide on the length of the forecast period you want to maintain (e.g., 12, 18, or 24 months). This horizon stays constant; as time moves forward, the forecast period rolls forward as well.

- **Determine Update Frequency**: Choose how often you will update the forecast. Common intervals include monthly or quarterly updates, depending on the volatility of your business and the effort required to gather and process data.

Step 2: Identify Key Variables and Assumptions

- **Key Business Drivers**: Identify the critical variables that influence your business outcomes, similar to driver-based forecasting. These will form the basis of your rolling forecasts.

- **Flexible Assumptions**: Develop assumptions for

these variables that can be easily updated as new information becomes available. The goal is to reflect the current business environment and outlook as accurately as possible.

Step 3: Develop the Forecasting Model

- **Build a Flexible Model**: Create a forecasting model that can easily accommodate new data and adjust forecasts accordingly. This model should allow for quick updates to assumptions and calculations.

- **Incorporate Historical Data and Trends**: Use historical performance as a guide, but focus on how recent trends and changes in assumptions will affect future performance.

Step 4: Implement a Process for Regular Updates

- **Data Collection**: Establish a routine process for collecting the latest data on key business drivers. This might involve collaboration across departments to gather sales data, market trends, cost changes, and other relevant information.

- **Forecast Update**: On a predetermined schedule, update your forecast to reflect the new data and any changes in the business environment. Adjust the forecast horizon forward, so it always covers the same future period.

Step 5: Analyze and Communicate Results

- **Review Trends and Variances**: Regularly analyze the forecasts to identify trends, opportunities, and risks. Compare forecasted results to actual outcomes to understand variances and refine your forecasting model.

- **Stakeholder Communication**: Clearly communicate the updated forecasts to stakeholders, including any changes in assumptions or significant findings from the latest data. This ensures that decision-making is based on the most current insights.

Step 6: Use Forecasts for Decision Making

- **Strategic Adjustments**: Use the insights gained from the rolling forecasts to make informed strategic decisions. This could involve adjusting budgets, reallocating resources, or changing strategic priorities.

- **Operational Planning**: Similarly, operational plans may need to be updated based on the latest forecasts, ensuring that the organization remains agile and responsive to changes.

Step 7: Continuous Improvement

- **Refine the Process**: Regularly review and refine the forecasting process, looking for ways to improve the accuracy of forecasts, reduce the time required for updates, and enhance the usefulness of the forecasts for decision-making.

- **Leverage Technology**: Consider using advanced analytics, AI, and forecasting software to streamline the data collection and forecasting process, improve accuracy, and provide deeper insights.

Rolling Forecasts offer a forward-looking perspective that can significantly enhance strategic and operational planning. By maintaining a continuously updated view of the future, organizations can navigate uncertainty more effectively, respond more quickly to changes, and allocate resources more efficiently, driving better business outcomes.

Made in United States
Orlando, FL
10 March 2024

44602072R00215